Overseas Chinese Christian Entrepreneurs in Modern China

Overseas Chinese Christian Entrepreneurs in Modern China

A Case Study of the Influence of Christian Ethics on Business Life

Joy Kooi-Chin Tong

ANTHEM PRESS
LONDON · NEW YORK · DELHI

Anthem Press
An imprint of Wimbledon Publishing Company
www.anthempress.com

This edition first published in UK and USA 2013
by ANTHEM PRESS
75–76 Blackfriars Road, London SE1 8HA, UK
or PO Box 9779, London SW19 7ZG, UK
and
244 Madison Ave. #116, New York, NY 10016, USA

First published in hardback by Anthem Press in 2012

Copyright © Joy Kooi-Chin Tong 2013

The author asserts the moral right to be identified as the author of this work.

Cover image © Shawn Ng Wee-Kian 2012

All rights reserved. Without limiting the rights under copyright reserved above,
no part of this publication may be reproduced, stored or introduced into
a retrieval system, or transmitted, in any form or by any means
(electronic, mechanical, photocopying, recording or otherwise),
without the prior written permission of both the copyright
owner and the above publisher of this book.

British Library Cataloguing-in-Publication Data
A catalogue record for this book is available from the British Library.

Library of Congress Cataloging-in-Publication Data
The Library of Congress has cataloged the hardcover edition as follows:
Overseas Chinese Christian entrepreneurs in modern China : a case
study of the influence of Christian ethics on business life / Joy
Kooi-Chin Tong.
   p. cm.
Includes bibliographical references and index.
ISBN 978-0-85728-353-5 (hardback : alk. paper)
1. Business ethics–China. 2. Christian ethics–China. 3.
Entrepreneurship–China. 4. China–Economic conditions–1976–2000.
I. Title.
HF5387.5.C6T65 2012
241'.6440951–dc23
2011045757

ISBN-13: 978 1 78308 056 4 (Pbk)
ISBN-10: 1 78308 056 6 (Pbk)

This title is also available as an ebook.

This book is dedicated to my parents,
Tong Geok Poi and Lee Siew Bee,
who have struggled throughout their lives to be honest in their
faith and business and who have set an example for me.
献给我的父母：童玉杯与李秀美

CONTENTS

Acknowledgments   ix

List of Tables and Figures   xi

Chapter 1   **Introduction: Studying Christian Ethics and Business Life in Post-1978 China**   1

     Religion and Economics   1
     China's Economic Reforms: The Transition to
         Capitalism, Foreign Investments and Business Ethics   5
     Reemergence of Religion: "Christianity Fever"
         in Post-1978 China   9
     Research Questions and Design   16
     Research Methods and Profile of Respondents   19
     Plan of the Chapters   29

Chapter 2   **Religion and Economic Life: The Protestant Ethic and Max Weber's Legacy**   33

     The Protestant Ethic Thesis: Calvinism and Capitalism   34
     Weber's Study on China and Confucianism   41
     Conclusion: Belief and Action   47

Chapter 3   **Overseas Chinese Christian Entrepreneurs in Post-1978 China (Shanghai): Business, Faith and Ethics**   53

     General Portrait of Overseas Chinese Entrepreneurs
         and Their Business Ventures in China   54
     Overseas Chinese Entrepreneurs in Shanghai:
         Investments and Relationships with Local People   58
     Christian Entrepreneurs among the Overseas
         Chinese in China   65
     Christian Ethics and Economic Life   70

Chapter 4	**Religious Motivation and Entrepreneurial Spirit**	73
	Religious and Entrepreneurial Spirit of Overseas Chinese Christian Entrepreneurs in Shanghai	73
	Success	74
	Self-Discipline	78
	A Sense of Calling	81
	Frugality	83
	Integrity	84
	Innovativeness	86
Chapter 5	**Business–Faith Integration: Three Types of Christian-Based Companies**	91
	Three Types of Business–Faith Integration	92
	Business as Mission (A "Christian" Company)	93
	Business or Mission	99
	Mission in Business	102
Chapter 6	**Communities of Faith: Fellowships for Overseas Chinese Christian Businesspeople in Shanghai**	107
	How Religious Community Affects Economic Behaviors: Networking and Mutual Accountability	107
	Communities of Overseas Chinese Christian Entrepreneurs in Shanghai	109
	Two Case Studies: Chinese Businesspeople Fellowship and Full Gospel Businessmen's Fellowship	112
Chapter 7	**Female Entrepreneurs: Four Stories**	123
	Gender Differences in Ethical Performances	124
	Women, Rational Business Behavior and Social Networking	125
	Formations and Expressions of "Female Protestant Ethics"	129
	Conclusion	141
Chapter 8	**Conclusion and Research Implications**	143
	Implications of the Research	144
Bibliography		151
Index		165

ACKNOWLEDGMENTS

I am significantly indebted to many people for helping me make this book possible.

First, I am indebted to my PhD adviser, Bryan Turner, for providing constant guidance and insightful comments to make this work possible. Bryan was the one who suggested that I take up a topic on China for my PhD research. And he consistently guided me through the writing process with his expert knowledge, even after he left the National University of Singapore.

I was also fortunate to benefit from the advice of Fenggang Yang of Purdue University. Without his encouragement and support, I would never have made the effort to work on this book project. I must also thank my former professors at the National University of Singapore, especially Douglas Kammen, for his patient and stimulating encouragement, Maribeth Erb, Duncan McCargo and Vineeta Sinha, for their valuable ideas and academic support, as well as my dissertation examiners, Jack Barbalet, Fenggang Yang and Robin Goh, for their critical and constructive feedback. I am also indebted to the three anonymous reviewers for their very helpful comments. It was partly through their suggestions that I arrived at the intellectual focus of this book.

Above all, I owe important debts to many people on my fieldwork in Shanghai. These are first, Jiaying (and also Guo An, as well as the sisters and brothers of the Songjiang Fellowship), Shain and Chad, Anxian, and Surina and Lawrence, who invited me to stay in their homes, participate in their lives and use their resources. I can never adequately express my appreciation to them. I am also very grateful to Prof. Liu Ping from Shanghai Fudan University for spending time to maintain a continuing dialogue and Pastor David Lin and Prof. Li Xiangping for their assistance on my research. My heartfelt gratitude belongs to the 60 entrepreneurs that I interviewed and other members that I talked to of the Chinese Businesspeople Fellowship (Huashang Tuanqi). They allowed me to pick their brains and listen to their sometimes very personal and difficult stories. I am deeply grateful for their generous help and trust in me. Most of them will remain anonymous here, but their help is greatly appreciated and will always be remembered.

I am also deeply grateful to my friends, Daniel and Taberez, for taking the pains to proofread the manuscript; to Shawn for designing the wonderful book cover; to friends who have known me for a long time – Jesse, Yimin, Constance, Yanhua, Agnes, Yuhao, Jianwei, Kuo and Wangyi – for their very faithful supports and prayers; and to a new but special friend, Charlie, who shared my anxiety yet managed to motivate me in a powerful way to press on.

The final and most important debt is to my family. My beloved parents and sisters – Christine, Ruth, Esther and Faith – have supported me at each stage of this research and constantly affirmed, encouraged and upheld me when I was about to lose hope. They share my joy and will be the happiest people to see me finish this research and embark on a new journey.

LIST OF TABLES AND FIGURES

Tables

Table 1.1	Foreign direct investment in China, 1979–94 (millions of US$)	6
Table 1.2	Profile of respondents	26
Table 3.1	Sources of foreign capital in China (cumulative 1979–93)	57
Table 5.1	Three types of business–faith integration in Christian-based corporations	105

Figures

Figure 3.1	Thanksgiving Church in Shanghai	67

Chapter 1

INTRODUCTION: STUDYING CHRISTIAN ETHICS AND BUSINESS LIFE IN POST-1978 CHINA

This book is a sociological study of religion which analyzes the influence of the Christian values of Overseas Chinese entrepreneurs on the emerging market economy of China. The purpose of the book is to examine how, and to what extent, Christian values and ethics, that is, how Christians see the world and interpret the meaning of their actions, affect the business practices of Overseas Chinese Christian entrepreneurs in China, as well as their possible social consequences. It is important in this introductory chapter first to discuss the uneasy relationship between religion and economics in general as groundwork for this research. Following this, the chapter moves on to provide the background for the economic and religious changes in China after 1978, emphasizing foreign investments, as well as Christianity in post-1978 China, to set these issues in context. This chapter ends with an outline of the purpose, methodology and chapter plan of the book.

Religion and Economics

The relationship between religion and economics is both controversial and complex. Many hold the view that these two areas are (or should be) separate, and at the extreme end, there are those who hold the view that religion and economics are incompatible and would likely create "a clash of civilizations" (Capaldi, 2005). Samuelson (1979, 718), for example, argues that "putting stress on these non-economic factors does not solve the problem of *explanation* [of economic issues]. It poses new problems." Also, according to Francis Fukuyama (2005), "It is safe to say that most contemporary economists do not take Weber's hypothesis, or any other culturalist theory of economic growth, seriously. Many maintain that culture is a residual category in which lazy social scientists take refuge when they can't develop a more rigorous theory."

Yet, despite such arguments that see religion as of no help to economics, sociologists have for most of the twentieth century been concerned about the economic consequences of cultural (including religious) orientations. Indeed, as suggested by Bryan Turner (2008), "The relationship between religion and economics, or more narrowly between religion and entrepreneurship has been, perhaps counter intuitively, a more or less persistent theme of the history of the sociology of religion." Of course, the most famous argument along this line is found in Max Weber's *The Protestant Ethic and the Spirit of Capitalism* (first pub. 1905), in which he argues that religious practices and beliefs have had important consequences for economic development in Western societies. Weber's thesis, although controversial, has provided an early and heuristic macro-level theory linking religion to the rise of capitalism and has invited a wide range of studies showing various connections between religion and modern economic life. Fernand Braudel (1966), for example, examines the role of minority religious groups, such as European Jews and Judaism, in developing economic institutions such as banking and finance across societies. Merton (1970) argues for a positive correlation between the rise of English Puritanism and the rise of German Pietism and early experimental science, which was integral to economic development. Collins (1997) explains how religious institutions, particularly Buddhist monasteries in Japan, provided a source of opposition to feudal domination and stimulated the emergence of capitalist enterprise.

Recent research has once again focused on religious influences on economic factors by situating theories in various contexts. Researchers such as Huntington (1996), Landes (1999), Inglehart and Baker (2000) and Barro and McCleary (2003) have argued that explanations for economic growth should go beyond narrow measures of economic variables to encompass political, social, and in particular, cultural forces. Notably, these studies have not merely been done by sociologists, as has been the case for decades, but also by economists. The works of Morishima (1982) on Japan and of Morawetz (1980) on Colombia are two examples of this sort. A more recent work by Harvard economists Robert Barro and Rachel McCleary has added to this body of research. Their research (2003) claims that religion affects economic outcomes by fostering religious beliefs, especially beliefs in heaven and hell as well as in rewards and punishments, which in turn influence individual traits such as honesty, work ethic, thrift and openness to strangers. Their findings, which largely confirm Weber's thesis, have been reached via a sophisticated analysis of a huge set of data collected in 59 countries between 1981 and 1999.

This result is perhaps surprising to many people whose secularization assumptions lead them to expect an opposite outcome, and which posit that economic development causes individuals to become less religious as religion plays a less vital role in the public sectors, including the economic sphere in Western societies. It might therefore be more striking if we notice how similar phenomena as described by Barro and McCleary are emerging, albeit slowly and minimally, in an Asian, communist society which has tried hard to eradicate organized religion and has a long and hostile history with Christianity – China.

Recently an article entitled "A Market Economy With Church and a Market Economy Without Church" appeared in the January 2006 issue of *Esquire*, a magazine published in China and targeting the business sector. In this article, the author, Zhao Xiao, one of the most active and influential young economists in contemporary China, claimed that a market economy by its very nature needs a certain type of ethics in order to bring out its greatest merits, "just like a good horse naturally needs a good saddle," as he puts it. Based on world history as well as Weber's *Protestant Ethic*, Zhao argues that Protestant ethics, possibly the most up-to-date and compatible model of ethics for the market economy, might be the answer to China's search for a moral vision in the midst of its rapid socioeconomic transition. Quoting data based on an empirical study of over one hundred nations on their varied relationships between religion and economics, Zhao says that the findings illustrate that more religious countries tend to have a stronger legal system as compared to secular countries, since legal regulation is more effective when placed under "the gaze of God." He concludes his claims by paraphrasing a popular Chinese poem, "Fear the power of God, fear lightning, and fear thunder in the sky, as only fear can save us and only faith can market economy gains its spirit."

Following this article, to illustrate Zhao's assertion, the magazine features stories of four Overseas Chinese Christian entrepreneurs in China, showing how they endeavor to integrate religious values with business ventures. One of the entrepreneurs was formerly CEO of Motorola China, the Taiwanese Shi Dakun. In the interview, Shi indicates his "5 F" priority (which is well known among his employees) to his Chinese readers from the various business sectors: the first F is Faith, followed by Family, Firm (or work), Fun and Future plans. This reasoning holds up the idea that faith is decisively the most important element in one's life, and because of that, it is as crucial in business activities as in private life.

Zhao's assertion and Shi's example might sound new and remote to many, whether Chinese or not, but these examples are not totally rare. In his famous book, *Jesus in Beijing* (2003, 31), David Aikman mentions, "In the coastal city of Wenzhou, Christianity in the 1980s seemed to surge proportionately to the success of Wenzhou retailers in making money.

In fact, more than a decade ago, some Chinese, thinking about capitalism, Christianity, and Wenzhou, were making the intellectual connection between religion and the rise of capitalism." Also, according to historian Daniel Bays (2003, 498), an authority on Protestantism in China, "There has been an increasing number of Chinese intellectuals who do research on Protestant Christianity…some believe that Protestantism was centrally involved in the overall process of modernization that fuelled the economic development, political democratization and worldwide expansion of the West in the past few centuries. Others have found Protestant ethics and patterns of community formation interesting or attractive. Some intellectuals have actively advocated China's adoption of some aspects of Christianity as part of its own modernization efforts, and a certain number of these intellectuals have themselves become Christians."

It is true that as China begins to ponder the question of "soft power" – through strengthening institutions and instigating a cultural renaissance – vis-à-vis the importance of "hard power," namely, economic power, more intellectuals including politicians and economists have come to see that religion might be able to contribute to the development of Chinese society. There is one question asked by many Chinese: "Is capitalism just a way of doing business, or does it come with concrete ethical and philosophical foundations?", as suggested by David Aikman (2003).Or, to phrase this intellectual concept differently, can we anticipate that Protestant Christianity will play a role in China's transformation to "capitalism with Chinese characteristics" as it did in the West?

Rather than testing the Weberian macro-level theory explaining the economic development of China based on religious prescriptions, this research aims to contribute to this larger issue by focusing on how religion influences both individual and corporate economic behaviors through ethical enforcements and religious training. The assumption is that religion is a determinant of economic behavior, but it is by no means the sole determinant and is generally not the prime determinant of the results of that behavior. The question of how large a part religion plays in the explanation of behavior is, in itself, intriguing. I discuss this more in the following chapter but it is necessary to assert here that faith is not seen as the only dominant cause of individuals' economic practices, obliterating other factors such as economic policy and structure. My concern is that since religion is clearly important to a growing number of Chinese Christian entrepreneurs, it deserves a respectable place in any attempts to understand their business activities and ethical practices. Before going into the details of their actual practices, it may perhaps be useful to first summarize the history of economic institutional change in China.

China's Economic Reforms: The Transition to Capitalism, Foreign Investments and Business Ethics

In the last three decades, China has gone through a series of startling changes that no one anticipated. These changes, especially China's decisive move to reopen its doors to the world, have probably been some of the biggest in the 5,000 years of Chinese history, which "could be as significant to China as the Renaissance was to Europe" (Gu 1991, 31). Of course, the impact of China's economic transformation on the modification of Chinese social and business structures is salient and complex; it is beyond the scope of this book to capture the whole picture. Instead, this section can only identify several aspects of the change that are related to this research.

The death of Mao Zedong in 1976, and Deng Xiaoping's assumption of control of the Party in late 1978, ushered in a new era in Chinese development. In December 1978 at the Third Plenary Session of the 11th Party Congress, the Chinese Communist Party, with Deng as its new leader announced the official launch of the Four Modernizations, which formally marked the beginning of the reform era. One aspect of the Four Modernizations included the establishment of a state-controlled agricultural market, the dissolution of the people's Communes, and the creation of special economic zones oriented towards exports with foreign investment and a partial liberalization of foreign trade. After some initial successful experiments were performed in agriculture in terms of the "household responsibility system," in 1985 the reforms were extended to the urban industrial sector, generalizing the autonomy of management of the enterprises, recourse to market mechanisms, and the strengthening of the financial and banking system. From October 1987 to early 1989, government policy determined that while the state regulated the market, the market in turn guided the operation of enterprises. By 1991, this policy had evolved to one in which the economy was determined to be a combination of state planning and market forces. In 1992, the 14th Party Congress announced that the objective of China's economic system was to establish a socialist market economy.

Particularly impressive and successful in China's economic reform have been the strategies designed to attract foreign capital (see Table 1.1). The symbolic example was the establishment of the four Special Economic Zones in Shenzhen, Zhuhai, Shekou and Xiamen in 1980, which aimed to attract foreign direct investment and to promote both exports and technological transfer. In order to achieve these goals, a relatively relaxed regulatory regime was established: tax holidays were granted; modern infrastructure, production facilities and logistics networks were built up; and land policies were implemented. The result was dramatic: Shenzhen, for example, was

Table 1.1. Foreign direct investment in China, 1979–94 (millions of US$)

Year	Contracted	Actual
1979–82 (cumulative)	6,999	1,767
1983	1,917	916
1984	2,875	1,419
1985	6,333	1,959
1986	3,330	2,244
1987	4,319	2,647
1988	6,191	3,739
1989	6,294	3,773
1990	6,987	3,755
1991	12,422	4,666
1992	58,736	11,292
1993	111,435	27,514
1994	81,406	33,787

Note: The data reported above are inclusive of foreign direct investment in equity joint ventures, contractual joint ventures, wholly foreign-owned enterprises and joint exploration as well as foreign investment in leasing, compensation trade, and processing and assembly.

Sources: Ministry of Foreign Trade and Economic Relations, *Zhonghua Renmin Gongheguo Duiwai Jingjimaoyibu Xinwen Gongbao* [The Bulletin of the Ministry of Foreign Trade and Economic Relations of the People's Republic of China], no. 2 (25 April 1994), 10; *Jinrong Shibao* [Banking Times], 26 January 1995, 1 (quoted in Lardy 1995, 1066).

a fishing village in 1980 with less than thirty thousand inhabitants but, in a few years, it became a bustling city of nearly 10 million (Fang et al. 2008).

As shown in Table 1.1, the flow of FDI declined temporarily following the Tiananmen crackdown in June 1989. But it was quickly restored with Deng Xiaoping's famous tour of Shenzhen in early 1992. Deng's slogans, "Let a few people get rich first," "To get rich is glorious" and "Development is the real truth," again boosted people's confidence in change and catalyzed China's unprecedented race to market. In the 14th Party Congress in October 1992, besides setting the goal of establishing a socialist market economy as indicated, the government generalized various strategies including those of special economic zones in more cities to attract foreign investment. The Shenzhen miracle was therefore duplicated in various coastal cities and inland provinces. Besides, China also opened up sectors such as retailing, power generation, property and port development that previously had been off limits to foreign investors. These combined efforts have led to particularly significant foreign capital inflows directed toward various parts of China. It is worth noting, however, that this foreign capital has been dominated by Overseas Chinese investors, namely those from Hong Kong, Taiwan and Southeast Asia. In fact, since China opened its doors in 1978, ethnic Chinese enterprises have been the largest investors in China, both in terms of total capital and number of firms established in China (see Table 1.1).

These reforms and investments have made China change from being one of the world's most isolated and backward economies to being its fastest growing and most dynamic (Fang et al. 2008). In the 1990s, China (after the United States) became the second-largest recipient of foreign capital investment, which accounted for more than 22 percent of all its investment. The average growth of its economy reached 9.7 percent per year (against 7.5 percent for the "Asian tigers"), and its exports grew by 19 percent per year (Huang 2008). China has become the most outstanding example of a "transitional economy" that the World Bank proposes to developing countries (Fang et al. 2008). Its entrance into the World Trade Organization in 2001 only accelerated the process of its reintegration into global capitalism.

Nevertheless, such a rapid economic growth has come with costs and problems. The reforms that were meant to enhance the authority of the Party-State have in fact undermined it and led to an element of social chaos. Deng Xiaoping's decentralization strategy has yielded considerable authority to the lower bureaucrats so that they can enjoy certain powers in making economic decisions and using tax revenues for local projects. As their authority grows, local bureaucrats form alliances with enterprises and often ignore central government injunctions against corruption, labor exploitation, product duplication or tax overcharges (Gu 1991). This reveals the huge gap between China's political and legal reforms as well as its economic reforms, leading to bouts of inflation and rampant corruption.

To be sure, it is quite evident that Chinese economic performance has been impressive. Yet, at the same time, some of its weaknesses such as the widespread exploitation and corruption have been widely reported. In Shanghai alone, for example, since late 2006 eight senior officials in charge of land management have been arrested. One of them, a deputy director of the land management bureau, amassed 10 million yuan, about US$1.25 million, in his bank accounts, as well as 26 apartments valued between 70 million and 80 million yuan (between US$8.7 million and US$10 million). Further, Chen Liangyu, the party secretary of Shanghai and a Politburo member, and Liu Jinbao, the head of the Shanghai branch of the Bank of China in the 1990s, were both detained on corruption charges. China also dominated the headlines in the world media in 2008 for a different reason. The melamine milk scandal that broke in July 2008 impacted an estimated 300,000 infant victims according to government reports. This scandal was referred to by the World Health

Organization (WHO) as one of the largest food safety events it has dealt with in recent years (Yu 2008). Events like these shock the world; in fact, the world is justifiably concerned about Chinese products and enterprises as well as its business ethics given the fact that China now manufactures or produces over 50 percent of the world's products. Perhaps, as argued by Redding and Witt (2007, 222), China is now facing one of its biggest challenges in its reformation, that is "the continued absence of institutionalized social capital" or institutional trust, which is limiting its growth and its role as a global player.

Here an issue which is important to this research arises: if we accept the importance of foreign/Overseas Chinese investments in driving the process of China's modernization – Lardy (1994) sees these investments, along with foreign trade, as the twin engines of China's economic miracle – we might reasonably ask, what kind of influence can we expect foreign actors to have on China's efforts to combat its ethical problems? Or, to put it differently, how can foreign enterprises help not only in building China's hard power, but also in helping build its "soft power"? Studies show that China's transformation would not have been possible without active learning from the West (Fang et al. 2008). They argue that foreign investments not only channel capital into China, but also provide China with technology, management know-how and access to international markets (Lardy 1994). Moreover, research on Chinese enterprise reforms finds that large enterprises formally related to multinational corporations tend to adopt rule-based procedures and practices and thus, through the spread of their rational-legal institutions, contribute indirectly to the stemming of corruption in China (Guthrie 1999). Indeed, after China entered the World Trade Organization, the need to comply with WTO rules has added impetus to China's development of business ethics (Yu 2008). This is expected if we refer to the neoinstitutional sociologists who have argued that when organizations interact with one another, their standards and practices tend to converge (DiMaggio and Powell 1991). They argue, in particular, that international actors can influence national actors through the spread of the norms they represent (Finnemore 1996; Risse et al. 1999). According to Wang and Chen (2005), norm diffusion can happen through a variety of mechanisms. First, it could occur through coercion; namely, the local organization changes its standards because of both formal and informal pressures from other foreign organizations. Second, it could happen when an organization imitates other successful organizations. Third, it could happen through normative pressures; often an organization changes its ways according to the larger normative context. Viewed from this perspective, we can expect foreign direct investors, especially those who transfer not only capital but also operations to China, would have some influence on the Chinese economic institutional environment.

Of course, the reality of China's economic development is much more complex than I have discussed. But the purpose here is to provide just a brief outline proffering some necessary background information for this research topic. Some of the issues will be picked up in greater detail in the following chapters. We now turn to another aspect of change in China after 1978, namely, the reemergence of religion in this nation, a phenomenon which is closely related to this study. Yet, as one can expect, the religious phenomena in China are, again, anything but simple and straightforward. Hence, the following section will only offer a selective background directly related to Christianity and to foreigners in a manner consistent with the theme of this book.

Reemergence of Religion: "Christianity Fever" in Post-1978 China

China's economic reforms have not only substantially transformed its social and political landscapes, but have also impacted its religious environment. One reason is China's open-door policy, a strategy which has directly contributed to attracting foreign capital and management skills to the country. This policy has also allowed the nation's elites to exit the country and has forced China to tolerate social diversity, competition and the exchange of information and values within its cultural sphere. Religion has thus had the opportunity to resurface openly in China. Moreover, as one might expect in times of such radical social transformation, which is akin to something like "the change of the human world" (*huan le renjian*) as described by a renowned Chinese writer, Wang Meng (quoted in Fang et al. 2008), the state and social actors are both seeking alternate competing belief-systems to keep up with the new challenges within China (Yang and Tamney 2005; Goldman 1986). The change in the religious sphere is thus a consequence as well as a reflection of the economic transformation in China.

The reemergence of religion in China has attracted the attention and interest of many sociologists of religion. Much pioneering sociological research on religion in contemporary China (see for example, Yang and Tamney 2005; Yang 2005 and 2006; Goldman 1986) has emerged as religion has gradually regained both its dynamics and legitimacy after many years of harsh political repression under the communist regime. In fact, the idea of conducting a sociological study of religion in China was close to impossible or at least could be viewed as irrelevant before the 1980s, and this can best be understood by the historical reality that by 1958, nine years after communist rule began, many religious institutions had been closed. In the case of Christianity, for example, there were no new pastors ordained after the 1950s, very few Christian publications or news of religion in the media and no religious education in the Chinese school structure (Hunter and Chan 1993). The persecution of religion reached its climax in August 1966 as the Communist Party issued a directive which marked the start of the Cultural Revolution – religious institutions were shut down, buildings were confiscated, leaders and believers were persecuted and religious life was dismantled (Hunter and Chan 1993). Many outsiders have assumed that religions, particularly Christianity with its "foreign" background, were basically extinguished from China (Hunter and Chan 1993).

The religious change, however "unintended" it might be, would not have been possible if the government had not relaxed its tight control over religious life. This change has been greatly fuelled by the state's lifting of the ban on the freedom of worship (Lai 2003). The first church was reopened in Ningbo in early April 1979, and it was soon followed by more churches in Shanghai and other large cities. The official church recovered much of its property and legal status and was revived as an institution (Hunter and Chan 1993). Of course, the reasons behind such liberalization of religious policies were manifold. One important motive which is directly relevant to this research was certainly to attract foreign aid, primarily from the West, but also specific aid from the Overseas Chinese in Hong Kong, Macau and Taiwan (Leong 2005). The subtle relationship between religious regulation and foreign investment can truly be seen from the following event: When China established diplomatic relations with the United States in 1979, President Jimmy Carter's private requests to Deng Xiaoping on the issue of Christianity were to permit the freedom of worship, in part by allowing for a distribution of Bibles and the return of American missionaries to China. Deng granted the first two requests but decisively rejected the third (Wehrfritz and Clemetson 1998). Obviously, Deng and his government knew that foreign relations and investment were directly affected by China's record regarding religion as well as human rights, noting how foreign direct investment had seriously decreased in 1989 and 1990 after the June 4th Tiananmen Square event. The new religious policy was therefore put into place to justify China's determined and long-term modernization policy (Leung 2005).

Under the pragmatic leadership of Deng, the regime moved away from the Cultural Revolution's destructive approach to religion to a more tolerant approach. Five religions, that is, Buddhism, Daoism, Islam, Protestantism and Catholicism, were granted legal existence under the government-sanctioned "patriotic" associations, and a limited number of Protestant and Catholic churches, Buddhist and Daoist temples and Islamic mosques were reopened for religious services. Freedom of religious belief was reaffirmed although it was limited only to "normal" religious activities. China has since then experienced a widespread revival of religious faith and practice. Many kinds of religions, including official and unofficial religions, have been reviving and thriving (Lai 2003). According to an April 2005 government white paper, there are "more than 100 million religious adherents" (Hamrin 2008). Yet, according to a BBC article published on 7 February 2007, a survey conducted by researchers in Shanghai and reported in Chinese state-run media concluded that 31.4 percent of Chinese citizens ages 16 and over, or 300 million people, were religious. In the February 2007 poll, approximately 40 million citizens identified themselves as Christians, compared with the official figure of 16 million in 2005, and 200 million identified themselves as Buddhist, Daoist or members of folk religions. Religious revivals are outstanding and visible – the number of church attendees and temple buildings, the number of religious venues, the number of clerics, the number of religious schools and colleges and the number of religious books and periodicals for all the five official religions have been rising rapidly (Lai, 2003). Growing alongside these official religions are folk religions, which include ancestor worship, local god worship, divination, *feng shui*, witchcraft and physiognomy, resulting in a significant growth in the number of new temples being built and a boom in sales of goods related to folk religious rituals and books (Lai 2003).

Christianity has grown at the fastest pace although it is not the largest group among the five officially tolerated faiths (Bays 2008).[1] This growth is remarkable to say the least, especially if we take into account the systematic persecution of Christians and the fact that there were fewer than 1 million Protestants in 1949. The total number of Christians increased to 3 million by 1982 and to over 10 million by the end of 1995 (Li 1999). As of 2005, Christians were approaching 4 percent of the population. Projections for 2020 show even more growth, with a jump to 10 percent or even more (Hamrin 2008). Indeed, as suggested by Bays (2003,488), "Protestant Christianity has been a prominent part of the general religious resurgence in China in the past two decades. Today, on any given Sunday, there are almost certainly more Protestants in church in China than in all of Europe." Recognizing this phenomenon, by 1989, Chinese research institutions began to label this "Christianity fever," and this term

---

1 According to a government census in the mid-1990s, there were 100 million Buddhists (including 7 million Tibetan Buddhists), 18 million Muslims (8.6 million Uighur, 7.2 million Hui), 11 million Christians (4 million Catholics, 7 million Protestants) and 50,000 Daoists (Lai 2003).

has since been used in official Chinese publications (Hunter and Chan 1993). Furthermore, research has also shown that Christians are not only expanding in quantity but also in variety; the church body now no longer consists primarily of female, elderly and illiterate people, but also includes a significant number of men, young people and members of the educated middle class (Chen and Huang 2004; Yang 2005). Moreover, new streams within the Protestant faith itself now exist, including urban house churches which no longer see themselves as "underground," divisions within official churches and international community churches (Hamrin 2008; Chen and Huang 2004).

The reduced hostility among China's opinion shapers – academics, economic and even political elites – to religion as well as Christianity has been equally remarkable. The central document of religious policy that was formulated by the Party's Central Committee in 1982, "The Basic Viewpoint and Policy on the Religious Affairs during the Socialist Period of Our Country," better known as Document 19, delineates the five natures of religion in socialist China: it has masses of believers, it is linked closely to ethnicity, it influences international connections, it will continue to exist over the long term, and it is complex. Therefore, religious questions should be handled with care; the mass of believers should be united for the common goal of building a modernized, powerful state; and the policy of religious freedom should be carried out (Yang 2005). In the National Religious Work Meeting, which was convened jointly by the Politburo and the State Council on 10–12 December 2001, Jiang Zemin, for the first time in the history of the People's Republic of China, acknowledged that religion could be a positive force for the stabilization of society and thus should be mobilized for national development (Leong 2005). At a high level meeting with China's top religious leaders which was held in Zhongnanhai on 1 February 2005, according to a *China Daily* report on 5 March 2007, Jia Qinglin (number 4 in the Chinese nomenclature) further stressed that religious morality played a positive role in both social development and harmony. Again, at the 17th National Congress of the Communist Party of China, which ended in late October 2007, Hu Jintao echoed Jiang's remark in affirming religion's positive potential in national development. The Party's attitudinal change toward religion, from the negative extreme of "social opium" to the positive extreme of "social capital," has indeed been both salient and significant; the positive functions and contributions of religion have finally been acknowledged and legitimized in the shifting philosophies of Communist China (Leong 2005).

Notwithstanding these official expressions, we should not be misled into thinking that religion has been freed from any political interference in post-1978 China. China's religious policy can be summarized as the toleration or promotion of "normal religious activities" that do not threaten the Party-State, with a remaining close control and crackdown on those that are perceived as a threat (Hunter and Chan 1993). While affirming the role of religion in China, Document 19 indicates that it is the professed duty of the Party, not religious believers, to decide on religious affairs including the location of religious activities, the teaching of doctrine, the education and appointment of clerics, relations with overseas religious groups and the propagation of faith. This is not surprising as the Chinese government has always defined religion as a part of public affairs or, rather, as a security issue (Chan 1992); religious personnel, activities and locations should therefore be subjected to civil control. This partly explains why the Chinese government is anxious about foreign involvement in its religious activities, which is seen as an "interference of internal affairs" (Chan 1992). In essence, it remains safe to say that the Chinese government's antireligious stance is softening, but overall this stance still plays an important role in the country's administration.

As this research is about Overseas Chinese in China, I shall now mention more in regards to the regulation of foreign people (anyone who does not hold a Chinese passport, including people from Hong Kong, Macau and Taiwan) in religious matters. Since there is an awareness that the Chinese diaspora has actively assisted the development of religion in China, new policies have been put in place reflecting the heightened desire to oppose the influence of foreign organizations. For example, Document 144 (1994) "Regulations from the Council of State on Managing Religious Activities" stipulates that one of the requirements for the registration of local religious institutions, besides a detailed financial report and approval from the civil authority, is proof of no connection with foreign organizations. The government has also restricted the entry of foreign religious people and activities and the involvement of foreigners in local religious affairs. As shown in Deng Xiaoping's rejection of President Carter's third request, missionaries are still officially forbidden and proselytizing is technically illegal. Also, the "Rules on Administration of Religious Activities of Aliens in China" states that foreigners are not allowed to develop religious followers among Chinese citizens or to conduct religious activities at places outside the lawfully registered sites for religious activities.

There is no question that China's government sees foreign involvement in religion, including the involvement of Overseas Chinese, as dangerous though useful. On the one hand, as in the area of economic development, China needs their resources. As far as Christianity is concerned, foreign money from the Hong Kong Christian Council for example, has been flowing in continuously for the rebuilding of 7,000 Protestant churches, mostly located in the countryside and with no pastor (Leung 2005).[2] The government has thus been saved from allocating money for repairing these Christian churches. Also, Overseas Chinese Christian communities based either elsewhere or within China, have worked closely with both registered and unregistered churches at the local level in providing the lay leadership with training as well as with various resources. Moreover, their good works are not merely church-related. In the May earthquake in western China last year, for instance, according to a *Business Week* report on 14 July 2008, a foreign company (Semiconductor Manufacturing International), led by the Christian Taiwanese American Richard Chang, alone donated US$140,000 to the victims. Yet, on the other hand, the Party is seriously aware of the possibility of "infiltration or manipulation" by "imperialists." Obviously, China's historical baggage in relation to Christianity has resulted in its current religious outlook. As Western imperialism in China was accompanied by the parallel penetration of Christian missionaries, the latter were typically seen as allies of Western colonizers and opportunists who played a part in China's "history of humiliation," which stretched from the eighteenth century until the establishment of the PRC in 1949.

But the government is also aware of the ineffaceable contributions of early as well as contemporary Christianity to Chinese society. By the early 1900s, much had been contributed by Western mission organizations to education, medicine, law, industry, military affairs and early forms of community building (Bays 2008). Christianity had also provided "models for moral renovation and social reform designed to address the challenges of industrialization" (Hamrin 2008) which include the campaigns against child labor, child marriage, infanticide and foot binding (Stockwell 2003). Religious voluntary associations such as the YMCA had also played a major role in developing China's civic sector. We might conclude that the relationships between the Chinese government and Christianity, especially involving any "foreign" actors, have always been complicated and tense. Following are some remarks concerning the current developments in China's religious sphere.

First, to summarize the overall situation in China, what is happening now can be seen as "limited toleration" (MacInnis 1994) or can be labeled "quasi religious freedom" (Hamrin 2008). It seems that the government is quietly and unofficially granting Christian communities, both local and foreign, the freedom to worship although they still need to be cautious about possible crackdowns which might occur at any time. As a result, Christianity

---

2 The rebuilding of these local churches by Overseas Chinese Christian communities was not meant to serve foreign people but to meet the needs of the rural Christian population. This evinces the potential impact of foreign Christians in China.

fever is also quietly expanding to other sectors of the society. For example, according to Hamrin (2008), local educators in Shanghai include readings from the Bible in their moral education curricula in primary schools, while university departments offer ethics and management courses which contain religious contents.

Second, as China's reform emphasizes rationalized modernity in which economic development is posited as the first priority, it is particularly intriguing to notice how a growing number of business elites, namely entrepreneurs and professionals, who are at the front line of this reform, openly describe the role Christian faith plays in their business life. This is certainly a novel and unprecedented trend in China. Many mainland Chinese businesspeople have converted to Christianity while studying or traveling overseas and, at the same time, increasing numbers of overseas entrepreneurs have seen their coming to China as a direct calling from God. These new phenomena are especially crucial if we take into consideration two elements. First, unlike commonly assumed, the conversion of Chinese businesspeople and the new emphasis on Christian business values are not to be regarded merely as efforts of Western missions or influences, but instead are mainly promoted by Chinese, both local and overseas. It is worth mentioning that Overseas Chinese, surprisingly, have played as crucial a role in this area as they have in the economic sphere. Second, and equally important, these Overseas Chinese Christian entrepreneurs are not the so-called "Confucian businessmen," who run their businesses by Confucian ideals. This is a fact which runs counter to what we normally assume about Overseas Chinese entrepreneurs. These Chinese entrepreneurs are as diligent, thrifty and proud of being Chinese as well as having their traditional culture as any "Confucian businessmen," but their motives are deeply rooted in their Christian faith. Also, significantly, the (overseas) Chinese Christian businesspeople groups, which sometimes function as a church but without the baggage of either the official church or house church, are mushrooming in big cities such as Shanghai and are providing business networks and Christianity-influenced management training courses to equip their members to play a positive role in China's economic and religious change.

Third, along with the progressive influence of Christianity, there are some commonly heard grievances of local and foreign Christians. For example, according to a *Christianity Today* article published on 1 February 2004, China's Public Security Bureau arrested fifty or more home church leaders and believers in 2004 following the release of the book, *Jesus in Beijing*, and a video which documented the huge growth among home church networks. As far as Overseas Chinese Christian entrepreneurs are concerned, some of the most common grievances have been related to the revoking of business licenses, the confiscating of business properties and their immediate expulsion from China.

For instance, a Guangdong-based ecological company called Enoch Group, owned by an Australian–Hong Kong Chinese couple, was forced to shut down and its assets and patents, which cost about 100 million yuan (US$13 million), were frozen by local government agencies in August 2007. A report by the China Aid Association[3] discussed this issue in detail and reported the suspicion that one main reason for this raid was the explicit Christian culture of the company – the high proportion of Christian employees and the company's mission statement about "love, peace, joy and faithfulness" that aimed to promote Christianity – which irritated the local authorities. According to the report, such a repression was meant to warn other foreign businesses in China owned by Christians with a similar strategy and mission.

This section has presented the opportunities and challenges that are faced by Christians, especially foreign Christians, in China. My concern here is whether or not Christianity can be one source and actor of a new public morality in contemporary China. To be sure, Christians will remain a minority in China, making up some 5–10 percent of the population in the decade ahead. But as Carol Lee Hamrin (2008) nicely puts it, "Perhaps this seed can grow into something with far greater impact than sheer numbers would predict." As indicated, China today faces a crisis of values that threatens not only to destroy its moral basis but to upset its economic and political reforms. But, in facing this crisis, as argued by Hamrin (2008), China lacks "widely accepted and effective moralizing agents. The family, village, and neighborhood all have been seriously weakened, first by socialism and then by urbanization; socialist values are seriously discredited; Confucianism as a philosophy lacks an organized mass base; and variants of Buddhism and folk religion have not proved to be modernizing agents." This explains why a growing number of intellectuals have advocated the idea of adopting Christianity as part of China's modernization efforts (Bays 2003). It is thus interesting to see how Christianity, with its institutional structures, strong moral values and size, could exert a latent capacity in playing a critical role in rebuilding China's moral order.

Research Questions and Design

Previous discussions have brought out two issues that explain my research questions: first, the relationship between Overseas Chinese investors and their possible influence on China's building of its hard and soft economic power. Second is the role of Christians, especially entrepreneurs, and Christianity as

---

3 See http://www.chinaaid.org/2007/11/large-australia-environmental-product.html (accessed 31 October 2011).

moral actors in China's modernization process. Now the question is, as posited by Zhao in his article in *Esquire* that we mentioned at the beginning of this chapter, whether or not Christianity can help China's market economy to gain its spirit or, quoting Aikman (2003), "If Christianity itself, which had been such a powerful, if not fully understood, ingredient in the global pre-eminence of Western civilization, could be a worldview that guides China's pathway into the twenty-first century."

These two broad issues are related but they are obviously different. If I were to deal with both, this book could be too long and complicated. Also, instead of testing the macro-theory explaining the relationship between China's capitalism and Protestantism, recognizing that China's reform was not initiated or motivated by any religious groups including Christians, I am more concerned with exploring the relationship between religious beliefs and economics from a micro-perspective, namely, from the point of view and the understanding of Christian individuals. Therefore, my research question will be limited to how, and to what extent, Protestant Christianity, in particular Christian ethics, has affected the business conduct of Overseas Chinese Christians and the "Christian-based firms" in China, and with what consequences?

The search for an explanation to this more specific question involves a set of three additional questions. First, how do beliefs affect actions? And what are the specific Christian values and practices that manage to generate certain economic behaviors in those Christian entrepreneurs? Second, what kinds of business activities as well as business firms result from these beliefs and values, how different are they from the others, and what kinds of influence do they have on society? Third, who are those Overseas Chinese Christian businesspeople that are working in China, what kinds of activities do they do within the nation, and how different are they from other Overseas Chinese businesspeople? This research is thus an attempt to examine these questions.

However, to make my stance clear, it is worth clarifying here that (1) the interest of this research is not to compare Christians and non-Christians, but mainly to look within the Christian community to see whether religion could make a difference in their interactions with surrounding people and the environment and, essentially, in their ethical attitudes.[4] (2) Having emphasized the role of beliefs in economic conduct, this research does not intend to prove

---

4 Therefore, the arguments of this research concerning the ethical behaviors of Overseas Chinese Christians in China should not mislead us into assuming that Christianity is the only religion that has a role in moralizing business dealings in China. Moreover, this research does not seek, based on the limited number of interviews among Christians, to argue for a "unique" contribution of Christianity to China when the discussion intentionally avoids quantitative measures.

Weber's Protestant ethics thesis or to argue that Protestantism was the spiritual cause of the development of capitalism in China. Evidently this was not the case; as just discussed, the reemergence of religion was a result, and not the cause, of the economic change and development in China. More of this will be discussed in Chapter 2, but it should be noted here that this research does not argue for a causal relationship between ascetic Protestantism and the rise of modern capitalism in China. (3) This research emphasizes the way values and ideas in the heads of key actors affect their conduct, but the research proceeds with a definite awareness that the conduct of workers/businesspeople is equally guided by multiple factors including political and social conditions. Values are merely one factor contributing to rational economic behaviors.

This research focuses on Overseas Chinese, who have become the largest group of foreign investors in China and are often used by Western companies as intermediaries to China. Their critical role in providing the capital and expertise to fuel China's economic takeoff, especially after the Tiananmen crackdown in 1989, is occasionally acknowledged but not adequately studied. As argued by Redding (1990, 227), "They have for too long been acknowledged as intriguing, seen as possibly powerful, but never really been understood outside their own sphere. Even inside their own sphere, remarkably little scholarship has addressed the question of their economic life. And yet they are clearly significant. As actors on the world scene they cannot be ignored." This research therefore aims to fill this knowledge void partly.

However, the use of the convenient phrase "Overseas Chinese" can be problematic.[5] In this research, I use it loosely to include those self-described Chinese who were born and raised outside of China, irrespective of their nationality and ability to speak the Chinese language. They include ethnic Chinese in Taiwan, Hong Kong and Southeast Asia, as well as those in the United States and Canada. It might be controversial to include people from Taiwan and Hong Kong in a list of Overseas Chinese, especially since the latter is now technically part of China. But, as argued by Redding (1990) in his study on Overseas Chinese capitalism, the business behaviors and culture of people from Taiwan and Hong Kong are generally more similar to those of the rest of the Overseas Chinese than to people from China. As this research is about entrepreneurs who have had different business norms, entrepreneurial

---

5 There are at least four views concerning the use of the term " Overseas Chinese" or *hua-chiao*: (1) Chinese living outside China on a short-term basis; (2) Chinese who are residents of foreign countries and who have not lost their Chinese citizenship; (3) Chinese who are citizens of foreign countries as well as their offspring born and brought up in those countries; (4) all persons who regard themselves as Chinese irrespective of their national status or their ability to speak the Chinese language (Wu and Wu 1980, 118).

culture, as well as religious experiences from those living within communist China, in order to study the impact of these Overseas Chinese on Chinese society, it is therefore seen as appropriate to include them in this research.

It should be noted here that this research has focused mainly on the particular group of Overseas Chinese residing in Shanghai. Shanghai was chosen as my field site for a few reasons: First, it has been one of the main cities for Overseas Chinese investments in China in recent decades and is therefore a suitable and important site for conducting such a research. Second, as we will discuss in Chapter 3, Shanghai has historically been a city famous for its large international communities and mission works. As was mentioned by the Presbyterian E. C. Lobenstine in the *China Mission Yearbook* of 1925, next to London and New York, "Shanghai is the most important center of missions in the world" (quoted in Clifford 1991). Its importance for Christianity in China today can be understood from the fact that both the Chinese Christian Three-Self Patriotic Movement Committee and the China Christian Council are headquartered in Shanghai. These are the only official religious associations based in Shanghai while the rest are located in Beijing. To be sure, Shanghai is the place in China where Christianity and foreign business ventures have met and produced fruitful results. But the decision to choose Shanghai as my *only* field site was mainly prompted by practical considerations. My ethnographical fieldwork was initially planned to cover Shanghai and another city in China to provide a comparative perspective. But the size and diversity of China and the nature of my research, which I will explain soon, have in fact forced me to limit my activities to just one city. The great differences in political and socioeconomic conditions, including the business and religious scenarios in various cities, as well as the practical constraints of time, energy and finance to travel among different areas have prompted me to narrow down my research to one location. Also, because of the difficulty in accessing the Overseas Chinese Christian groups, given their unregistered nature and the religious controls placed on foreigners in China as has been indicated in the earlier paragraphs, it has taken me an extensive period of time to gain access to the contacts and more importantly, their trust. It was thus practically difficult to cover two cities in my limited 8-month stay in China. But, as expected, Shanghai can be unique in its development; one should therefore be careful when generalizing from the case studies of this research in making broader conclusions.

Research Methods and Profile of Respondents

This study is based on data gathered through participation observations and in-depth interviews with Overseas Chinese Christians. Ethnographic methods were selected as an appropriate way to examine both the individual and corporate expressions of faith in China, given religious controls that make alternate data collection methods on religious activities difficult. Most important, these methods facilitated my main purpose of discovering the understanding, practices and outcomes of the combination of faith and business (Berg 2009; Denzin and Lincoln 2000) and helped me to capture the context in which those perceptions and behaviors took place, as justified by John Van Maanen (1979, 10):

> No matter what the topic of study, qualitative researchers…claim forcefully to know relatively little about what a given piece of observed behavior means until they have developed a description of the context in which the behavior takes place and attempted to see that behavior from the position of its originator. That such contextual understandings and empathetic objectives are unlikely to be achieved without direct, firsthand, and more or less intimate knowledge of a research setting is a most practical assumption that underlies and guides most qualitative study.

Throughout my fieldwork in Shanghai from December 2007 to July 2008 (several interviews were conducted in Taiwan in October 2007), I conducted 60 face-to-face, semistructured and open-ended interviews with a diverse group of Overseas Chinese Christian investors and high-ranking managers, 20 of whom were women. I also carried out 17 interviews with their employees or colleagues. In addition, I conducted extensive participant observation by attending various activities held in my respondents' companies. These mainly included religious activities offered to employees, such as prayer meetings, Bible study sessions, Sunday services and company Christmas celebrations, as well as nonreligious social gatherings that included company picnics, luncheon meetings and employees' family gatherings. In several cases, I was allowed to spend one or two days in my respondents' offices to observe how people interacted or worked, although I was not able to attend any formal business meetings. Businesspeople are generally guarded about their own companies, seeing their business practices and decisions as confidential and private. Beyond that, these respondents were being asked to talk about things, such as their failures or struggles in business or relationship with their employees, which many businesspeople, even the most confident and neutral professionals, might be reluctant to disclose. This explains why they were reluctant to allow me, an outsider who was trying all means to examine their business behaviors, to join in their business meetings. Besides this, I participated in as many activities as I could that were conducted by Overseas Chinese businesspeople fellowships, including their committee meetings, men's and women's groups, marriage conferences, baptisms, etc.

A snowball sampling method, that is, recruiting interviewees through existing networks of friends, acquaintances and interviewees was used for three main reasons. First, since no comprehensive list of Overseas Chinese Christian businesspeople in Shanghai has been found to exist, initial contacts were mainly based upon my personal network in Taiwan and Shanghai. This contact choice explains why Taiwanese composed slightly more than half of my sample. Second, since questions related to business and religious activities are either private or very sensitive in nature (if we remember how foreigners are regulated in their religious activities), an effective means of getting more truthful answers was through referral from a middle person (mainly from an entrepreneur who had already been interviewed) that both parties would know and trust. Most people could trust my identity, or rather the motivation and purpose of my research, more readily because they could trust the individuals who referred me to them. Third, snowball sampling served my purpose of exploring the social networks of Christian businesspeople as well as finding out their moral reputations, which might be an indicator of their ethical performance among their peers. In most cases, respondents would be asked to suggest another suitable Christian interviewee. Some people would indicate that they could not think of any, but most would suggest one or two names after some consideration. In so doing, I managed to make a list of people who held a higher level of concern for business ethics in the eyes of their peers than did others.

However, as is to be expected, some people did not wish to be interviewed. In fact, at the outset, gaining access to both business groups and individual entrepreneurs was a formidable task. The main reason was the religious restrictions that were placed on them; they were cautious about the risks that might be involved in disclosing their business and religious practices. On one occasion, I was scolded by an academic-turned-manager of a Taiwanese company for the possible threat of "exposing the secret of Christian groups to the communist government." He refused to listen to my explanations but instead said that I should not try to deceive him as, he said, "I was a professor and I know what you guys are doing." Others began to worry, or show regret, after the interviews were conducted. For instance, one interviewee requested me to delete his contacts from my phone after the interview; another wanted me to send my interview data out of China, with the immediate concern that it would otherwise be stolen by others and thus expose the interviewees' identities. Another interview which was conducted in a restaurant with a Christian leader as well as a businessman was abruptly terminated because he suspected somebody was spying on us and overhearing our conversation. Also, many were reluctant to be questioned about business or ethical issues or their private faith. In particular, when I came to the more sensitive part of the research regarding actual business practices which were ethically problematic, I faced the difficulty of finding an appropriate stance that would convince those with whom I spoke that I understood their situations and "was thus a person with whom they could 'feel comfortable' enough to trust," as Jackall (1988) described in the entry issues that plagued his fieldwork. Another problem was the frequent travel and hectic schedule of these individuals and the lack of a clear reward, which made some of them reluctant to spend time being interviewed.

However, after spending significant amounts of time in these circles and making many explanations and attempts, including assurances of confidentiality, I managed to interview a few key people and, through their referrals and reputations in the community, other businesspeople were willing, or felt secure, to accept my request. Many would first ask detailed questions about my background and purpose for the study before answering my questions. The fact that I am a Malaysian Chinese who previously studied in Taiwan, then later in Singapore, as well as my ability to speak Cantonese, probably influenced the way some people, especially those from Malaysia, Taiwan, Singapore and Cantonese-speaking Hong Kong accepted me. More importantly, my identity as an evangelical Christian (some people would ask me about my denominational background) made my access into their community much smoother. Yet this might occasionally have affected the reliability of some of their responses as they tended to give me what are perceived as "theologically correct" answers. This is to be expected in all varieties of human research where the people involved generally like to cast themselves in a positive light. In my research, this happened occasionally with interviewees who were highly confident in their religious and business experience and saw my interview as a God-given opportunity to convince me and my readers of their "correct" understanding regarding certain issues. It also happened with some people who seemed to have problems in understanding me as a "disinterested" and objective researcher who was prepared to accept all kinds of responses, rather than a fellow believer, during our interview. It is therefore conceivable that a non-Christian might have been able to gather somewhat different replies from the same set of respondents on the nonfactual questions. In this regard, the information gathered is supposed to be seen as the product of certain interactions and relationships between my respondents and myself, as suggested by Mishler (1986, 82): "The interviewer's presence and form of involvement – how she or he listens, attends, encourages, interrupts, digresses, initiates topics and terminates responses – is integral to a respondent's account."

The inherent limitations of the interview-based approach and snowball sampling, such as self-delusion, as well as the smaller and nonrandom sample, have already been acknowledged. Recognizing this, I have made certain efforts to enhance the validity and reliability of my data. First, to cross-check the information and to guard against self-delusion, I checked, as far as possible, the consistency of the respondents' answers with that of their employees or colleagues or other respondents in the same community. For this, I completed 17 interviews with my respondents' employees, half of whom were nonbelievers, and conversed with their family members, pastors and church members.

Second, as my purpose was to seek understanding and theoretical insights into the relationship between faith and business, I did not need a sample of subjects representative of the whole population of Overseas Chinese businesspeople in China. Yet, I tried to select interviewees of different nationalities, gender, age, business type and size to increase the variety of my samples. In order to do this, I conducted participation observation at the nine Overseas Chinese businesspeople fellowships that I could find in Shanghai and attended the two international churches that existed then.

Third, I relied on my intensive participation observation to provide additional information. As mentioned, I participated as much as I could in their religious and corporate activities in order to check the consistency of their answers, as well as to look for examples of behaviors to examine their answers and ask for justification if questions arose. Also, I was fortunate to have the opportunity to stay with several of my respondents during my fieldwork. Upon my arrival in Shanghai, I stayed with a business couple from Taiwan through the recommendation of a mutual friend. My stay with them gave me plenty of time to ask questions and talk through many issues which were not initially included in my interview questions, but nonetheless were very important to my understanding of their lives in China. Then I moved on and stayed with a woman pastor, who was in charge of several Overseas Chinese businesspeople fellowships in Shanghai. I had met her several years before in Singapore while she was studying at Singapore Bible College. Because of our friendship, she was happy to host me and introduce me to her friends. I was then able to interact with many businessmen and women who came from different countries and I started to recruit future subjects from the acquaintances that I made there. Thus, the snowball began to roll. I also had a valuable opportunity to stay at the workers' dormitory owned by one of my respondents, who operated a hair salon. Given the fact that I knew their boss, the ten female workers were quite reluctant to share with me about their feelings and opinions in relation to their work or faith. But after a week of eating and staying with them, they began to trust me more and tell me their stories. This allowed me to gain a better knowledge of the feelings or thoughts of people working under a Christian boss. For the rest of my time in Shanghai, I stayed with two Overseas Chinese entrepreneurs' families, with one for a few weeks and the other for several months. My daily interactions with them as well as with their families and friends allowed me to have a closer and more realistic look at the fabric of what they were thinking and seeking in business and faith. Additionally, I interviewed several of the subjects two or three times to track the progress of some of their decisions and practices. As far as I could, I attempted to find examples of behavior and to challenge my respondents for justification so as to guard against self-delusion or wishful thinking. In reporting the results of my findings, I have attempted to allow the interviewees to speak in the first person, as much as the page limitations allow, in their own words. This is one of the ultimate guarantors of validity in studies utilizing the interview method (Mishler 1986).

Most of the interviews were conducted in Chinese, though a few were in English, based on a semistructured questionnaire with open-ended questions. I interviewed the 60 respondents and their 17 colleagues or employees myself, and I then recorded and transcribed all the interviews verbatim. Many quotations throughout this book are my own translations. The interviews usually took from two to three hours and were basically divided into four main parts. The first two parts dealt with religious background and the career profiles of the subjects; the third was concerned with their business and managerial practices; and the last part contained the faith–business relationship as well as ethical values and their relationship to personal faith.

The interviews included these questions:

1. When (before or after coming to China) and where did you become a Christian?
2. Are there any people, events or books that had an important impact on your conversion?
3. What kind of religious activities do you participate in? How often? Any change over time?
4. What kind of jobs or businesses have you had before and after coming to China?
5. Why did you decide to work in China?
6. Why did you decide to enter the present business?
7. What is your purpose in doing business? Why do you want to be an entrepreneur or manager?
8. How would you define a successful (Christian) entrepreneur and an organization?
9. What are the key elements that affect the organization's survival?
10. What kind of corporate culture do you intend to build?
11. Is there anything written down when you are in the process of making a large-scale decision?
12. Is there a guiding principle which affects your choice of what to do with the business?
13. How did you pick up ideas about business behavior?
14. Do you have a mentor? What are the influences that he/she has on you?

15. Are there any reference groups you identify with?
16. Were there any specific support systems that assisted you in getting started? What support systems do you have now?
17. According to your understanding, what are the ethical norms that Christian faith requires you to follow?
18. Do you see any conflict between your faith and business (past and present)?
19. Does your faith have a direct or indirect influence in your business? Is it helpful for doing your business (past and present)?
20. If you were not a believer, would you do things differently in your business?
21. Before and after your conversion, how did you deal with people at work: with fellow workers, with supervisors, with subordinators, with customers, with government officials etc. In these relationships, how do you decide what to do or not to do? Can you provide examples of events, incidents, and issues that have affected your interactions with others?
22. Are there any other guidelines (besides Christianity) you use, such as traditional values, etc?
23. How did you pick up ideas about integrating (or not integrating) faith and business?
24. Describe a recent business failure and explain why it happened.

I conducted most interviews at people's offices during business hours. In this way, I could observe business operations and the corporate culture. However, I conducted a few of the interviews at the subjects' homes because the entrepreneurs preferred to be interviewed in a place separated from their employees. Further, I conducted a few of the interviews at church after Sunday services, on the way to immigration offices or in other places when the schedules of individuals were too tight for an interview in their offices. These respondents are referred to by their initials or pseudonyms in order to protect their identity and security.

The methods, procedures and limitations of the research have already been acknowledged. But there is another issue that has affected this research and the final presentation of the research. It is related to the difficulties in obtaining accurate data and the lack of a previous sociological study on Christianity, business ethics and Overseas Chinese. Any analysis of the religious community and activities in China is expected to face this problem, as noticed by Hunter and Chan (1993, 10): "In the modern era there is no readily available set of provincial or district level surveys to which one can refer for accurate data with regard to religion." If the task of obtaining useful data regarding the local religious community can be that arduous, it is clear that my attempts to find accurate data about Overseas Chinese religious groups in China could be extra-laborious if not impossible. The main reasons are two: the limited number of official publications as well as social science research on religion in China typically ignore the Overseas

Chinese, because they are foreigners, a category which is not included in the imagination of the indigenous "Christianity fever" in the minds of academics, and also because the number of Overseas Chinese in China is small, and they are thus presumed to be insignificant. Furthermore, again, because of the religious restrictions in China, these foreign Christians tend to keep a very low profile in their activities and are happy to be ignored or excluded from any public or scholarly attention. In fact, they have endeavored not to expose their activities "unnecessarily" to outsiders. This adds to the difficulty of any attempt to understand them and have access to their influence. Noticing all these problems, this research is thus to be seen as a preliminary study of a long-ignored yet increasingly important group.

Profile of respondents

The profile of respondents is summarized in Table 1.2.

Table 1.2. Profile of respondents

	Female	Male	Total
(a) Nationality			
Taiwan	14	21	35
Singapore	3	4	7
United States	2	5	7
Malaysia	1	4	5
Hong Kong	0	3	3
Canada	0	2	2
Korea	0	1	1
(b) Age group			
31–40	5	5	10
41–50	11	20	31
51–60	4	11	15
>60	0	4	4
(c) Marital Status			
Married	5	37	42
Divorced	6	2	8
Single	9	1	10
(d) Years in China			
Up to 5 years	11	10	21
6–10 years	8	13	21
11–20 years	1	17	18

(Continued)

Table 1.2. Continued

	Female	Male	Total
(e) Position in company			
Owner	10	15	25
CEO/ GM or equivalent	1	16	17
High-ranking manager or equivalent	7	9	16
Professional	2	0	2
(f) Business type			
Manufacturing	7	19	26
Trading	3	5	8
Construction	2	5	7
Retailing and wholesaling	3	1	4
Food	1	1	2
Cosmetics	0	2	2
Professional services	4	6	10
Finance	0	1	1
(g) Years of being a Christian			
Up to 5 years	8	8	16
6–10 years	2	5	7
11–20 years	2	4	6
>20 years	8	23	31
(h) Conversion			
Before coming to China	14	33	47
After coming to China	6	7	13
(i) Charismatic tendency			
Charismatic	9	16	25
Pro-charismatic	3	5	8
Against/noncharismatic	2	10	12
Unclear	6	9	17

Respondents were recruited from Overseas Chinese Christian entrepreneurs who attended religious services regularly and resided in Shanghai. In this research, I followed a broad definition, as suggested by Campbell (1992, 271), that an entrepreneur is "the head of a business who takes an active role in decision making, risk-taking and day-to-day management of a business in which he or she has majority ownership." It thus can refer equally to someone who has started a one-person business, to someone who is a principal in a family business or partnership, or to someone who is a shareholder in a joint venture company which he or she runs. I extend this category to include high-ranking managers who have played a similar role as entrepreneurs, that is, are in charge of decision making and management, except for holding ownership of the company. The requirement that the respondent had to be in a "business enterprise" ruled out those in nonprofit organizations. The profit motive and thus business ethics in these nonbusiness organizations were seen to be less of a burden.

The nationality composition of the respondents appeared to be relatively reflective of the overseas population in Shanghai and those attending the religious communities I visited. More than half (58 percent) were Taiwanese, followed by Americans (12 percent), Singaporeans (12 percent), Malaysians (8 percent) and Hong Kongers (5 percent). Hong Kongers were underrepresented in this sample as I only managed to access the Cantonese community at the final stage of my fieldwork.

The backgrounds of the Taiwanese respondents represented two potent streams of cultural upbringing. One group was the migrants who went to the United States through their tertiary studies. They were normally in their late forties or fifties, with children still studying or staying in the US and were therefore traveling frequently between the two countries. Most of them went to China as CEOs or senior managers of multinational corporations assigned to head the Chinese office because of their familiarity with the language and culture. They had generally converted to Christianity through campus ministries in the US and had served actively in local churches before returning to China. The second group was people trained in Taiwan, individuals who brought with them knowledge and experience directly from Taiwan. Most of these people were younger, in their early to mid-forties, generally self-employed and typically having their families with them in Shanghai. A large number of them were new converts and had certain charismatic backgrounds. While people from the latter category constitute the majority of people in the Christian business communities now, the key leaders remain people from the former category.[6] This is mainly because they went in earlier through the first wave of China's open-door policy in the 1980s, and also because they already had experience serving in churches in either the United States or Taiwan.

In terms of positions held by these people within a company, about 40 percent were business owners, while 30 percent were in top management as CEO or general manager or other positions. Another 12 percent were high-ranking managers, such as the human resource director or chief engineer.

---

6 This is understandable as the US investments in China declined dramatically after 1989 while the number of Overseas Chinese, especially those from Hong Kong and Taiwan, rose in 1990s. This explains the increase of the second group of people and the decrease of those from the US.

In terms of age as a Christian, half of the respondents had been in the faith for more than 20 years. 26 percent had been Christians for five years or less. Among the 13 respondents who became converts to Christianity after they entered China, 10 of these individuals converted because of family or business problems. Among the 47 respondents who were already Christians before entering China, about 30 of them indicated that they went with a calling or a mission, whereas 12 mentioned they received their calling, an issue that we will discuss in the following chapters, after entering China through their involvements in church and religious activities. About 81 percent of such people were either charismatic Christians or had a strong tendency toward charismatic teachings although they might belong to conservative groups. This would have a certain influence on some of their business behaviors and values, as I will explain in the following chapter. In summary, the sample represented a group of relatively spiritually mature Christians, if age as a Christian is to be taken as indicative of spirituality.

Plan of the Chapters

In this chapter I have presented the general economic and religious backgrounds of this research, the methods employed in collecting the data and the central questions that I would like to answer in this book.

In Chapters 2 and 3, I will try to lay a theoretical foundation for the following empirical studies. Chapter 2 is a critical review of Weber's works on the Protestant ethic and Confucianism, explaining how they provide a general backdrop and framework for this research. The chapter ends with a discussion on the relationships between beliefs and actions, aiming to trace how beliefs affect, nourish, redirect or mutually encourage economic behaviors.

The task of Chapter 3 is to analyze the overseas communities in China in general and in Shanghai in particular. As discussed, ethnic Chinese from Asia are the greatest foreign investors in China and one of the most effective bridge builders in helping China's modernization process. Most studies on Overseas Chinese have attributed their business success, inside and outside of China, to the efficacy of Neo-Confucian ethics. This chapter provides a different picture. Through a review of previous research and my empirical examples, it becomes clear how a significant group of Overseas Chinese Christians exist and how they systematically apply their faith to economic activities. It also provides evidences showing how personal piety, which seems to be unrelated to, or best, excluded from economic behavior is in fact one of the primary forces in the formation of certain Overseas Chinese' business ethics and behaviors in a secular society such as China.

Chapters 4 to 7 are the empirical extension of the previous theoretical analysis on beliefs and business behaviors among Overseas Chinese Christians. Chapter 4 goes into detail about the worldviews of Christian businesspeople, exploring the broader attitudes inherent in their religious ethos which induce and influence their economic motives and activities. Attitudes, including a strong drive to succeed, self-discipline, frugality, a sense of calling, integrity and innovativeness are highlighted through an analysis of the 60 Christian businesspeople that I interviewed in Shanghai.

Chapter 5 moves on to a detailed analysis of the organizational expression of the Christian business ethic in China. Following on Chapter 3's discussion of how Christianity has closely been integrated into some of the Chinese believers' values, practices and relationships, this chapter asks: How do those influences manifest themselves in the present-day mentality and behavior of Christian entrepreneurs? What kinds of organizations result? This chapter focuses on the second question through examining three types of "Christian companies" (owned or run by Christian owners/managers), in part by emphasizing their collective values, their culture and their role as moral agents as well as bearers of ethics and duties. The result is an institutional/corporate expression of the Protestant ethic.

Chapter 6 is a study on the relationship between religious communities and Christian ethics, which is inspired by Weber's work, "The Protestant Sects and The Spirit of Capitalism" ([1906] 1946b). According to Weber, the early Protestantism within America affected economic productivity through two channels: The first channel was through the rise in productivity directly because of more diligent work attitudes, more rational lifestyles and higher motivation to accumulate economic capital, a topic that we have discussed extensively in the previous chapters. The other channel was indirectly through the formation of universal trust, norms and regulations which were built on the "superior community of faith" such as Puritan sects in the West. It is the second channel, namely the formation of Christian communities, which will be dealt with in this chapter. It highlights (1) how Christianity helps generate social networks for its members; (2) how these networks of mutual aid and trust help strengthen economic activities; and (3) the effects of Christian fellowships in shaping values and inducing moral obligations.

Chapter 7 is a study on women and Christian business ethics. Research has shown that more women have become entrepreneurs in China lately. A recent report by the Xinhua News Agency on 4 July 2002 claims that women entrepreneurs make up about 20 percent of all the entrepreneurs, and 41 percent of them work in the private sector. What appears to be intriguing and equally if not more important to this research is that such numerical significance of women not only exists in the business field but also in the religious field.

Gender imbalance in church attendance is certainly an undisputable fact in China; it is now estimated that 80 percent of the Christian members are women. The consequence of this fact, namely, the growing importance of women in both business and religious fields, is the indispensable importance of the issue of gender in our discussion on Christian businesspeople in China.

However, perhaps unsurprisingly, knowledge about these Chinese women in general and Christian women in particular remains very limited. The purpose of this chapter is thus to provide a detailed account of the ethical performances and personalities of Overseas Chinese Christian businesswomen to fill a gap in our knowledge about the "female Protestant ethic." It is hoped that such an account will help to answer the following questions: How are "ascetic practices of the self" expressed through these businesswomen? Are there any distinctive features of the female Protestant ethic, habitus or personality? It is worth emphasizing that Weber did not have gender on his mind when he wrote about the Protestant ethic. This discussion, therefore, hopes to shed light on a neglected aspect of an old topic.

In the final chapter I intend to provide a few implications from this research.

Chapter 2

RELIGION AND ECONOMIC LIFE: THE PROTESTANT ETHIC AND MAX WEBER'S LEGACY

This study is about how religion and, in particular, Christianity, is influencing both the economic practices and the orientations of Overseas Chinese Christian entrepreneurs in China. The topic and primary focus of this study clearly pay tribute to Max Weber's work on the economic ethics of world religions in general and *The Protestant Ethic* in particular.

The main concern of the study is not to test or apply Weber's thesis concerning Protestantism and the rise of the spirit of capitalism to China. Nor does it aim to confirm or refute Weber's argument on Confucianism or to search for any equivalent or a Chinese religious ethic analogous to Weber's type case in modern China. The main purpose of this research is instead to apply Weber's motivational approach, that is, to explore the consequences of religious motivations in the realm of economic activity in a study of the Christian ethics of Overseas Chinese Christian entrepreneurs in China. This research is an investigation of the importance of religious values and commitments to gain an understanding of economic actions. Such an approach is rare as most research on Weber and Chinese society is either concerned with refuting or refining the Weberian thesis on Confucianism and China or with searching for equivalents for the Protestant ethic in China. This typical approach has been important in calling attention to the role of Asian religions, especially Confucianism, in promoting economic development in East Asia. Nevertheless, it has unavoidably neglected the actual role and influence, if any, of Protestantism as well as Christian ethics within the Asian context. Thus, in what follows in this book, I will attempt to contribute to the research that aims to fill this gap. This chapter starts with an overview of Weber's analysis of the Protestant ethic and the evolution of this issue. It then moves on to Weber's work regarding China and Confucianism. The chapter concludes with a discussion of the relationship between beliefs and social action, which is the theoretical framework of this research.

The Protestant Ethic Thesis: Calvinism and Capitalism

The Protestant Ethic and the Spirit of Capitalism, which was first published in 1905 and later revised in 1920, has remained controversial and critical, and has become, as believed by sociologist Daniel Bell, "probably the most important sociological work of the twentieth century" (1996, 287). Weber's account has been reiterated on countless occasions, so it is unnecessary to repeat it in detail. I shall focus, instead, only on what I consider to be the central propositions of his argument which are more related to my research.

In his original essay, Weber embarks initially on identifying the origins of the historically unprecedented business ethos or "the spirit of modern capitalism," that is, the distinctive moral attitude toward economic activity and the methodical style of life which was demonstrated by early Calvinist capitalists (Baehr 2002). The new attitude, which Weber illustrates with quotations from Benjamin Franklin, possesses certain traits which are uniquely "modern," includes both an understanding of moneymaking and work as a moral and religious obligation and not a meaningless chore as well as an understanding of calling that is central to one's identity and deserves one's best capacities. It is this feeling of responsibility to moneymaking which Weber sees as the most significant difference between modern capitalism and the forms of capitalism of the Middle Ages, in which "money-making was regarded as socially degrading and morally and religious[ly] dangerous" (Fullerton 1928, 163). But what is the origin of this modern spirit? Weber suggests that it may have originated from the Calvinist ethic, a product of the Protestant Reformation of the seventeenth century.

Weber argues that the Reformation changed Western Christianity substantially. From a religion that promoted rejection of the world, it was then turned to one that supported inner-worldliness. Standing in a direct and unmediated relation to God, the lay believers were freed to live their lives solely under the scrutiny of individual conscience and the Bible, with the removal of the Catholic Church and its priests and sacraments as the bridge between man and God. However, Calvinism's individualistic soteriology and doctrine of predestination (God by his grace had predestined each man's eternal destiny and there was nothing one could do to change it) had left its adherents with the psychological tension of "salvation anxiety" as believers sought to prove to themselves and others that they were among the chosen. As it was believed that the elect differed externally in this life, the most important kind of activity for believers was one that produced visible evidence of God's blessings. Material success was therefore a tangible and convenient indication that provided evidence of salvation and inner worth. As hard work assured success, it was therefore believed that endless labor could glorify God.

With this mentality, as well as the moral obligation to work, Calvinists created a work ethic – one that emphasized unremitting diligence, thriftiness and delayed gratification – which brought an unprecedented degree of rationalization and systematics into social and economic affairs.

As each believer was in practice a priest on his or her own, the disciplines that were practiced only in the pre-Reformation monastery were then transferred to both the family and factory, where every believer was expected to exert ascetic control over his or her daily life in order to live up to the status of being saved. It was in this direction that the Protestant ethic contributed to the ethos of capitalism in Weber's scheme. The religious responsibility imposed on the believers made them not only diligent, but also moral and ascetic. According to Weber, this motivation of being honest in business was simply a religious motivation initially. It was because of their belief, motivated by their concern for their eternal salvation, that Protestant businessmen were willing to offer services with good quality and better prices. Yet such practices ended up bringing about economic benefits; the Protestant businessmen acquired loyal and long-term clients and their businesses grew. It should be noted that the Protestant code of ethics, historically speaking, was not new (Weber 1992, 121–8). But the provision of a psychological sanction to enforce adherence to this code was, however, exceptional (Weber 1992, 197).

> The essential point…is…that an ethic based on religion places certain psychological sanctions (not of an economic character) on the maintenance of the attitude prescribed by it, sanctions which, so long as the religious belief remains alive, are highly effective…only in so far as these sanctions work, and, above all, in the direction in which they work, which is often very different from the doctrine of the theologians, does such an ethic gain an independent influence on the conduct of life and thus on the economic order. This is, to speak frankly, the point of this whole essay, which I had not expected to find so completely overlooked.

It is also important to elaborate here the Calvinists' new understanding of work as a calling ordained by God. As originally conceptualized by Luther, the idea of "calling" (*Beruf*) was that the highest expression of Christian morality came not through monastic asceticism and withdrawal from the world, but in the fulfillment of earthly obligations and roles that were assigned to each individual. For Luther, all people were equally obligated to fulfill the commands of the gospel, and this fulfillment was not to be accomplished apart from the world but in the sphere of the secular life itself. Weber sees this conception of the calling as the first and most important step toward a new understanding of the secular life. Nevertheless, as Weber argues, Luther's idea of calling remained conservative and traditionalistic as it did not possess a "world-affirming" attitude. "For the Catholic, 'calling,' or 'vocation,' was to live the religious life apart from the world. 'Calling' for Luther was to live the secular life religiously, to serve God within one's calling (*in vocatione*). The final step remained to be taken, namely, to serve God by one's calling (*per vocationem*)" (Fullerton 1928, 102). It was in Calvinism that this final step was accomplished; behavior toward secular work which had previously only been tolerated was now ideologically justified (Marshall 1982, 155). For the Calvinist, the greater glory of God was the supreme motivation for work. Therefore, it was intrinsically important for the faithful not only to work, but also to work in an extremely diligent and systematic manner. Also, one should seize opportunities for self-improvement in work, viewing it as God's invitation to join in his ministry on earth. In essence, to have "virtue and proficiency in a calling," as explained by Weber, individuals were required to work effectively and to live a disciplined life that emphasized a methodical character of worldly asceticism with the sole intent of glorifying God. Work, as part of this disciplined life, was not merely an economic means but had a spiritual end; the fervent pursuit of wealth was no more an advantage but a duty.

> The increase of his profits and possessions was a conspicuous sign of God's blessing. Above all, his worth could be assessed in the eyes of men and of God through success in his calling, provided it was achieved by legal means. God had his own good reasons for choosing him for economic prominence…in contrast to others…who had been singled out for poverty and drudgery. (Quoted in Parkin 1982, 49)

This idea that success reveals a blessing from God was not unknown before Protestantism. Judaism had it too (Weber 1952, 223). But Calvinism gave it a central place by linking it with the idea that success may very well be a sign of salvation. Hence, the salvation anxiety released a vigorous energy into the economic field. The practical outcomes of this idea were inevitably significant: It was an impoverishment of lifestyle, a single-minded ascetic concentration on rational-methodical profit making and a keen desire to accumulate capital. Also, it was a change in attitude toward the surplus of the Protestant workers' labor. Calvinists dared not waste their profits on self-indulgence, but rather should reinvest their profits to achieve greater profits in the hope of gaining a little more assurance of being among the elect. They could only spend their money if it was practical and necessary and brought glory to God. Therefore, as Weber argues, their radical drive to reinvest and their pursuit of economic rationality transformed capitalism into its modern bourgeois variety. Yet, when the capitalist system was firmly established, Weber also mentions, there was less of a need that everybody accepted the notion of a vocation with an explicitly ethical dimension because people had to work in a systematic and relentless manner anyway if they wanted to survive economically.

In short, in his work concerning the paradoxical relations of religion to capitalism, Weber argues that it was religion and its asceticism which encouraged the emergence of a new type of capitalist mentality. Yet, such asceticism would inevitably disappear by the time capitalism became an iron cage. Utilitarian industriousness, which was induced by Protestantism, would then replace the search for salvation and eventually undermine the Protestant ethic and Protestantism itself (Turner 1996). It would then be a time of, in Weber's words, "specialists without spirit, sensualists without heart."

For a more complete picture of what Weber attempted to accomplish with *The Protestant Ethic*, we need to take into consideration his article, "The Protestant Sects and the Spirit of Capitalism" ([1906] 1946b), which explores the relationship between the ascetic sects and economic life. As this article will be discussed more in the following chapter on religious networks, it is enough to highlight here that the new information it supplies on the Protestant ethic is that Weber indicates a new mechanism, namely, the voluntary association or the religious sect, which had helped turn the "impulses of individuals to engage in inner-worldly ascetic behavior into a character trait that was favorable to economic rationalism" (Swedberg 1998, 128). Swedberg (1998) suggests, "This is a novel twist to Weber's previous argument by examining the manner in which a certain kind of group discipline, as distinct from an ethic (and its psychological inducements), nourishes and actively shapes the formation of the capitalist 'spirit.'" According to Weber, because sect membership conferred on its members an ethical proof and "a certificate of moral qualification" required in business matters (Weber 1946b, 305), it was highly valued by its members. Similarly, the sect community would ensure that its members maintain high ethical standards and succeed in business, for failure to do so would damage the credibility of the group as a whole. In *The Protestant Ethic*, believers were concerned to prove to themselves and to God that they were among the elect; in "The Protestant Sects," they were eager to prove to their fellows that they were hardworking, disciplined and trustworthy (Weber 1946b, 321):

> To repeat it, it is not the ethical doctrine of a religion, but that form of ethical conduct upon which premiums are placed that matters. Such premiums operate through the form and the condition of the respective goods of salvation. And such conduct constitutes "one's" specific "ethos" in the sociological sense of the word. For Puritanism, that conduct was a certain methodical, rational way of life which – given certain conditions – paved

the way for the "spirit" of modern capitalism. The premiums were placed upon "proving" oneself before God in the sense of attaining salvation – which is found in all Puritan denominations – and "proving" oneself before men in the sense of socially holding one's own within the Puritan sects. Both aspects were mutually supplementary and operated in the same direction: they helped to deliver the "spirit" of modern capitalism, its specific ethos: the ethos of the modern bourgeois middle classes.

In short, Weber's initial thesis as presented in the two essays on *The Protestant Ethic* and "The Protestant Sects" is, to quote Gordon Marshall (1980, 20): "The Protestant ethic caused the development of a unique attitude toward everyday (including economic) activities, namely, 'the spirit of modern western capitalism,' due to the psychological consequences of the doctrine of proof which operated to enforce rigid adherence amongst the faithful to the ascetic Protestant code of ethics."

Criticisms and Weber's responses

It is not surprising that Weber's revolutionary thesis has created a great deal of debate since it was originally published. Criticism and arguments emerge partly because of the complexity and ambiguity of Weber's arguments and illustrations, given that the essay exists in two versions, interspersed by the polemical rejoinders to Fischer and Rachfahl and by its complex relationship to Weber's other writings on capitalism and religion (Baehr 2002). It has to be recognized that there have been considerable differences of opinion over the correct interpretation of the Protestant ethic thesis (Turner 1998b). To present the major arguments and counterarguments in the debate arising over the past one hundred years is not possible in this chapter. I shall instead mention a few words about Weber's own participation in the debate and several criticisms which are more important to my research. Briefly, the following arguments and counterarguments serve merely to provide a simple background of what has been going on surrounding the Protestant ethic controversy.

As expected, most critics took issue with Weber's analysis of the origins of capitalism and the causal relationship between ideas and economy, in general, and with Calvinist beliefs and modern capitalism, in particular. Rachfahl and Fischer, Weber's principal critics, accused him of proposing an idealistic interpretation of history in opposition to Marx's historical materialism. Others reduced Weber's thesis to the proposition that "ascetic Protestantism caused modern capitalism" and criticized him for such a crudely monocausal argument (Trevor-Roper 1963). Still others, such as Tawney (1926), Robertson

(1935), Fanfani (1935) and Samuelsson (1961), argued that Weber's focus on the influence of religion, however important religious factors could be, is one-sided, artificial and overstrained; it is a result of an ignorance of developments not connected with religion. One typical example is H. M. Robertson's (1935, xi–xiii) critique which claimed that Weber "sought a psychological determination of economic events" that "saw the rise of 'capitalism' as the result of the rise of a 'capitalist spirit.'" He continued that he "wish[ed] to show that the spirit of capitalism has arisen rather from the material conditions of civilization than from some religious impulse." For Robertson and others who held similar views, Weber had ignored the many factors besides religion which were important for economic development in the West, for example, the Renaissance, the discovery and exploitation of the Americas and of sea routes to the Far East, and the influences of Roman law and of improvements in techniques of production and exchange.

Other theorists, such as Hartwell (1971), have pointed to the fact that capitalism existed prior to and has occurred independently of ascetic Protestantism. To take but a few frequently cited examples, capitalism existed in Italy, France, Spain and Portugal long before the Reformation era, whereas ascetic Protestantism seems to have given no impetus to capitalist development in Scotland, the Netherlands or Switzerland. Others have also argued that Weber underestimated the significance of Catholic, pre-Reformation merchants and bankers as vehicles of capitalism. Further objections concerned Weber's interpretation of *Beruf* (calling) and the theoretical weight to which he accorded this. Weber was also criticized for his failure to see that the ethic of capitalism, especially where it embodied frugality and self-discipline, was not peculiar to Protestantism. For example, Fernand Braudel found many of these qualities both in Catholic merchant and in banking families in the Italian city-states. Robert Bellah (1957) found them in Japan's Tokugawa Buddhism, Clifford Geertz (1960) in Java's Santri Moslems, and McClelland (1961) in India's Jains and Parsis. Twentieth-century social scientists have also found similar ethics in Eastern civilization. We shall soon return to the issue of Confucian ethics when we discuss Weber's legacy concerning China and Chinese religions.

In responding to his critics, Weber was progressively being drawn into a wider discussion. His initial question about the origin of the "spirit of capitalism" was expanded and shifted more toward the significance of this spirit (or ideology), together with other elements, in the development of a modern capitalist economy. In his four replies to his critics (1907–10) and in his second revision of *The Protestant Ethic* (1920), he argues that he was not suggesting that an affiliation to a religious belief-system alone would be sufficient to invoke a given economic system. He insists that his argument was rather that ascetic Protestantism had played an important role (though not causal) during the late sixteenth and seventeenth centuries in the creation of a new kind of economic mentality (but not modern capitalism itself).

This change of focus of Weber's thesis can also be seen from his lecture course known as the *General Economic History*, in his *Economy and Society*, as well as his essays on China and India. In the *General Economic History* (1950, 286), for example, Weber recognizes "as characteristics and pre-requisites of capitalistic enterprise the following: appropriation of the physical means of production by the entrepreneur, freedom of the market, rational technology, rational law, free labor and finally the commercialization of economic life." Given these necessary conditions, Weber argues, it could then be asserted that a rational, this-worldly ascetic ethic was crucial for the emergence of modern capitalism. It is now clear that Weber's thesis concerning the relationship between "religion and the rise of capitalism" encompasses two separate issues. Initially, he wanted to prove a more direct causal relationship between the Protestant ethic and the development of the "spirit" of modern capitalism. He was concerned to describe the origins of a unique "modern" attitude toward profits and work; capitalistic acquisitions related to other attitudes are acknowledged by Weber as long having predated Luther and Calvin. In this regard, the existence of "pre-Reformation capitalism" could not refute Weber's case. In the latter stage, Weber was more concerned instead to argue that religion was merely one of a range of factors that was responsible for the development of the modern capitalist order. Just as Weber assumed that the existence of a religious worldview was important for economic development, he also assumed that other objective factors were equally so. His examples about Siberian Baptist wholesalers and Arabian Calvinist manufacturers exhibited his concerns about the social, political and economic conditions under which modern economic developments might occur besides the "capitalist mentality" arising out of Protestantism. Herein rests the critical and complex issue about the interrelationship between religion and social change or between belief and action. I will go into more detail regarding this issue in the concluding section of this chapter.

But before I close this section, let me single out briefly one of the recent contributions and supplementary angles to the debate on the Protestant ethic which is of special interest to my research. It is Gordon Marshall's (1980, 1982) attempts to use empirical measures to examine the extent of the influence of Protestantism belief-systems on businesspeople. According to Marshall, the "spirit of capitalism" or the "capitalist side" of the argument in *The Protestant Ethic* had been ignored both by Weber himself and by subsequent commentators. He argues that Weber based his account entirely on Franklin's texts and thus failed to "corroborate empirically his assertion that the orientation towards economic activity allegedly induced by the belief-systems of ascetic Protestantism was, in fact, adopted by seventeenth-century businessmen" (1980, 17). To rephrase Marshall's comment, the question is then: What exactly are the economic consequences of the ascetic Protestant ethic for Christian capitalists?

Marshall's comment is relevant to this research as it shows the weaknesses of most studies that have attempted to apply the Protestant ethic analogy to Chinese contexts. As mentioned at the beginning of this chapter, most studies of this type are interested to prove or disprove the functional equivalent of Confucianism for the Protestant ethic. They thus practically ignore the applicability of the Protestant ethic to the daily business practices of its adherents and its significance in promoting voluntary associations in China. This is partly due to the fact that Protestantism was virtually insignificant in number and influence in the past decades in China. Yet, with the changes after the economic reform of 1978 and the revival of Protestantism especially in the city, we should now respond to Marshall's comment with more empirical studies on Protestant ethics within China. This research is an attempt along this line, investigating empirically (although not quantitatively) the economic consequences of the Protestant ethic for the new Chinese Christian entrepreneurs and managers.

Marshall proposes several ways of establishing whether the Protestant ethic has indeed had the economic consequences that Weber claimed it did. He suggests that we might expect these entrepreneurs to be honest and diligent, to reinvest rather than to consume, to expand systematically their businesses and to feel impelled to use their time and money efficiently. My research, in examining the dynamic of the Protestant ethic in contemporary China, has modified Marshall's list to include other elements such as innovativeness, self-discipline (to restrain from unethical business behavior such as accepting bribes), the feeling of being impelled to integrate religious values and business and seeing such an integration as part of their calling as entrepreneurs.

Weber's Study on China and Confucianism

Weber's study on Confucianism and Daoism, which is the first study in *The Economic Ethics of the World Religions*, is partly an extension of his work on the Protestant ethic and partly an independent inquiry into the sociological conditions which underpin the major differences between Occidental and Oriental civilizations (Eisenstadt 1968). To prove his thesis in *The Protestant Ethic* more convincingly, Weber turns to a comparative study of Asian cultures, and more especially Asian religions, to examine why their economic development differed so fundamentally from Occidental paths. He notices that other societies, in different historical periods, had the materials necessary to industrialize but had not yet done so. There clearly need to be certain circumstances for the rational variety of modern capitalism to emerge. He is thus concerned to find out the factors that brought these special circumstances into being. In the case of China, by comparing Chinese and Western societies, and more particularly Confucianism and Protestantism, he seeks to show how the latter stimulated and the former slowed down the rise of modern capitalism.

In contrast to his approach in *The Protestant Ethic*, Weber starts with a typological difference in the social and political structures between European and Chinese societies in *The Religion of China*. In order to characterize the more enduring aspects of Chinese society, Weber focuses on the distinctive features of Chinese cities, Chinese patrimonialism and officialdom and Chinese religious organizations. China had, according to Weber, no urban independence and no bourgeoisie of the Western type. Its legal system and the state were patrimonial in nature and therefore not conducive to industrial capitalism, which demanded a high level of predictability and calculability from the political system. There was little rational technological, scientific, accounting or economic policy. The Chinese economic mentality was thoroughly traditionalistic and conservative as the economic prosperity of the cities relied on the centralized government. So were the various forms of religion in China: As the emperor was the supreme ruler and high priest of the realm, his religious function was never challenged. Traditionalistic mentality expressed as much and was further strengthened through the kinship system, which rested on the belief in the power of the ancestral spirits and in the need to sacrifice individual desires. The kinship system was consolidated by the large number of social and economic functions that were regarded as familial obligations. In return, it protected its members from adversity but in doing so discouraged a work discipline and the rationalization of work processes.

Viewed from this perspective, according to Weber, China was in essence dominated by traditionalism in all spheres of life. This mentality was reinforced by the Chinese "ethos," which Weber characterizes as the status ethic of the literati. Classical Chinese education aimed at cultivating men "for a certain internal and external deportment in life" (Weber 1951, 120) instead of the specialized training of the expert official. Weber observes, "Confucianism, like Buddhism, consisted only of ethics and in this *Tao* corresponds to the Indian *dharma*... Confucianism meant adjustment to the world, to its orders and conventions. Ultimately it represented just a tremendous code of political maxims and rules of social propriety for the cultured men of the world." In essence, Confucianism was based on ethical maxims serving mainly to ensure the tranquility of the social order and the inner man. Its supreme virtue, upon which all other virtues were dependent, was piety toward parents and superiors.

According to Weber, the conservative nature of Confucianism was mainly due to its lack of a concept of salvation, which was presented as the pivotal element of Protestantism. Because of its lack of "any tension between nature and deity, between ethical demand and human shortcoming, consciousness of sin and need for salvation, conduct on earth and comprehension in the beyond, religious duty and sociopolitical reality," Confucianism could not support "conduct through inner forces freed of tradition and convention" (Weber 1951, 235–6). As the "Confucian had no desire to be 'saved' either from the migration of souls or from punishment in the beyond" (Weber 1951, 156), Confucianism deterred man from forming a personality which was "placed methodically under a transcendental goal" (Weber 1951, 235). Missing also in the Confucian tradition was the notion of asceticism. According to Weber, "Asceticism...was not only unknown in Confucianism but was despised as parasitism" (Weber 1951, 229). The Confucian way of life, though rational, was "determined, unlike Puritanism, from without rather than from within," resulting in "mere sobriety and thriftiness combined with acquisitiveness and regard for wealth" but "far from representing and far from releasing the 'capitalist spirit' in the sense that this is found in the vocational man of the modern economy" (Weber 1951, 247).

As a result, for Weber, Confucianism and Protestantism represented two comprehensive but mutually exclusive types of rationalism: While Protestantism formed a rational mastery of the world, Confucianism was a rational adjustment to the world (Weber 1951, 248). Therefore, the typical Confucian practiced ethical behaviors to attain and preserve "a cultured status position," and he used this as an adjustment to the social order, as self-perfection, and, above all, to fulfill familial obligations, whereas for Calvinists, the systematic control of one's nature was a tool in the service of God that led to a mastery of the world. For Weber, it was this difference in the prevailing mentality that contributed to the rational capitalist development in the West but the absence of a similar development in China. Nevertheless, despite the uniqueness identified in Confucianism which was seen as incompatible with the development of rational capitalism, Weber argues that in the case of China, values were not the decisive factor in explaining why capitalism failed to develop; the main reason was instead the patrimonial structure of the Chinese state. In short, Weber sees the role of religion and values in the case of China as secondary and dependent on social conditions.

Criticisms and evolution of the issue

Weber's study of Confucianism has received considerable scholarly attention (Bellah 1963; Eisenstadt 1985; Sprenkel 1964; Turner 2008) and has become a crucial point of controversy among scholars of Chinese studies (Berger and Hsiao 1984; Tu 1984). Basically, it has gone through different phases in the Chinese studies application of Weber's argument. Initially, in line with Weber's argument, research (Levenson 1958 and Fairbank 1979) found that Confucianism did not possess certain important elements similar to the Protestant case and that it thus hindered the modernization of China.

However, economic growth in East Asian countries such as Japan, Hong Kong, Taiwan, South Korea and Singapore, which was seen as "Confucian society" influenced by Confucian cultural tradition, has attracted worldwide attention and shed new light on Confucianism (Berger and Hsiao 1988). As Ronald P. Dore (1996, 17) wrote: "All of those economies which can be described as 'of Confucian culture' have experienced periods of rapid economic growth – at rates of ten per cent or more – and all the other countries have not." Many scholars claimed that they found counterparts to a Protestant ethic in Confucianism and took Weber to task for his Eurocentric and erroneous analysis of Asian religions. One prominent example is Yu Ying-shih's (1987) *Zhongguo Jinshi Zongjiao Lunli yu Shangren Jingshen* (The Religious Ethic and the Spirit of Merchant in Early Modern China), in which he tried to demonstrate that one can detect in both the Neo-Confucianism of the Song and Ming Dynasties and in Zen Buddhism a turn toward an inner-worldly asceticism that was similar to the Protestant ethic. Also, the "Way of the Merchant" practiced by a strata of scholar-merchants during the Ming and Qing Dynasties matched Weber's portrayal of the spirit of capitalism. In essence, Neo-Confucianism, which was critically different from the classic Confucianism in *The Religion of China*, had reinterpreted the role and practice of the merchant class which was directly related to the underdevelopment of traditional Chinese capitalism (Yu 1997). Others (for example, Berger 1988; Tu, 1984; King 1983) have criticized Weber for not recognizing that Confucianism, like Protestantism, demanded self-control, frugality and unrelenting effort, and that these defining qualities underpinned the modern development of East Asian capitalism. King, for example, in his paper (1983) "Rujia Lunli yu Jingji Fazhan: Weibo Xueshuo Chongtan" (The Confucian Ethic and Economic Development) proposes that the impressive Asian economic miracle has posed the greatest challenge to Weber's thesis on China and in particular his comments on the Confucian ethic. He suggests that the "Confucian ethic is the cultural explanation to the puzzle of East Asian socioeconomics" (King 1983, 75). Tu has since delineated the content of Confucian ethics and discussed how they might have contributed to the rapid growth of these East Asian countries (1991, 31):

> These include the idea of the self as a center of relationship, a sense of the community of trust modeled on the family, the importance of established

ritual in governing ordinary daily behavior, the primacy of education as character building, the importance of exemplary leadership in politics, the aversion to civil litigation, the belief in consensus formation and the practice of self-cultivation. The value system that seems to be most compatible with these features is commonly labeled "Confucian ethics."

Also, others have felt that Weber misunderstood the nature of Chinese patriarchy (Hamilton 1984) and that his construction of a purported ideal type of traditional China was problematic (Hamilton and Kao 1990).

In short, it is generally agreed by scholars that Weber's analysis showing that Confucian ethics had inhibited the growth of an entrepreneurial spirit and thereby the development of capitalism in China has been empirically falsified (see for example Berger 1988). The simple fact that capitalism is now flourishing in various parts of East Asia has seriously challenged Weber's thesis. Clearly, Weber had failed to notice the rational asceticism aspect of Confucianism and overlooked the potential role of Confucian ethics in the process of capitalist development. He had also neglected the fact that there is probably more than one route to capital formation than the one he found in Western Europe and the United States.

However, having said that, there are several reasons that Weber's thesis still attracts scholarly attention. First, his questions concerning the religio-ethical roots of capitalism are still highly important, even if some of his answers have to be discarded. As argued by Wei-Ming Tu (1984, 78), Weber's thesis about the "motivational component of a belief system" is generally correct. His sociological approach to examining the relationship between motivational values and a particular form of economic ethic is very useful in helping us to clarify our interpretations of the entrepreneurial spirit. This contribution of Weber is particularly crucial to my research as I have employed his motivational approach as an explanatory model in attempting to understand the economic behavior of Overseas Chinese entrepreneurs. I will go into this in the following section.

Further, in explaining the emergence of East Asian capitalism, to be fair to Weber, we cannot ignore the fact that first, as many scholars have pointed out, Weber's concern was not how capitalism spread to non-Western cultural areas once it had emerged, but how the West generated capitalism and the rationalization process. Thus, Weber's thesis on China might not necessarily be challenged by the Asian economic miracle as it was a historical fact that Asian societies, including China, did not generate capitalism on their own and out of their own cultural content (Ku 2010). Second, as implied by my first point, part of the explanation for the Asian economic miracle lies in the distinction made by Weber himself between the problem of origin and the problem of diffusion or transplantation of capitalism. Weber (1951, 248) argues that there were inherent obstacles, of which Confucianism was not the main one, preventing capitalism from emerging on its own in traditional China. But Weber believes that the Chinese would be quick to adopt the capitalist form of business once it had been invented and "taken-off," that is, once capitalism had developed as a self-sustaining business ideology independent of its religious origins in the West. According to Weber, "The Chinese in all probability would be quite capable, probably more capable than the Japanese, of assimilating capitalism which had technically and economically been fully developed in the modern culture arena" (Weber 1951, 248). This is particularly true in explaining the case of Overseas Chinese capitalism. As argued by Godley (1981), we can anticipate a great number of Overseas Chinese entrepreneurs, Christian or not, to have caught the spirit of Weber's elusive Protestant ethics due to their unique social and historical conditions. Being born and raised outside of China, many Overseas Chinese have assimilated Western values and business practices to a significant degree. This assimilation is accelerated by an English language education and the frequent necessity to work with or to compete with European competitors in overseas settings. The need to conform to the colonial policy and rules of commercial law in some overseas societies, as suggested by Godley (1981), has become a crucial factor stimulating in Overseas Chinese an awareness of basic Western business values. This situation obviously provides them with an opportunity and encouragement to absorb the Protestant spirit that may well have been absent in China. It is therefore not surprising to see Overseas Chinese displaying a certain rational business ethos akin to Protestant ethics.

Moreover, as argued by Hamilton (1991), it is understandable if we find Confucianism seems to be able to legitimize modern capitalism; all religions and value systems have the function of legitimizing what is going on. The issue is not whether Confucianism can legitimize industrialization or not but whether it has the transformative potential (this is what Weber saw as its critical downside) to redirect the process of industrialization.

It should be mentioned here that in my attempt to explain the behaviors of Overseas Chinese Christian entrepreneurs, I am aware that however important Christian belief may be in my findings, I do not intend to imply that Christian worldviews or ethics have no relation with Confucianism or traditional Chinese values but are rather solely a result of the Christian faith. It is well accepted among scholars that Confucianism is the bedrock or foundation of Chinese culture, as has been argued by Fenggang Yang (1999), for certain Confucianism ethical values are indeed the "habits of the heart" of ordinary Chinese. It is therefore practically impossible to disentangle Confucian values from Christian values in the modern Chinese Christian businesspeople, as both sets of values are deeply instilled and integrated in them. In other words, it is very difficult to show a "totally independent" Christian effect on Chinese Christians. A study on Korea, an Asian country with 25 percent of the total population classified as Christian, might illustrate my concern. This study shows there is an unusually strong tendency for "Confucian values and practices" to be found among Korean Christians (quoted in Koh 1991: 193). According to this research, most of the Christians are identified as at least "marginal" adherents of Confucianism due to their convictions and practices of filial piety, deference to seniority, prohibitions on endogamy, ancestor worship and so forth. This therefore proves positively that Christian beliefs and certain Confucian practices coexist in Korean Christians' lives. We can expect a similar situation exists in Chinese Christians' lives too.

Yet, on the other hand, there are also ample counterarguments suggesting that Confucian values have not been as strong in the Overseas Chinese communities, especially among the Southeast Asian Chinese, as they have been more inclined toward Buddhist or Daoist beliefs (Wang 1988). The idea of "post-Confucianism," as raised by Wei-Ming Tu (1990), also suggests that Confucianism no longer dominates the Sinic world, as "these societies have been so Westernized – or more appropriately 'Americanized' – that the presence of the Confucian heritage can no longer be taken for granted."

It is beyond the scope of this research to solve this puzzle. But it is probably safe to conclude here that Confucianism as an integrated ideology is fading in the Overseas Chinese Christian community but not to the extent that the deeply embedded values and daily practices are being eradicated totally. As we have seen in the case of Korean Christians, the legacy of Confucianism continues to have a hold, though in a much diluted form, on the minds and behavior of Asian Christians, especially in issues related to family practices and relationship building. For many Chinese Christians who possess both value systems, now the issue is how Chinese traditional values are selectively preserved or reinterpreted to coexist with their newfound faith (Yang 1999).

Conclusion: Belief and Action

Weber's work on the Protestant ethic remains influential, despite the extensive criticisms that have been raised against its principal conclusions, because, for one thing, this work has provided us with an intriguing understanding of the problems of meaning and action in historical and sociological analysis (Turner 1999). It points to the importance of motivational factors and to subtle and non-obvious connections between cultural and religious beliefs and behavioral outcomes, which historians, economists and sociologists have often neglected (Bellah 1963). Peter Baehr, in his introduction to the new translation of

The Protestant Ethic and the "Spirit" of Capitalism and Other Writings (2002, ix), has aptly summarized Weber's contribution to sociology: "Weber's achievement was not to definitively answer a riddle but to stake out a territory fertile of new puzzles at the heart of which is the claim that religious forces, not simply economic ones, paved the way for the mentality characteristic of modern, Western capitalism." Not surprisingly, then, after 100 years of publication, *The Protestant Ethic* is now undergoing another intensive phase of study (Whimster 2005); centenary conferences on Weber's work have been held in London, Madrid, Buenos Aires, Montreal, Heidelberg, Munich and other places. Moreover, new translations based on historical principles by Peter Ghosh as well as new translations by Stephen Kalberg, Peter Baehr and Gordon Wells have all demonstrated the ongoing scholarly interest in Weber's work (Whimster 2005).

In this final section, I will trace the relationships between belief and (economic) action to formulate my theoretical framework. There are a number of different ways in which one could phrase the question and bring out the various interpretations of Weber on this issue. One way to raise the question, as suggested by Turner (1999), could be: Is the relationship between belief and economic behavior causal, contingent, analogous or one of "affinity"? Weber appears to change positions among diverse, sometimes overlapping, but in other respects, contradictory lines of argument.

The strong thesis presented by Weber is that beliefs are a cultural precondition which facilitates economic change. Calvinist values were a direct causal factor in the creation of the capitalist spirit. In *The Protestant Ethic*, Weber concludes that modern capitalism would not have originated without the Protestant ethic, and there was also evidence showing that the absence of such an ethic held back economic development elsewhere. In Weber's words (1958, 174),

> As far as the influence of the Puritan outlook extended, under all circumstances, and this is, of course, much more important than the mere encouragement of capital accumulation, it favored the development of a rational, bourgeois economic life; it was the most important, and above all the only consistent influence in the development of that life. It stood at the cradle of the modern economic man.

This direct causal argument suggests that the Protestant ethic was not only a historical coincidence existing before rational capitalism but that it was *the* decisive force in forming its spirit. Modern economic conduct is seen as "born" from the spirit of Calvinist asceticism.

This strong monocausal argument, which is labeled by Weber in his later work as "foolish and doctrinaire" (Turner 1998b, 10), has earned him the reputation of an idealist. Weber's attempt to demonstrate a direct link between religious ideals and values and a capitalist mentality has often been thought of as a critical response and alternative to Karl Marx and historical materialism (Salomon 1945; Wiley 1987; Antonio and Glassman 1985). Whereas Marx treated values and beliefs (the "opiate of the masses," as he put it) as byproducts of class or material interests, Weber has been seen as showing that ideology was what had made the modern capitalist world possible.

Yet, it is safe to say that most scholars now do not think such a direct and "mechanical" causal approach, "that one thing results from another in a simple linear way like one billiard ball pushing another" (Redding 1990, 7), is capable of explaining social change. Clearly, there have been other factors, however important religion may be, involved in the explanation of the emergence of modern capitalism. They obviously include structural, economic and political factors. A monocausal approach is thus not convincing.

A second thesis presented by Weber, a weaker one, is that the capitalist spirit could be shown to have a "special affinity" with the Protestant ethic, namely, that the moral value of the early Protestants was highly congruent with the economic value of the rational capitalists. Because of mutual reinforcement, rational capitalism led to religious success, and religion stimulated capitalist success. A more cautious approach to this weak thesis is summarized by Weber (1992, 91) as below:

> In view of the tremendous confusion of interdependent influences between the material basis, the forms of social and political organization, and the ideas current in the time of the Reformation, we can only proceed by investigating whether and at what points certain correlations between forms of religious belief and practical ethics can be worked out.

This interpretation of Weber suggests that his main concern was to explore historical connections between meanings which were embedded in economic actions. It rejects the criticism against Weber that he was an idealist, and argues that for Weber, the idea was not *the* factor but one of the many factors in a complex situation and might be identified as one of the crucial, yet often neglected, factors (see for example Aron 1970; Besnard 1970; Warner 1970; Moore 1971). This interpretation of Weber is also shown in Gerth and Mills's (1957, 60–1) introduction to their selection and translation of Weber's works. They refer to Weber's thesis: "By such a comparative analysis of causal sequences, Weber tried to find not only the necessary but the sufficient conditions of capitalism...in his pluralism, he naturally did not consider this type of personality the only factor involved in the origin of capitalism; he merely wished to have it included among the conditions of capitalism." Scholars such as Ling (1991) and Turner (1998b) have also suggested that Weber in fact rarely talked about causal explanation and was more willing to think about the "elective affinity" between circumstances, which took into account the complex relationships among a variety of factors – material, geographic and economic circumstances, and the importance of interpretation rather than explanation. Thus, according to these scholars, Weber was concerned to elaborate and discover complex "affinities" or "congruencies" between meaningful actions. As Peter Berger (1963, 950) has observed:

> Weber's understanding of the relation of ideas to history can be seen most clearly in his concept of "elective affinity" (*Wahlverwandtschaft*) that is, of the way in which certain ideas and certain social processes "seek each other out" in history.

This interpretation, which views the relationship between religion and economics as not one of causation but of congruence, links closely to the third interpretation in which Weber describes ideas as having the function, not to directly influence action, but to redirect interests and actions like switchmen through providing worldviews. In his famous metaphor, Weber argues that it was "not ideas but material and ideal interests [that] directly govern men's conduct. Yet very frequently the 'world images' that have been created by 'ideas' have, like switchmen, determined the tracks along which action has been pushed by the dynamic of interest" (Weber 1946a, 280). Based on this understanding, people's actions are driven by their desire for ideal interests – which include religious benefits such as a desire for salvation and to escape the sufferings in hell – as well as material interests. But even though interests propel the actions of people, Weber adds, these interests do not necessarily determine the exact direction of people's actions. It is religion that creates "images of the world" which conditions the direction in the manner of "switchmen." In *The Economic Ethics of the World Religions*, Weber provides several examples of such "world images" conditioned by various religions, including Confucianism which we just mentioned and shows how these had set similar ideal interests on very different "tracks."

Lastly, while Weber is concerned with subjective meaning, he also realizes that the effects of human actions were typically not their intentions and that history was, in fact, the "unintended consequences of actions." Weber argues that it was not simply that purposive actions had consequences which were not recognized by social actors, but that "the outcome of human actions often worked against social actors in such a way as to limit or reduce the scope of their freedom" (Turner 1996, 10). This aspect of Weber's argument finds its dramatic expression in *The Protestant Ethic*, where he argues that the spirit of capitalism was the unanticipated consequence of Protestant faith (Baehr 2002, xiii):

> Between action and consequence lies a chasm that no one can bridge, let alone control. The Puritans of Weber's story did not know, could not know, what they were doing; people can only know what they intend to do, and even then their self-knowledge is highly imperfect. More precisely, the Protestant radicals, inspired by a powerful sense of the divine, helped unwittingly to create a social and economic order its pioneers would have seen as godless, materialist, and devoid of any ultimate purpose.

Obviously, these four aspects of Weber's argument concerning belief and its behavioral outcomes are not wholly consistent. All of them seem to be empirically possible but they are not mutually exclusive. Weber has invoked, in short, pluralistic explanations for the direction and influence of religion on economic change. Nevertheless, precisely because of their ambiguities, these explanations are helpful in underlining the complexity of the economic situation and the difficulty in locating the interrelationship between belief and action. It might be worth mentioning here two caveats to our discussion on belief and action. It is common knowledge that what people believe and what they actually do may not always coincide. For example, there is a difference between believing that work is a God-given task and treating it as such. A Christian entrepreneur may be ideologically committed to the doctrine of work as a calling to express his love to God, but he may, in the daily organization of his enterprise, treat his work as an opportunity to make quick money and exploit his workers. What this research could do to reduce this inevitable problem is to look for the *consistent* patterns of someone's practices, such as the business strategies and corporate policies of a person's corporation, against his or her belief to understand more effectively the connection between his or her belief and action. An added caveat in tracing the behavioral outcomes of religious belief is that it is likely to be difficult to uncover what someone really believes in his or her mind. Belief can motivate people to act in certain ways but it can also be used as a convenient way of legitimating an attitude, or it can be both. To solve this problem, this study focuses on religious practices and habitus, not only on doctrines and ideas, to uncover people's fundamental commitments in religion.

A critical issue which has arisen in Weber's sociology of religion, and now arises in this chapter and this book, is the contingent nature of the connection between religious values – especially in terms of their motivational significance – and economic behavior. Understandably, this research does not argue for a direct causal relationship between Christianity and economic development in China given the fact that multiple and complicated factors are involved in China's political and economic transformation process. Also, it would be unwise to make a stronger case about Christian ideas and economic development in China because of the restricted religious conditions in China and the cultural influence of Confucianism among ordinary Chinese.

This research, instead, aims to examine the indirect and sometimes non-obvious consequences of Christian belief in adherents' attitudes, practices and strategies in business. It therefore tends more toward the second and third interpretations of the Weber thesis, that is, that religion (including its beliefs and practices) can nourish, redirect, mutually encourage and support economic actions. As has been mentioned, I am aware that however important religion may be, it is merely one factor, albeit a crucial and frequently neglected one that affects economic activities. Within this research, then, it is assumed that in alliance with other important socioeconomic factors, religion can influence and has influenced individuals' behaviors and the formation of the ethics of modern economic life. This research has, in doing so, indirectly assumed the congruence and affinity of Christian ethics to the modern economy.

The findings which this study provides can only be of a preliminary and exploratory nature, keeping in mind that a vast network of connected elements is involved in the issue. They can therefore be seen as part of a more complex explanation. As suggested by David Martin (1990, 206) in his study on Pentecostalism and the economic activities in Latin America, "The posited linkages and plausible likelihoods" of religion and economic behavior have to be couched in terms of "frequent concurrence and mutual reinforcements": Evangelical religion and certain economic behaviors "do *often* go together, and when they do so appear mutually to support and *reinforce* one another" (italics in original). Based on Weber's insights into the role of values in action, the following chapters provide a reasonable amount of evidence for exploring and examining the multiple relationships between individuals' piety and their business activities.

Chapter 3

OVERSEAS CHINESE CHRISTIAN ENTREPRENEURS IN POST-1978 CHINA (SHANGHAI): BUSINESS, FAITH AND ETHICS

Over the 30 years, Overseas Chinese, returned compatriots and their families showed their tremendous love of their hometown and motherland... Overseas Chinese will be written into history for their role in supporting the opening-up and reform, in the creation of a positive international environment and in the nation's social development...
—Yang Xiaodu, Head of the United Front Work Department of Shanghai, 2008 (quoted in Wang 2008)

Overseas-Chinese community is the mother of China's (economic) revolution.
— Cheng Xiyu (1994, 3–4)

Research has shown that the number of ethnic Chinese in China who came from Hong Kong, Taiwan and Southeast Asia grew significantly with China's open-door policy in the 1980s, and they soon became the biggest foreign investors in China (Huang 2003). According to official reports, more than 80 percent of the total foreign investments in China came from Overseas Chinese sources (see Table 3.1) (Chen and Hu 1997; Huang 1998). Studies also revealed that in China, 18 to 20 million people were employed by Overseas Chinese–owned or Overseas Chinese–invested enterprises by the end of 1994 (Tracy and Lever-Tracy 1997). Both of the quotations at the beginning of this chapter show that Overseas Chinese have been seen by politicians and intellectuals alike as bridge builders who, especially after the Tiananmen crackdown in 1989, have emerged as an important group in providing the capital and expertise for fueling China's rapid economic growth.

It is therefore reasonable to ask what kind of impact we can expect the Overseas Chinese to have on China's business environment, particularly in the area of business ethics. But to be able to discuss the influence of the Overseas Chinese, we need first to understand these peoples. This chapter will provide a brief review of the Overseas Chinese entrepreneurs within China, in general, and in Shanghai in particular. It also discusses their daily lives and their relationships with local people. This is important and relevant to our purpose since ethics, including business ethics, are firmly embedded in their personal relationships and the communities to which they belong.

General Portrait of Overseas Chinese Entrepreneurs and Their Business Ventures in China

The number and influence of the Overseas Chinese in China has grown dramatically in recent decades. Yet, such an involvement is not totally new as the Chinese diaspora has been playing an ongoing role in the economy of communist China, except during the Cultural Revolution (1966–76) period, since the founding of the People's Republic of China in 1949. But their influence has only very recently become more obvious and outstanding.

The groundwork for the involvement of the Chinese diaspora in China had already been laid long ago. As early as 1870, the Manchu government had stipulated policies to attract both the capital and the expertise of the *Nanyang* (Chinese in Southeast Asia) capitalists (Godley 1981). Following the Hundred Days Reform in 1898 and China's efforts to modernize its government, the consulate officials of China in Singapore, Tokyo and San Francisco further promoted an exchange of trade between local Chinese businessmen and China (Wang 1995). The Overseas Chinese businessmen that seized these opportunities were conferred titles that raised their status to that of *shangshen* (official merchants) (Wang 1995). These were the people who were initially forced to leave their homelands and move to Southeast Asia, East Asia and the United States due to famine, population pressure and revolutionary upheaval and typically started their lives in the foreign lands as poor coolies or small shopkeepers. Over time they began to play a role in China's economic development through their remittances and investments.

Their contributions to the motherland were in fact due partly to the unique character of "overseas" Chinese which was created by historical circumstances. Taking up residence in foreign lands, Overseas Chinese had grasped the chances provided them abroad and achieved an economic preeminence far out of proportion to their actual numbers. They also learned business values and skills through their daily interactions with colonial powers and European trading houses while maintaining their loyalty to the homeland and their traditional values, as described by Godley (1981, 173):

> As Westernized Chinese, men with practical knowledge of foreign ways who still desired to identify with elements of the traditional civilization, returning merchants came as close as anyone to maintaining that precarious balance between Western techniques and Chinese principles... they served alien masters, followed Western laws and developed a taste for certain aspects of a non-Chinese style of life. The nationalist awakening as experienced in the Chinese communities of Southeast Asia, however, helped revive interest in traditional moral teachings... as Confucian-capitalists and gentlemen-merchants, the Overseas Chinese may well have seemed to combine the best of both worlds. They brought capital and Western ideas but, unlike foreigners, they spoke Chinese, quoted the classics and were willing to elevate their own social position. Furthermore, they were not openly backed by gunboats. The existence of an independent base of wealth and power beyond the control of the Chinese government also set the Nanyang capitalists off from the rest of the merchant community and permitted these individuals much of the freedom usually granted foreign business interests. The throne needed their talent, initiative and capital not only to begin new enterprises but to pave the way for local merchants who continued to have little faith in government sponsorship. It was willing to pay the leading Overseas Chinese figures almost any price in terms of prestige, tax advantages and monopoly rights.

This lengthy quotation explains how historical and social conditions have promoted an unusual character in the Overseas Chinese, preparing them to be effective merchants and intermediaries in China's initial opening to the outside world and then to play an essential role in China's early modernization.

The situation is quite similar today. Although Overseas Chinese investments were "generally unwelcome, certainly suspect and eventually penalized" (Wang 1995) in the early period of the PRC, the situation changed following the third plenum of the 11th Communist Party Central Committee meeting in late 1978, a watershed moment in China's move down the path of economic reform. China again started to mobilize the ethnic Chinese to assist in its economic reforms. The Communist government now perceives ethnic Chinese as supreme sources of capital and expertise needed to assist China in its move from self-reliance to a more open policy, for two reasons. First, as just mentioned, Overseas Chinese are experienced traders with substantial wealth. Their "ungrounded commercial empire" has expanded rapidly and with significant success. More importantly, they are interested in investing in China. Second, their involvement is considered to be more favorable than that of non-Chinese foreigners by the Communist government because of China's policies of self-determination and its fear of foreign exploitation (Bolt 1996). Also, their established networks and their skills in converting Western market rationality into Chinese social mores have made them the effective bridge between China and global business (Bolt 1996). However, despite China's invitation, there were no serious investments by Overseas Chinese in China's commerce and industry until 1987 when they became more certain that the Communist government was firmly committed to the market mechanism and its market socialism was working.

The number of Overseas Chinese is, in fact, quite small when compared with the total population of China. There are an estimated 60 million Overseas Chinese individuals: 80 percent of them live in Asia, about 6.5 million live in North America, and the remainder, about 4.4 million, are scattered across South America, Europe and Africa (Ambler and Witzel 2003). However, these communities have been known for their commercial success and entrepreneurial drive and have exercised an economic power out of proportion with their numbers. Statistics show, for example, that in 1995, they had a gross domestic product in excess of US$500 billion and assets of approximately US$2 trillion, amounts significantly greater than can be found in China and nearly two-thirds of the level of the assets in Japan (Ambler and Witzel 2003). It is thus not surprising that the Chinese government has targeted Overseas Chinese through so-called patriotic appeals and various special policies and preferences. Ross (1988, 168) calls this preferential treatment a "reminder of their ethnicity and of their responsibility to their fellow Chinese on the mainland." One example of this kind would be the "Temporary Preferential Measures Regarding Investments by Overseas Chinese and Hong Kong and Macao Compatriots in Guangzhou." The special treatments given to Overseas Chinese include a reduction in land-use fees and tax fees, provision of special titles or cash awards to the investors and allowing their relatives to move from rural areas to the city (Bolt 1996).

Overseas Chinese investments have increased rapidly as China's reforms have deepened, especially when its economic ties with Asian developing countries (such as Malaysia, Singapore and Thailand) were strengthened in the 1990s. Among Southeast Asians, Singaporeans have been one of the largest investor groups in China. This is mainly due to its government's regionalization project by 1990 to encourage Singapore businesses to invest abroad. Consequently, its investments in China increased from US$53.28 million in 1990 to US$1.180 billion in 1994. Similarly, the Malaysian Chinese investment rate in China grew by 53 percent in 1994 after its government promoted an economic exchange

Table 3.1. Sources of foreign capital in China (cumulative 1979–93)

Source country	Percentage of total number of enterprises	Percentage of total value of foreign direct investment
Hong Kong	63.7	69.1
Taiwan	12.3	9.3
Macao	2.5	2.8
Singapore	1.8	2.2
Thailand	0.8	1.2
Subtotal	**81.1**	**84.6**
US	6.9	5.4
Japan	4.2	4.8
Other sources	7.8	5.2
Total (%)	100.0	100.0
No.	167,500	US$68.7 billion

Sources: State Commerce Bureau, *FDI in China: Analyses of Trends and Future Directions*, 1993; *International Trade News* (MOFTEC), 16 May 1994, 1.

with China in the early 1990s. The combined investments from Malaysia, Indonesia, the Philippines and Thailand rose from US$10.83 million in 1990 to almost US$692 million in 1994 (Bolt 1996).

Businesspeople from Hong Kong have always been China's largest foreign investor group. Hong Kong investors were moving factories and investments into China, mainly Guangdong, beginning in the 1980s. One main reason was the cheaper labor and land in China. It made good economic sense for Hong Kongers to move production into a low-wage area just across the border as soon as this became feasible under the "reform and opening" policies of the central government in the 1980s. It was also important that Hong Kong businesspeople, who speak Cantonese, could easily deal with local officials and suppliers in Guangdong and knew how to do business with them. Also, most Taiwanese invest in China through Hong Kong because of Taiwan's restriction on direct investments. Overseas Chinese from Southeast Asia have also used Hong Kong as a base for investing in China because of its dynamic environment.

The case of Taiwan is more complex due to competing claims over its sovereignty with mainland China. Yet, despite the political constraints, the Taiwanese continue to be actively involved in China's economy. The Chinese government has especially welcomed Taiwanese businesspeople as it sees the high levels of economic exchange as a means of providing China with an extra advantage in dealings with Taiwan. However, understandably, many in Taiwan are fearful that such dependent relationships could undermine its sovereignty. Therefore, limits are placed on exchanges of trade, investment and communications, which must then be directed through a third country or territory such as Hong Kong. Table 3.1 shows the importance of Overseas Chinese investments for China. It shows that more than 80 percent of the total investment in China was made by the ethnic Chinese in Asia.

Overseas Chinese Entrepreneurs in Shanghai: Investments and Relationships with Local People

Shanghai has long been a city known for its large international expatriate communities. In 1925, the census listed 37,638 foreigners in the city. This is remarkable given that other foreign cities in China such as Hankou and Tianjin had only perhaps 2,500 and 8,700 foreigners, respectively. Even British Hong Kong had only about 13,000 foreigners (Clifford 1991). The foreigners that occupied Shanghai were not just Westerners, but also Overseas Chinese. Reports show that Shanghai, as the country's prime manufacturing, commercial and financial center, had attracted large-scale investments from the Overseas Chinese since the late nineteenth century. Although Guangdong ranked first in volume of Overseas Chinese investments because it had the largest number of natives abroad, Shanghai was also successful in attracting a large proportion of Overseas Chinese industries, including tobacco, textiles and sugar production as well as commercial enterprises and finance (Lim 2006). The amount of Overseas Chinese investment in Shanghai reached 2,146,940 yuan in the period from 1900 to 1949 – a remarkable success given that Fujian, another region with a large number of natives from abroad, had only managed to reach half of that amount (Lim 2006).

Today Shanghai continues to serve as the headquarters for many foreign ventures. This became more so after its successful sponsorship of the Asia Pacific Economic Cooperation Conference (APEC) in October 2001 and the World Exposition in 2010. Significantly, according to a *China Daily* report on 7 October 2008, almost half of the foreign-invested companies in Shanghai were funded, fully or partly, by Overseas Chinese. The report mentions that in the years between 1978 and 1995, 60 percent of the projects and 56 percent of the capital of Shanghai's foreign direct investment came from Overseas Chinese and compatriots of Hong Kong and Macao. Another report shows that in 2005, the main foreign investors in Shanghai were from Hong Kong (24 percent), Japan (11.5 percent), the United States (9.8 percent), Singapore (5.5 percent), Germany (4.7 percent) and Taiwan (4.2 percent) (Wang 2006). Although investors from Hong Kong have composed the largest group of investors in China as well as in Shanghai, the importance of other Overseas Chinese, especially the Taiwanese, as just explained, should not be neglected.

In view of the growing amount of foreign investments in Shanghai and this city's ambition to regain its position as China's "global city," especially after Shanghai's Pudong was granted similar special privileges in 1990 that other special economic zones had, we can expect that more and more Overseas Chinese will settle in Shanghai (Tian 1999). Many of them first came as business investors or managerial professionals for multinational companies that were in need of Mandarin speaking professionals to handle cross-cultural issues. For foreign and especially Western investors, cross-cultural management issues, ranging from the interpersonal level relating to communication and negotiation, to the organizational level relating to human resource management practices and liaison work with government institutions, have been some of the hurdles that have seriously affected their business expansion. Thus, Overseas Chinese from Southeast Asian countries, Taiwan and Hong Kong are considered favorably by multinational companies in China as suitable candidates to solve these issues (Bjorkman et al. 2008). Their language expertise, their common Confucian heritage which might be similar to that of the mainland Chinese and their dietary habits have all created advantages for these Overseas Chinese in adjusting quickly to the local society.

The Taiwanese populace constitutes the largest Overseas Chinese community in Shanghai. According to a *Xinmin Weekly* report on 9 July 2001, there were about 300,000 Taiwanese living and working permanently in Shanghai and the surrounding area. This figure does not include businesspeople moving between Taiwan and Shanghai, estimated at about 10,000 people per month. The milestone "cross-traits" flight agreement that was signed by the leaders of Beijing and Taipei on 4 November 2008 has certainly increased this number dramatically. In comparison, there were only about 6,680 Hong Kong residents working in Shanghai in 2003 according to Shanghai municipal government statistics (Hong Kong Trade Development Council 2004), along with 35,000 long-term Japanese residents in Shanghai (Farrar 2005). In fact, in the random interviews which I conducted in Shanghai, the Overseas Chinese entrepreneurs whom I came across most frequently were Taiwanese. Among my 60 respondents, 35 of them were Taiwanese. The rest were Singaporean, American Chinese, Canadian Chinese, Hong Kong residents and Malaysian and Korean Chinese. But it should be noted that the great majority of the American Chinese that I met in Shanghai were in fact born in Taiwan and had then migrated to the United States after their tertiary studies there.

As mentioned, because of the common language and cultural heritage that the Overseas Chinese share with the local people, they usually consider themselves as having been well integrated into Shanghai society in comparison to other foreigners. In the case of the Taiwanese, the self-identified term "Shang-Tai-nese" might show their confidence in this (in Chinese "Shang Tai Ren" is an expression with a double meaning: one is "Taiwanese in Shanghai," while the other is "man in power") (Shen 2004). Yet, besides business connections, most Overseas Chinese socialize mainly within their own circles. The richest individuals remain in exclusive expatriate communities, while the rest live in upscale communities with guards at the main entrances. They play golf with their expatriate friends on weekends and sing karaoke at bars owned by foreigners, while their children attend the few and costly international/American schools or the international section of local Chinese schools, and they go to private hospitals run by Singaporeans when they are sick. Also, they join businesspeople's associations for Overseas Chinese which provide services from business networking to permit applications.

Yet this is not to say that they do not seek closer links with the local society. Indeed, relationships with local Chinese businesspeople as well as officials are critical in helping to maintain their enterprises in China. Also, in terms of daily life needs, they seek help from local Chinese for babysitting or helping with the housework and driving them to work or to school. They are eager to build *guanxi* with local people at all levels, yet they still find ways to keep their distance so as to protect their interests, as a Taiwanese businessman explained, "This is their place, we have to be good to them. But you can't be too close to them, if not they will take advantage of you." The example of *daibao* that I learned in my fieldwork in China as well as was mentioned by Shen in her study on Taiwanese capitalists in China (2004) displays the tension between the Taiwanese and local peoples. *Daibao*, or "foolish compatriots," is a common expression which the Chinese use to taunt the Taiwanese for their ignorance about both the local culture and prices of Chinese goods. It has become an open secret that some Chinese take advantage of this ignorance and purposely raise prices on the Taiwanese. But the Taiwanese are aware that they are treated differently or cheated, as was mentioned by my respondent who has been in Shanghai for more than ten years: "They call us *taibao* (Taiwanese compatriots) when they want us to come over for investment, but in reality they treat us as *daibao* (foolish compatriots)." Many people like her are upset over the fact that Taiwanese, despite being called "compatriots," are actually not only treated as foolish, but also as foreigners; they are charged much higher fees than are the local people in many respects including for their children's school fees in local Chinese schools and even for a down payment for a telephone line. This exemplifies an aspect of the mutual reliance, yet tense relationship, between the overseas people and the local Chinese.

After giving a few details of overseas daily life in Shanghai, I shall now return to the main subject of this research: the issue of business ethics. I will in the following paragraphs examine three specific relationships which exist between Overseas Chinese businesspeople and local people and the consequences for business ethics: (1) the relationship with local bureaucrats and the issue of corruption, (2) the relationship with local employees, which relates to the issue of labor exploitation, and (3) the relationship with Chinese women and the issue of sexual immorality that follows.

Relationship with local bureaucrats and clients

Most investments of the Overseas Chinese in China, especially those of Taiwanese, represent a new pattern of foreign direct investment which is characterized primarily by small- and medium-sized independent manufacturing firms, with 400–800 employees and an average investment of US$1.5 million (Hsing 1998). This is different from the common practices of multinational corporations that involve huge amounts of investment and therefore deal directly with the national government. By keeping their initial investments small, the Taiwanese investors negotiate mainly with low-ranking local bureaucrats. The effectiveness of their investments therefore results largely from the linguistic and cultural affinity, including an understanding of saving face and gifts between the investors and the local officials (Hsing 1998; Huang 1998).

Taking advantage of such privileges, these investors have endeavored, frequently engaging in acts of corruption, to cultivate interpersonal relationships with local officials so as to avoid much of the bureaucratic red tape. Their success depends not on the quality of the service or products, but on the relationship with local officials of various agencies including the public security bureau, the custom service, the tax bureau and so forth (Tracy and Lever-Tracy 1997). This situation obviously has become a great advantage for lawless businesspeople, while for others it has turned out to be one of the hardest ethical struggles. American anthropologist Aihwa Ong's (1999, 47) description of her research trip to Xiamen in 1993 exhibits the former situation. Ong mentions that local people frequently complain that Taiwanese investors and managers "have the local policemen in their pockets" and "tend to exploit their women, create corruption, and intensify unequal relations in the province across lines of gender, class, and nationality." My own experiences in Shanghai exhibit the latter situation. The Taiwanese chief executive of a semiconductor manufacturing factory told me that he had repeatedly received calls, or "threats," from competing local agencies asking him to give the very costly leftover materials to them in exchange for various privileges. As a Christian, he was caught in this dilemma as he was personally unsure of whether he should even release these materials or to which agency he should give them if he decided to do so.

A deviant type of *guanxi* is equally widespread in the dealings with local clients and suppliers. In an environment where business contracts are often decided by connections, especially political connections and bribes, activities such as social eating and money giving are typical and are seen by many as unique in Chinese types of networking. In essence, one's ability to deal shrewdly with the corrupt practices is thus at the heart of one's business success as well as of the particular ethical challenges faced in China itself.

Relationships with local employees

Another aspect of the tension between foreign investors and local Chinese lies at the heart of industrialization, that is, the relationship between employers and workers. There is much talk in China about Overseas Chinese factory owners, who exploit workers and mistreat them. Many respondents mentioned that local Chinese ranked the Taiwanese as the worst bosses with which to work, with Japanese and Americans following. In a study of a team of Hong Kong managers operating two factories on both sides of the Hong Kong–China border, Lee (1998) finds that labor control in China is military-like and punishment-oriented, while in Hong Kong, it is an open and contested process. Other research (Huang 1998) shows that many employers in China have adopted an authoritarian and military style of labor management. The recent spurt in suicides by workers of Foxconn, a manufacturing plant owned by a Taiwanese, at its Shenzhen facility highlights the seriousness of this problem.

The reasons behind such an unequal and exploitative relationship are complicated. It should be noted that it was only after 1979 that China allowed the existence of various private enterprises. As a result, as Schak (1997) argues, many Chinese have yet to develop the values of hard work, the initiative and the concepts of quality production for a market. Such behaviors are usually interpreted as resulting from a "big rice pot" mentality, which developed under a communist system that assumes the state would guarantee jobs for life, regardless of performance. Furthermore, workers in factories are virtually all farmers from poor inland provinces in China. Most of them are young, low-educated and female (Huang 1998). This also explains why they are not socialized or trained into being "modern" workers that can satisfy their result- and profit-oriented foreign owners. They are thus frequently seen by foreign owners as people who are "irresponsible, unreliable and lacking motivation," and who deserve to be controlled in a mean and often unethical way.

Relationships with Chinese women

Another tension, which often does not relate directly to business ethics but can be linked closely with business life, is the sticky relationship between foreign businessmen and Chinese women, or more concretely, sexual exploitation of Chinese women by foreign businessmen. A Chinese medical doctor's furious response toward my casual question regarding his impression of Taiwanese men might exemplify this tension: "All Taiwanese businessmen are lecherous. They leave their wives behind so that they can sleep with their Chinese secretaries and employees. Chinese women are equally stupid because they are seduced by money. Or maybe they are smart. If you work for him, you only get a minimum pay; but if you go to bed with him, you get a house which your salary will never be able to afford." His response obviously echoed Ong's comments on Taiwanese businessmen's "unequal relationship with local women."

Stories of Taiwanese men and Chinese women frequently came out during my fieldwork. Shen (2004), in her empirical study on Taiwanese businessmen mentions, "As Taiwan has become a new investor in the contemporary global economy, Taiwanese masculinities have simultaneously transnationalized. China and Chinese women have become the feminized bodies economically and sexually penetrated by masculine Taiwanese capitalism and businessmen." However, it should be emphasized that the businessmen of other nationalities are no exception in this matter. A report in *The Nation* on 5 July 1997, for example, shows that men from Hong Kong control the Shanghai sex industry. My own contacts seem to confirm many of the stories that I have heard. In December 2007, I was introduced to a young Malaysian couple, with their two little children, who had just arrived in Shanghai for a new post. A few months later when I met with the wife again, I was surprised to learn that the husband was involved in an affair with a Chinese girl. What turned out to be more serious was that the husband was in fact involved in multiple such relationships. The wife said, "It is hopeless for him to change as all the male (Singaporean) colleagues do the same thing. I can't believe that they actually went together and are very proud of it." Eight months after our first meeting, they were on their way to a divorce. This story is repeated over and over again among Overseas Chinese entrepreneurs. An important reason behind this is the custom, practiced in business communities in China, of making connections with clients or local officials through the practice of offering sexual entertainment.

My main purpose of delineating the relationships of Overseas Chinese businesspeople with the local Chinese is to show how these relationships become the hardest challenges that they face in doing business in China. Individuals' responses toward these problems can therefore be seen as an indicator of their values and ethical positions, which are presumably derived from diverse social, cultural, moral, and, more essential to this research, religious influences. More discussion on these ethical issues will be put forward in the following chapters as here my concern is to provide a general background of the business environment.

In thinking about the values or ethics of Overseas Chinese businessmen, some scholars as well as popular and business writers have somewhat automatically linked these ethics to Neo-Confucian ethics, as discussed in the previous chapter (Hicks and Redding 1983; Berger 1988; Hicks 1989; Redding 1988, 1990). As argued by Redding in his famous study on Overseas Chinese capitalism (1990, 2), "Directly Confucian ideals, and especially familism as a central tenet, are still well enough embedded in the minds of most Overseas Chinese to make Confucianism the most apposite single-word label for the values which govern most of their social behavior." Along the same lines, researchers (see for example Barton 1983; Landa 1983) have provided lists of the Neo-Confucian ethics, namely the capacity for hard work, frugality and high saving rates, family and kin-group solidarity, respect for education and commercial networks based on interpersonal trustworthiness, which are all regarded as absolutely necessary for the business success of Overseas Chinese, although there has been no consensus as to how far such values account for their business performance and entrepreneurial capacity.

The fashionable thesis claiming the extraordinary influence of the Confucian ethic on Overseas Chinese enterprise is contestable. Scholarly literature over the last decade or so has argued that significant differences, including identity and class, exist among Overseas Chinese (Gomez and Hsiao, 2001) and they have even challenged the "unique Chinese characteristics" (Chu, 2010) and the "vagueness of the notion of 'Chineseness'" (Dirlik, 1996). Indeed, the Overseas Chinese community cannot be taken as a homogenous unit; to do this is to demonstrate a common lack of adequate attention to the various subgroups as well as to the different set of values that exist and are mixed within the communities. This study attempts to show how Christian values exist and are not uncommon among the Overseas Chinese and how these values contribute to the heterogeneity of the group.

To conclude this section, I quote Huang's (1998, 68–9) study on the Overseas Chinese management style in the southern part of China to show how, in Huang's words, "a new way of management in Overseas Chinese invested enterprises," one which intriguingly combines Christian values with Confucianism, has emerged:

> There was an interesting case in the study in which a different method in labor management was employed. An overseas Chinese manager,

educated in the United States, believes that good management is based on proper moral standards established in the factory. He adapted moral teachings mainly from Confucianism and some from Christianity and inculcated them in his factory. In the factory, posters on the walls tell workers how to become good human beings, in which achieving such qualities as sharing, modesty, tolerance, and generosity are strongly encouraged. Rules and regulations are written in a literary format, which is thought to make workers feel comfortable about accepting them. Quotations related to morality are printed and distributed to workers. Meetings with workers are regularly arranged to discuss problems and to share decisions made between managers and workers. A local labor official told us that the turnover of workers in this factory was the lowest in the district though its wage level was also fairly low compared with most other foreign-funded enterprises. The reason workers stay on was related directly to the atmosphere of the factory and the way that the workers were treated. This case demonstrated that the Chinese cultural tradition seems to be nicely blended with Western ideologies in the management practice in China. Although it was the only case in the study, it represents a new way of management in Chinese TNEs [transnational enterprises].

Huang might be correct in saying that this case as such is indeed rare among the Overseas Chinese, if we remember how most foreign employers would prefer a military and controlling management style as just mentioned. Yet, if we focus only on Christian entrepreneurs, as I will show in the following chapters, Huang's example is not an isolated case. For many Christians who decide to invest their money and time in China, like the Overseas Chinese manager in Huang's story, the business provides extra responsibilities beyond just making money. Their religious values obviously play a role in making them different from others in constructing a more humanitarian corporate culture and management style. We might expect this "new way" of business management to become more common and to gain momentum gradually as more Christians come to play a significant role in China's modernization.

Christian Entrepreneurs among the Overseas Chinese in China

A study by Backman (2001) suggests that church membership is now "a new mode" (again, a "new" way) of networking among the younger generation of Overseas Chinese in Asian. To quote Backman (2001, 217):

> Though dialect and family links are still important among the older generation of Overseas Chinese businessmen in Asia, they are less so

among the younger generation. This isn't to say that networking and relationships are no longer important. They are, but it is the modes that have changed. Many Asian families now select the business school in the United States to which to send their children on the basis of the connections they might make there with the sons and daughters of other Asian business families…classmate connections are important, but one of the most important venues for fervent networking among Overseas Chinese in Asia has become the church. A growing number of Overseas Chinese business people are Christian – and often they are fundamentalist.

Indeed the number of Chinese Christians is growing steadily in various Asian countries including Malaysia (9.6 percent of its Chinese population is Christian), Singapore (10 percent of its total population is Christian) and Hong Kong (10 percent of its population is Christian). Similarly, another study (Yang 1998) shows that Christianity is now the main religion of the Chinese populace in the United States. Taking into account this growing number of Chinese Christians in Asia and the US, we can expect an increasing number of Overseas Chinese investors or high-ranking managers who enter China to be Christians.

Consequently, there have emerged a growing number of self-described "Christian" companies in China, owned by both overseas and local Chinese Christians. These companies have beliefs which are a successful merging of biblical principles with business activities. As was indicated in Chapter 1, it is particularly intriguing to note that a magazine published in China, *Esquire*, featured a special article in its January 2006 issue entitled "God is the Chairman of My Board of Directors" (*Shangdi shi Wo de Dongshizhang*), which depicted four Overseas Chinese Christian bosses' experiences of living out their faith through their business in the marketplace in China.

One of the four interviewees was Richard Chang, the Taiwanese American chief executive of China's largest chipmaker, Semiconductor Manufacturing International (SMIC), which is based in Shanghai. His story, although not totally representative, might serve as a useful illustration of the Overseas Chinese Christians in China. Chang is well known in Shanghai not only because he established China's largest chip making company, but also because he initiated and funded the only "private" yet officially approved church in Shanghai. Thanksgiving Church (see Figure 3.1) is the third government-sanctioned international church in Shanghai besides the Shanghai Community Fellowship and Abundant Grace international fellowship. It was opened on Christmas day in 2005, five years after SMIC was established, and now claims to have over 800 regular attendees (including local Chinese) at its Sunday

Figure 3.1. Thanksgiving Church in Shanghai

Source: http://www.songzan.org/yellow/corpinfo.asp?corpid=2789 (accessed 9 December 2011).

service. In a country where churches are required to sever ties with Western influences, it is surprising to see a "foreigner-initiated" church that is allowed and officially recognized. This shows the potential influence an Overseas Chinese entrepreneur can have in China.

On 14 July 2008, the New York–published *Business Week* had a story on Richard Chang. In the report, Chang openly admitted that he and his colleagues "were called to China to share God's love" and that spreading the gospel was a main part of his work. A key business partner of Chang told me this personal story of Chang. She and her husband had met Chang and his wife in Los Angeles several years before when Chang was just returning to the US after a rather unsuccessful business venture in Taiwan. As the business partner described things:

> I remember during our conversation his wife said, "We should now retire since we have had enough money to spend for the rest of our lives, we should return to Texas (Chang spent many years at Texas Instruments) and do something we really enjoy." But Richard said he had a strong vision for Chinese people and he had been longing to come to China. I didn't agree with everything he did, but I was very sure that he has a heart for God. So I decided to be one of his small partners in the SMIC.

Thanksgiving Church is only one of the several churches that Chang has helped to fund in China. One of his employees explained this: "Richard makes it clear to the Chinese government and all of us that wherever he goes to establish his factory, there will be a church." In fact he has successfully built churches in each of his factory compounds in China.

Chang's efforts can be seen as representing a growing interest in mission work in China on the part of Christians from the West as well as Asia. His vision is indeed fairly common among many Overseas Chinese Christians that I met in Shanghai. Some of them have managed to start a "Christian" company like Chang's, although not as big as his, while others have worked under like-minded Christian bosses who have a similar mission to live out their faith and to run their businesses in a different way. Indeed, Chang has helped draw many other foreign Christians to his Shanghai office. Their efforts are an endeavor of Overseas Chinese Christian businesspeople to influence Chinese society, not merely by investing money and creating work opportunities, but also by integrating business with moral ventures.

Interestingly, there is a parallel development among local Chinese Christian businesspeople. Recent research by Chen and Huang (2004) on Christianity in China shows that there is a group of "boss Christians," who have both religious enthusiasm and financial influence, emerging in some of China's economically more open coastal areas such as Zhejiang province. Contrary to the stereotypical understanding of Chinese Christians as old, female and low-educated peasants, this new group of Christians consists of owners of private businesses who are more educated, mainly male and willing to proclaim their faith openly through their business activities. There was also an article about Wenzhou in Zhejiang province, published in the *Wall Street Journal* in 1995, that made a similar observation: "Just as they [Chinese Christians] drink Coke and carry Motorola pagers, entrepreneurs show off their cosmopolitan savvy by erecting the finest houses of worship. Taxi drivers sermonize passengers. Factory foremen lure their workers to Sunday services" (quoted in Bays 2003). Yet, besides these preliminary observations and some tentative conclusions about these Christian entrepreneurs, it is very difficult to know with certainty their identification and activities. One thing that can be more certain is that, as mentioned by Chen and Huang (2004), they are "steadily gaining momentum."

As discussed in the previous chapter, it is nevertheless important to make clear that these Christians are not in any sense less Chinese nor should they be regarded as less influenced by Confucian and Chinese cultural values. In fact, they see both Christianity and Confucianism as their cultural repertoires, although they would prioritize the former, and they are keen to emphasize the complementary nature of both value systems in meeting the perceived crisis of morality in an emerging market society such as China. Christian business ethics, they may argue, should be introduced to Chinese people as they can contribute, in alliance with other cultural resources, to the construction of a moral framework and fill the ethical vacuum that comes along with drastic economic transformations.

Integrated values: Confucianism with/under Christianity

A great majority of Overseas Chinese, especially those of older generations, have grown up in Asian societies with a background of Chinese religion as well as Buddhism and Daoist beliefs (Tan 1995; Wong 1988). In the case of my respondents in Shanghai, most of them converted to Christianity at a later age, and then became aware of their new identity and the requirements of their new faith. They rejected Chinese religion, Buddhism and religious Daoism after their conversion to protect the integrity of their Christian faith. Interestingly, their identity as a Christian became particularly acute when they arrived in China, not only because the practice of religion was seriously restricted and their faith was challenged within China's borders, but also because of their awareness of their minority status, both as foreigners and Christians, in a foreign and atheist land. Compared to other Overseas Chinese, their sense of being foreigners, namely, "Westernized Chinese," as described by Godley (1981), has indeed become more heightened and apparent. Nevertheless, they are concerned to exhibit crucial elements of "Chineseness" at every level of their lives. After all, being a "Chinese" individual, who shares a common cultural background with the local people, is one of the crucial factors as well as great advantages for conducting business in China. As in the case of Yang's (1999) study on Asian Christians in the US, Overseas Chinese Christians in my study embraced a great many Chinese traditional virtues, which might also be identified as "Confucian ethics," including filial piety, diligence, tolerance and harmonious relationships. They generally agreed that Confucianism was a part of their cultural heritage and perceived some major Confucian values, such as *ren* (love or benevolence) and *xiao* (filial piety), as being compatible with Christianity.

Although Max Weber argues that Protestantism broke the traditional importance of family and kin, while Confucianism perceived filial piety as the supreme virtue, the Chinese Christians in my study did not seem troubled by this dilemma. They argued for the importance of filial piety in Christianity as it is the only commandment of the Ten Commandments that comes with a blessing.[1] Yet, because of the exclusivity of Christian belief, they hold a higher value for Christianity than Confucianism. When conflicts occur between the two worldviews, Christianity always remains superior and must be given uncompromising priority. For example, as my respondents argued, when laws, such as the Communist government's restrictions on spreading Christianity, contradicted biblical commands to evangelize, they would generally stick to

---

1 It is mentioned in the Bible, Exodus 20:12, to "Honor your father and your mother, so that your days may be long in the land that the Lord your God is giving you."

their evangelizing beliefs, even if such incurred a cost. Therefore, although Christianity emphasizes obedience to the authorities, as does Confucianism, Christians are willing to disobey if the government goes against biblical principles, as "Confucianism is a system of moral values, whereas Christianity provides transcendent beliefs and spiritual guidance" (Yang 1999). With this mentality and categorization, Chinese Christians negotiate between the two worldviews and make the best of both the Chinese and Christian worlds. As suggested by Yang (1999), the integration process of the two identities and value systems is selective and negotiable, but based solely on the absolute ground and superiority of Christianity. In this regard, their value-system could probably be seen as one of "Christian Chinese ethics."

Christian Ethics and Economic Life

In the previous chapter, I discussed Weber's thesis on the Protestant ethic and especially the relationships between beliefs and actions. I concluded that religious values could nourish, affect or mutually reinforce economic behaviors in various and probably indirect ways. Since we are aware that recently there have been more empirical studies on the Christian ethical and spiritual foundations on which economic life rests, it is perhaps necessary and worthwhile to review some of these literary studies here.[2]

Fenggang Yang's (2007) pioneering study on Christian ethics in China is one of the very few sociological efforts to apply the Weberian Protestant ethic thesis to contemporary China. His study proves positively Weber's thesis concerning the congruence of the Protestant ethic and the "spirit" of a market economy, and he underlines the importance of Christian ethics in China today in motivating and switching the Chinese economy toward a direction which is modern, rational, legal and moral. According to Yang, a market economy which is rational and moral, arguably based on Christian business ethics, should not be seen as contradictory, but rather as an important component of a real socialist society. Recently, Li and Yang's (2008) study on Christian companies in China, which forms the first part of a series of studies on contemporary religions and social trust in China, displays an abiding belief in Protestant ethics in general and integrity and trustworthiness in particular among the Chinese Christian entrepreneurs. Again, it shows an elective affinity between the two powers, Christian ethics and the market economy.

---

2 There has been a sizeable volume of literature on normative or theological aspects of economic problems and policies. Interested readers can refer to Hawtrey (1999) for a good review of this topic.

Research on religion and business ethics in other countries seems to show a similarly positive relationship between the two. Hong's (2007) study on Malaysian evangelical Christian businesspeople shows a degree of differences in the ethical attitudes of Christians with different levels of religiousness and argues that those longer in the faith are less accepting of unethical behavior. Two studies by Ibrahim at el (1999) and Ibrahim and Angelidis (2005) on the long-term performance of "Christian-based" companies and their secular counterparts in the United States show that the former have higher growth rates in sales and lower growth rates in their workforce, which suggests a higher level of productivity. Factors responsible for this are, according to them, the characteristics and practices of these Christian companies, which notably include emphasizing more strongly (1) organizing regular on-site religious activities such as devotionals and the reading of scripture for their employees; (2) making profitability, competitiveness and productivity the central concern of the companies; (3) promoting employees' integrity, cooperation and compliance with the "golden rule"; (4) guarding the company's reputation as well as customer satisfaction; (5) actively supporting their communities by donating goods, services or funds to both secular and "Christian" organizations; and (6) having loyalty toward and fair negotiations with suppliers.

Laura Nash's book *Believers in Business* (1994) shows a similar result. Nash interviewed 65 evangelical Christian CEOs in the United States about the constant struggle between Christian faith and business, and yet their great enthusiasm for this challenge. She argues that faith continues to play a significant role in business practices and ethics in the United States today. Backman (2001), in his similar study on the Indonesian Chinese, illustrates how the businessman Ferry Teguh Santosa conducted regular prayer meetings at the Jakarta headquarters of his Ometraco Group, as did Mochtar and James Riady at the offices of their Indonesian Lippo Group. According to Backman, Hong Kong's Thomas Kwok and his family, who collectively control Sun Hung Kai Properties, one of the special administrative region's four major property developers, are also staunch Christians who do not shy away from showing their faith through their business activities.

Another part of the literature is an issue of *Business Ethics Quarterly* which was devoted to the various religious perspectives on business ethics. Among them, Roels's (1997) study on evangelical business ethics argues for the central role of personal piety in evangelicals' perceptions of moral business behavior. Evangelicals, according to Roels (1997, 114), believe that "moral business behavior is first rooted in faith-based behavior, not rational analysis, and that the modeled behavior of other business Christians is much more crucial to business ethics than policy handbooks." In practice, Roels' evangelicals have generated four emphases in their business ethics: (1) piety – regular

Scripture reading, prayer and worship; (2) witnessing – to bring non-Christian businesspeople to the Christian faith; (3) tithing – many of them have decided that a tithe of their profits should be used for church related causes; and (4) neighborliness – showing a real concern to others. These people turn directly to the Bible and prayer for answers to their business questions, encourage Bible study and prayer groups on the business premises, and believe strongly in moral absolutes which are based on both the Ten Commandments and one's own conscience.

Similar to the findings of previously mentioned research, Roels' evangelicals emphasize conducting religious activities on business premises as they assume that Scriptural understanding and prayer among the employees will result in pious living, and will help in cultivating Christian character and preventing immoral behavior in the workplace. This explanation seems consistent with our assumption, mentioned in the previous chapter, that beliefs would affect individuals through religious training, which in turn produces a certain personality and life order (Turner 2008).

This chapter gives a general picture of Overseas Chinese entrepreneurs, their business activities and their lives in China. It also shows, through the research and examples mentioned, first, that personal faith and ethics can be and have been applied to workplace behavior. It seems that business practice could mirror religious beliefs. As mentioned by Dorff, "Religion will not allow the attitude, 'Business is business,' for that asserts that business exists in an isolated realm, free of any ties imposed by other aspects of our life" (Dorff 1997, 31). Second, this chapter provides a picture of how the personal piety of Christian entrepreneurs, including Bible reading, prayer, Christian witnessing and giving tithes, which seems unrelated to, or best, excluded from, economic behaviors is in fact one of the primary forces in the formation of business ethics and behaviors. This is somewhat of a surprise to nonbelievers or the larger business culture, which tends to separate personal faith from workplace behavior. Third, this chapter has shown that, perhaps even more surprising, there are concrete examples of boss Christians such as Richard Chang who bring their faith into their business practices despite the very secular society of China. This shows that Chinese economic activities are not necessarily a departure from or a denial of Christian values; they can in fact be an implementation of certain interpretations of them, as the following chapters will discuss in more detail.

Chapter 4

RELIGIOUS MOTIVATION AND ENTREPRENEURIAL SPIRIT

> Market capitalism that compels people to work harder can only produce the prettiest, largest and sweetest fruit when it is combined with strong faith (ethics) that compels people to not lie and not harm others.
> —*Esquire* (2006)

China has in recent years witnessed the rapid growth of religion in general and Christianity in particular. A great number of young, educated and well-off Chinese, including entrepreneurs, have declared their new faith in the Christian God. Research has also shown that there are a growing number of "Christian" companies, ones that declare their active pursuit of combining Biblical principles with business activities, emerging in cities such as Wenzhou and Shanghai (Chen and Huang 2004). It seems for more and more people in modern China, economic success, hard work and Biblical values are societal components capable of existing together in harmony. This chapter goes into detail about the worldviews of Overseas Chinese Christian businesspeople, exploring the broader attitudes and values inherent in their religious ethos which induce and influence their economic motives and activities.

Religious and Entrepreneurial Spirit of Overseas Chinese Christian Entrepreneurs in Shanghai

There are inevitably different views among Christians, as we shall see later, but there remain certain values which are manifestly seen among them. In order to better understand the following chapters on Christian business organizations, religious networks as well as Christian women's business performances, it is necessary to first delineate the underlying values and economic motivations of those Overseas Chinese Christian entrepreneurs whom I interviewed. As important as these values are, they will reappear frequently in the following chapters, sometimes in mere passing remarks while at other times in more concrete and detailed ways. The accounts here are thus general. The values and attitudes that will be discussed include a strong drive to succeed, self-discipline, frugality, a sense of calling, integrity and innovativeness.

Success

The values that motivate people to behave in a certain way also influence their sense of success. The ideas of success that mainly concern us here are those that affect the attitudes toward material gains from business activities, as well as how individuals think wealth can be honestly acquired. But before going into the details behind this idea of entrepreneurial success, I will first discuss the notion of success in general.

My respondents have been relatively successful in terms of educational and career achievements. Most have tertiary degrees while a few have master's or even doctoral degrees from Western universities. This is especially the case for the top executives of multinational corporations. But this should not mislead us into thinking that all Overseas Chinese Christian businesspeople in Shanghai are successful in their business. This is clearly not the case. Many respondents could easily list some names, including those of Christians, who left China because of failed investments. Some were struggling with grave problems in their businesses or careers when I met them. Yet, what is more important to my discussion here is that, even if they have been or are suffering from business problems, they continue to be success- and goal-oriented people who highly value their achievements.

My findings were very much in line with Yang's (1999) study of Chinese Christians in the United States. The situation among Overseas Chinese Christians in Shanghai has been similar to that of their counterparts in the US but, if anything, worse in the former when it comes to competition for resources among peers. The continuing emphasis on success and achievement is demonstrated at every level of the community, most overtly and unabashedly by those who have school-aged children, a situation which is again similar to Yang's (1999). It was very common to hear them, mostly women, asking one another about their children's exam results. On one occasion after a Sunday service, I had the opportunity to listen to a typical conversation between a couple, their 11-year-old daughter and the daughter's friend, a 10-year-old boy, in a Mercedes while we were on our way to a restaurant. The wife said to the boy: "How did your sister manage to get direct enrollment into the high school? I still remember how we prayed for her exams." The boy replied that his sister worked very hard until late at night every day. Trying to justify this "unbelievable success," the husband commented, "See how God answered our prayers! I think it is also because she has good teachers." The wife sighed,

"Your mom looks so happy and proud of her!" The girl interrupted suddenly, "But hers is not the best school in Shanghai; it is very hard to get straight A's in my school." The wife looked at those in the back seat and said, "This means we have to work harder."

The straightforward reason behind this success-oriented mentality is that these Overseas Chinese Christian individuals are eager to send their children out of China to Western countries for further study; getting excellent results is thus the first necessary step. This seems reasonable and important but might not be the ultimate purpose; studying abroad in Western universities does not necessarily require "straight A's." Instead, the mentality that one will have to be the "best," or find success, is the underlying motivation that is taken for granted. During my stay in Shanghai, I came across a few incidents that illustrate this point dramatically. A 16-year-old boy attempted suicide after he failed his exams. He did very well academically in Taiwan, but after transferring to Shanghai he faced difficulties in adjusting to his new life. He told his mother that he felt worthless since he was no longer the top student among his new peers. Another incident was about a woman who was paralyzed from the neck down and at risk of dying at any time due to a serious car accident. She arranged to be sent back to Taiwan for treatment but she refused to let her son accompany her through this difficult journey because "he will have his final exams at year's end." While we were visiting her in the Shanghai hospital to say goodbye to her, her son burst into tears: "I am so afraid that I will not see her again." Although the pastor tried to change her mind, she insisted that the son's successful future should not be interrupted by anything, including her serious illness. What is more revealing to me is that many of her peers seemed to agree with her intention and decision; success is, therefore, an uncompromising value.

Such a desire for success is also emphasized, although less overtly for some people, in business ventures. These Chinese Christians admitted readily that success brings material rewards and secures prestige, but equally important, they emphasized the religious significance that was attached to their achievement. It is a God-given duty to excel in one's business, so the expression of good stewardship was prevalent in their talks. Other common reasons that they used to describe their desire for success were "to glorify God," "to bear witness to Jesus," "to prove that obedience to God's principles brings blessings," "to exemplify that Biblical principles are relevant and applicable," to bring "God's kingdom to the marketplace" and so forth. Their eagerness to excel in business "for God's sake" is without doubt. Yet what exactly the meaning of success is can be critically different for people with different denominational backgrounds. For some, success is, in a crude way, equated with material gain or prosperity; the wealthier a person is, the more successful that individual becomes in both a worldly and spiritual sense. But for another individual, success can mean a lot of different things – including being faithful to one's calling regardless of the results, having a more personal positive influence on society, being able to serve others' needs through business efforts and so forth. It is impossible to make a clear and definite line between these two camps as a great number of people show a combination of both, but we can still discover some general differences between them, which have certain implications for their business practices.

Charismatic-influenced Christians, who made up about 50 percent of my respondents, showed a greater tendency toward the first category. They were more likely to claim that prosperity is good and desirable as it is the manifestation of God's goodness and blessings. Unlike Weber's Puritans, these Christians do not understand their achievement as an assurance of salvation. They are people who are optimistic about their salvation – salvation is by grace alone and its assurance is certain for those who believe – and more importantly, they trust God's desire in blessing his children who are faithful to him in their lives. The central message is simple: Christians who act as the Bible tells them, who are "doers of the Word," will prosper, not just in the next life but in the here-and-now. Their core belief is that God does not intend to have any of his children remain poor. Some believe that God will actually channel wealth to them, while most would say that they trust God will empower them to achieve wealth.

Nevertheless, these successes come at a price. To be successful, individuals need to work hard. Equally important, they should receive divine blessings by discovering God's principles and obeying them so that they can reap the fruits of their investments in higher returns. For example, some of these Christian businesspeople have committed to giving a certain amount of their companies' profit as an offering to the church. A few of them have, in fact, committed to set aside a tenth of their companies' profit for their churches, mission work, Christian social service agencies or needy community organizations. This is usually an extra offering besides their personal commitment to paying tithes, as prescribed by the Bible. Others think that giving the company's profit as an offering is too large a commitment to make, so they only give their own personal tithes consistently. What is apparent is that they see giving money to God as an important Biblical principle that needs to be followed if they desire prosperity for themselves.

I remember my first experience of attending an Overseas Chinese charismatic Christian group prayer meeting in Shanghai. It was held in a business office owned by a Christian on a weeknight and had about forty participants. Before the meeting started, they projected all their prayer items on a screen. Immediately, I saw that "prayer for business blessings" was high on the list. When it came time for this, they invited each participant to share their business goals for the coming year. The leader started by sharing his personal testimony about how God had blessed him financially over the past years. He finished his sharing with a loud claim, "In the name of Jesus, I proclaim success for my business! I claim that my business will have a new breakthrough in the coming year, the turnover rate will reach 15 percent and the sales will increase 20 percent! Praise the Lord! Amen!" The congregation's members were excited and responded with a big loud "Amen!" Another woman who shared after his testimony requested that the participants pray specifically for one of her big Australian clients (who seemed to be slow in making decisions) that "the spirit of delaying will be cast out from this client." After a short period of intense prayer, a woman from Hong Kong stood up and said that she had received a vision from God: "God wants to assure you that he desires you to be successful, and he will transfer wealth to you. He will take away your problems and transfer money from the sons of this world (nonbelievers) to his children who are faithful to him."

It should be noted that such a straightforward and open claim for business success was not invented by these people in Shanghai. The so-called "Prosperity Gospel" or "Gospel of Wealth" is commonly seen among some charismatic Christians in the United States, Taiwan, Singapore and elsewhere (Tong, 2008). Presumably, the Chinese Christian businesspeople who made such claims had adopted this kind of theme from their overseas Christian experiences and exposure to this kind of preaching. Also, it is impossible for us to tell if the act of tithing could result directly in an individual's prosperity; however, as argued by Miller and Yamamori (2007), the Prosperity Gospel does often serve to help believers develop entrepreneurial talents through providing a hope for future advancement and provoking people to think in new and creative ways.

But such a Prosperity Gospel was not welcomed among the noncharismatic Christian people that I met in Shanghai. Although they also aim for prosperity in their businesses, they are less confident about their motivations. This lack of confidence does not relate to their abilities, their actual achievements or their experience; instead, it is a product of their theological understanding about material things, as my first interviewee in Shanghai, who was a director of a human resource company, said, "It is all too easy to confuse our desire for a comfortable life with God's will." Some of my noncharismatic Christian respondents showed a certain suspicion toward wealth and this-world gains. A few of them even expressed a sense of guilt when talking about getting rich. My first interviewee mentioned that she was troubled by pessimism and a feeling of doubt when faced with the question of whether a business can truly be "Christian." She never asked the church members to pray for her success in business. She said, "Whenever I face problems in my business I would think automatically that maybe it is because of my sins, maybe I have focused too much on material things instead of spiritual things or maybe I do not spend enough time in doing God's work." They see more their duty to work diligently in whatever calling they might have chosen; but they consider that their God-appointed task as businesspeople is relatively risky as it is too close to money. For them, success and wealth are good but they have to come with God's blessings through hard work. While theology may have an effect on one's propensity for economic gain, a person's attitudes should also be considered as a product of his or her environment as well as experiences. Some noncharismatic Christians whom I interviewed indicated that they started to have an interest in charismatic teachings after encountering business or health problems in Shanghai; charismatic groups' dynamics expressed through an easing of rigor and an acceptance of prosperity along with health as God-given rewards have been shown to be supportive and attractive to struggling businesspeople.

However, in the cases of both charismatic and noncharismatic Christians, success in the secular world, as important as it is, is said to be less valuable to God than ministry. Many of these entrepreneurs are therefore active members in their religious communities despite their tight schedules and heavy responsibilities. A newly converted Canadian Taiwanese businessman told me that he would retire early in order to achieve "things which are more meaningful and have eternal value." He has a plan of what he could do as a new believer to contribute to God's kingdom, which is to offer free business consulting to other Christian businesspeople in Shanghai. A similar idea is well captured in another respondent's comment about success: "I wanted success in terms of money when I was young, but now I see success as living a significant life that 'glorifies God and benefits others (*rongshenyiren*).'"

In short, both charismatic and noncharismatic Christian businesspeople, in general, exemplified two main attitudes toward success in Christianity, which do not necessarily contradict each other but have a very different focus. On the one hand, as shown by most charismatic Christians, Christianity is keen to show that Christians can be successful within the faith, and the desire to succeed must not be dampened. Yet, on the other hand, Christianity emphasizes that loving money more than God is an open door to evil of all kinds, and the desire for worldly gain and greed should be restrained. The challenge for Christian entrepreneurs is therefore how to succeed in a "Christian" way.

Self-Discipline

Self-discipline, or sobriety, is a value frequently cited by Christian businesspeople to evince their strong emphasis on individual responsibility for one's body and life. They see religious holiness as an individual commitment that needs continuous endeavors of self-discipline. One aspect that they linked most often to the practice of self-discipline was sexual behavior. Christians can also be lured by sex and greed and a fun-loving life; and because of this, they take extra care in teaching and practicing self-control in this area, which is usually seen as the "first temptation for businessmen."

Almost every businessman with whom I talked in China had his own stories of "sexual temptation." While some are more common, such as being "forced" to go to karaoke by their clients, others are more unique. A Taiwanese factory owner recalled an experience when he first went to Guangzhou 10 years ago. One night when he was sleeping in the factory office, he was woken up suddenly at midnight by a sound and, to his shock, a naked female worker was sitting beside his bed. KH, a 37-year-old Malaysian businessman who frequently travelled between Shanghai and Zhejiang, mentioned he was first "lured" by his beautiful "local secretary" in Zhejiang, a woman offered by his Chinese business partners who was capable of meeting both his business and physical needs. Feeling guilty after several trips, he decided to seek the help of his pastor and, after some consultations, he chose to reduce the length of his travels and also carry piles (hemorrhoid) medicine in his pockets to prove that sex was inconvenient for him. "This strategy is so far so good," the businessman laughed. Another man who was a new believer told me how he was mocked badly and ignored by his business partners after he indicated his intention of "not going to those places anymore." He concluded his story by asking me a question, "Why is it so troublesome to be a Christian?"

This question is rightly raised in an environment where the morality of sex is rather relative and lacking. Many Christians point to the teachings in the Bible as well as specifically the requirements of the Ten Commandments, that is, the teachings about not committing adultery, to justify their self-restraint from extramarital relationships. Also, these individuals understand God as omnipresent and therefore "he knows every act of us," implying that divine blessings and punishments will come as a result of one's own actions. The story of XG, a handsome 38-year-old owner of a computer business, might illustrate this point. Before conversion, XG had been sleeping around with many women including his secretary and some of his other employees; at least five of his babies had been aborted by different women. But after a horrible incident in which he was robbed and nearly stabbed to death, he realized his wrongdoing and turned to God. With the help of a group of brothers in the businesspeople's fellowship, he gradually left behind his previous lifestyle and settled down in a marriage with a Christian. But their baby died prematurely. He interpreted the loss as a punishment for his sins. His regretted past has nevertheless made him more diligent in his faith; now he often travels to different Christian groups to share his testimony:

> I used to go to karaoke every night. If I didn't go, I felt very uncomfortable. But I decided to go less after my conversion. I tried very hard to reduce it to two nights per week, spending other nights in attending church activities, etc. Then after a few months, I slowly reduced it to twice a month, once a month, and finally once a few months…I don't go anymore now. It is about submitting my body to my will.

It appears that those who have been living longer in the faith generally display stricter attitudes toward self-discipline (Hong, 2007). Perhaps those younger in the faith have not absorbed enough of Christian ethical teachings. The man mentioned above who questioned the value of self-discipline was in fact a new convert. Mature Christians would be sterner in practicing self-control; common practices among these people include not going out alone at night with a member of the opposite sex, not traveling with secretaries or female employees, calling home every night when they are on business trips and informing their church members about their whereabouts so as to hold each other accountable. In addition, 7 out of 60 of my respondents, all Christians for more than ten years, mentioned that they not only practiced self-discipline, but also institutionalized it through implementing certain policies within their companies. For example, in one case, the company established that an employee would be fired, regardless of his position, if he was caught having an extramarital relationship. True enough, one of its best salespeople was recently fired because of this action. Another company required its managers to bring their families along when they were assigned to a new city. The company made sure that each manager would not be required to travel on a business trip for more than a week each month. In another case, a company did not encourage its salespeople and employees to entertain clients at either a karaoke or a bar; expenses at those places were thus not allowed to be reimbursed. In addition, most companies emphasized family values as part of their corporate culture; activities such as seminars on family values, company family trips and counseling and assistance with family problems were occasionally provided.

The continued practice of the faith through Sunday church attendance and personal devotions over a longer period of time may also explain why people who have been longer in the faith can have a higher motivation and ability in practicing self-discipline. As explained by XG, "It is very hard to remain in a sin (immoral sexual relationship) and still continue on with your church life. Three times a week, in the Sunday service, cell group meeting, and prayer meeting. Unless you don't participate in any one of these, if not it is even harder to maintain a double life than a Christian one." Despite the importance of participation in religious activities, a great majority of my respondents emphasized that it was mainly through their daily devotions, that is, reading the Bible and prayer, that they managed to keep an awareness of the moral requirements and had the motivation to be a "good" Christian.

A Sense of Calling

The Christian businesspeople whom I interviewed often used the term "*shiminggan*" (a sense of calling) to describe their conviction that "doing business in China" was a vocation given by God, an understanding of calling which is similar to that of the Calvinists. It is seen as basically a career path, a profession or a moral duty, in which all one's best capacities are to be engaged that God has placed in one's life (Fullerton 1928). Yet, their interpretation of such a calling can be different from that of Weber's Protestants in the sense that calling is not so much about "money-making" per se, but rather about achieving it in "China." Attending a conference organized by Overseas Chinese Christians for their colleagues in a hotel in Shanghai one weekend, I observed how they were hotly discussing the issue of calling. The leader started by asking the participants a question, "Why are you here in Shanghai? Who called you here, God, your boss, or yourself?" For an outsider or a nonbeliever, this question might sound foolish because, like anyone else, Christian investors went to China either because of internal economic changes in their home countries or because of China's open-door strategy; after all, not many corporations could afford losing the world's biggest market. The answer sounded even more obvious if it was directed toward those executives or managers, as they were basically assigned or sent by their headquarters to work in China. Yet, judging from the heated discussions that went on among the hundreds of participants, the answer seemed to be not as straightforward as first suggested.

Some have a clear and strong calling from God to invest or work in China; and their companies' assignments that often came later merely served as a confirmation of their calling. Some even indicated that they purposely looked for a job that would send them to China or they took the initiative to inform their headquarters of their "China dream." Their calling typically came through a pastor's revelation, prophecy, or personal experience, a topic which I will later note in the following chapter. Others received their calling after many years of working in China. They first saw themselves as either being sent by the office or pressured by business needs to enter China. Yet, after some years of working in China and serving in local religious communities, they gradually gained the feeling that they were on the right path that was set by God. The expression, "Although that was my decision, God was behind it and directed it," was frequently mentioned by some interviewees. Still, there were some people who were confused and directionless. This appeared more commonly among people who were struggling with their business or facing critical problems in their work. But the main point is they were clearly conscious, or anxious, about seeking a sense of calling or working it out through their efforts.

Why does this sense of calling seem so important to them? Two possible reasons include, first, the many difficulties and challenges that these businesspeople face in China which have caused them to seek eagerly for deeper meaning and to justify decisions in religious terms. A clear "calling" from God is obviously one important legitimizing force sustaining them in times of difficulty. This is aptly showed in the remark of a Singaporean manager, "I was a businessman in Singapore, but during that time I never thought of calling or what. It was a natural choice. You graduated, you worked and you decided to do business. I don't need a calling but I can survive well. But now the situation is different [in China]; I don't know how long or how good I can survive if I don't feel it is because of God's calling that I am here." Such a response to a new environment, nevertheless, is not unique to Christian businesspeople in China; in fact, it is common among immigrant entrepreneurs elsewhere (Yoo 1998). Secondly and more importantly, the unique religious situation in China has intensified these individuals' need of a calling. As there is still a strong degree of religious control in China, which is seen by Christians as hampering the growth of Christianity, those who manage to enter China would typically see it as a God-given opportunity to evangelize the Chinese, who have probably not heard of Jesus throughout their lives. The role of businesspeople is particularly significant in this regard as they are welcomed by the Communist government. Compared to missionaries who have had problems in obtaining a long-term visa and are seen as illegal in doing evangelism in China, businesspeople have a safer environment and more natural opportunities to get in contact with many Chinese, such as their employees, in day-to-day interaction. In some cases, the number of their employees could amount to thousands. A sense of calling is thus important for these people to face the challenges as well as the unique opportunities that they will encounter in China.

While more examples will be provided in the following chapters regarding this issue of calling, here I will only mention a typical case to show how it works in Christians' daily lives. Richard Chang, the famous Overseas Chinese Christian entrepreneur in Shanghai, once mentioned, "I have come across incalculable difficulties [in doing business in China]; I prayed to God many times asking for his help. Miracles did happen and I thank God for his blessings…during that difficult period, it was our *shiminggan* that strengthened our faith to face all kind of problems" (*Esquire* 2006).

Frugality

Local people in Shanghai can easily locate areas where most foreign businesspeople live; they can specifically point out which areas are designated for the Japanese, Taiwanese or Koreans. The exclusive and expensive lifestyles of foreigners in Shanghai is a well-known fact: a big house located in an affluent neighborhood in places such as Gubei and Pudong (which might cost over 3 million yuan with more than 2,000 yuan monthly maintenance fees), luxurious cars with drivers, golf club memberships, a maid taking care of house chores and so forth.[1] Similarly, a great majority of the Overseas Chinese Christian businesspeople that I met in Shanghai have a good income and live comfortably; they did not look different from other expatriates upon first sight. Yet a deeper look into their lives led me to rethink my answer. I first experienced their frugality when I attended a monthly gathering of a group of Taiwanese Christian businesspeople. More than a hundred people attended the evening meeting, which was held at a ballroom in a business building. I was told that dinner would be served before the program started, so I expected to see at least a buffet as most of them were wealthy entrepreneurs. But to my surprise, the only food served was *zongzi*, a kind of dumpling made of glutinous rice wrapped in reed leaves (which cost about 2 to 3 yuan each), several simple Chinese cakes and tea. The attendant politely explained that each participant could only take one *zongzi* and a cake. This was surprising as the group was very rich; one of the people in charge told me that they did not actively encourage their members to give tithes and offerings as they were reluctant to handle such a large amount of money if every businessperson really were to give a monthly tithe. Also, similar to what Yang (1999) observed among Asian American Christians, the church life can be frugal. Like Yang, I too, in a few of the committee meetings, witnessed how the budgets of ministry as well as Christmas evangelism meetings were subject to item-by-item scrutinizing by the members.

Talking to several local Chinese who interacted frequently with my subjects, for example, their Chinese maids, drivers or employees, I found them readily agreeing with my observation that these Christians are frugal, and even mean. Many of them own villas in brand-new gated communities in neighborhoods selected mainly for the reasons of safety or convenience; they want their families to live close to their friends or colleagues as the husbands are always away on business trips. Also, equally important, as in the case in Yang's study (1999), they justify the purchase of a large house because of the benefit of hosting

---

1 See http://61.129.65.8:82/gate/big5/pinglun.eastday.com/eastday/node127047/node127048/node127160/node127179/node127181/userobject1ai1089912.html (posted on 12 May 2005; accessed 2 November 2008).

fellowship group meetings. An American Chinese who came to Shanghai alone told me that he had rented a luxurious house in the Songjiang area which belonged previously to a high-ranking local governor. Inquiring about his purpose for living in a big house by himself, I found out that the main reason was for religious functions. His house, with a big living room and five bedrooms, was opened to church members for Sunday worship and weekly meetings even when he was not actually there. This was not uncommon among my respondents; in fact, several of them duplicated and provided their house keys to church members so that others could use these houses for religious functions when the respondents were away. As they frequently justified their wealth as given by God, and saw themselves as stewards of God, there were adequate reasons for them to be cautious and sometimes calculating about their money.

Here I will quote a report again on Richard Chang published in *Business Week* on 14 July 2008. In the report, Chang was described as "eschew[ing] the expensive suits, flashy watches, and other bling favored by China's new business class…" In an international stockholders' meeting of his company, Semiconductor Manufacturing International (SMIC), which was held in Shanghai, he arranged for his big investors to stay at a small hotel near the office; many of them were then forced to find a five star hotel for themselves (*Esquire* 2006). Presumably, not many Christians would display the same degree of frugality as Chang, but they were nevertheless thrifty in many ways. Most did not have golf club memberships although they could afford them, and most did not go after expensive goods such as branded hi-fi systems, golf equipment and antiques, which were normally seen among businesspeople in Shanghai. I visited about thirty big houses during my fieldwork in Shanghai and I found some of the most everyday equipment or "luxuries" that they have were a piano, a wide-screen TV, an overhead projector screen scrolling up on the wall, a long dining table and comfortable sofas. This is not to say that there was no lavishness, but this only means that extravagance or showoffishness was not encouraged. But still, when compared to the standards of the local Chinese, their lives can be considered luxurious, especially when it comes to their children's education. It is common that an American school would cost about US$20,000 per year for a student. This does not include other expenses for children, such as costs for a music course, individual tuition and so forth. But this is an understandable and necessary investment if we take into account the success mentality.

Integrity

The significance of trustworthiness has been noted commonly as a key component of economic exchange for the Overseas Chinese (Silin 1976; Barton 1983). Its importance in reducing the cost of economic transactions is not to be neglected. In the same vein, Overseas Chinese Christian businesspeople think highly of the value of integrity. But they regard it not merely from an economic perspective, but also as both closely related to their religious calling and to their desire to be successful in this life as well as the afterlife. Integrity is expressed in a person's intention to want to act according to moral standards in general and Biblical principles in particular in business transactions. In practice, most people explain it as withholding oneself from practicing immoral behavior towards one's clients, business partners and employees for personal gain. It is about being honest to others and ultimately to God.

Linda's story might reflect what most Christians think of the test of integrity for businesspeople in China. A Singaporean businesswoman in her early fifties, Linda started her interior design business in Shanghai in 2000. In March 2007, she was engaged in a serious bid for three big projects in Beijing. Although she provided the best quotation she could, she was informed that other bidders were prepared to pay bribes. She knew that such business opportunities did not come frequently and she did not want to lose that important client. So she wrestled with the idea of using the same tricks to play the game. "It is embarrassing to say that I gave in finally." She sent a middleman to pay the under-the-table money. But she was not at peace with her decision and felt particularly guilty when she was with her church friends. The struggle was so strong that she had to make a swift and decisive move eventually. She called the middleman to find out if he had paid. When she found out that he had not met with the client yet, immediately she said, "Don't give. I have changed my mind. If I get it, great, if not, it is ok. It is up to God!" Such a decision sounded absurd to many people surrounding her, and the result was almost predictable; she lost the three projects. But six months later she was surprised to see that the client visited her office in Shanghai from Beijing. The client asked if she would still be interested in taking over the projects. They had been started but the contract was broken prematurely because of poor service and bribery scandals. Trying to avoid further legal problems, the client decided to find someone who was "clean and professional." She was therefore very proud of her decision. "If I had compromised, I could definitely get more big business, but the thing is I will have to continue to compromise and to sin against God. The rule of the game is that as long as you do it once, you can't say no the next time. People expect you to do more. Then I will be forever stuck in this routine." It appears from her talk that people like her do not perceive immoral practices as merely an unpleasant business culture; neither is it simply an illegal or unethical conduct. It is seen as a sin – to refrain from it is not a preference, but a determining substantive religious duty. With this idea of religious sanction, perhaps it is more understandable why people like her would want to pay the high cost to keep their integrity when they see the rules of the kingdom of God and those of the sinful earth clashing.

Manifestly, to keep one's integrity in financial matters would mean to resist the excessive love of money, a moral lesson which is easy to teach but difficult to practice especially when it involves large amounts of money or when grey areas exist. A Malaysian procurement manager of a construction company, Shawn, described his wrestling between his conscience and his love for money when suppliers tried to bribe him for contracts. "It is especially hard when you know everybody takes it, and why should I say no? But if I take it, I am not being honest with my boss and my clients, because I might decide something which is not in their best interests. I am not honest with myself either; I have to compromise on the quality of products if I accept their favorites."

Shawn's struggle is not uncommon especially to those who deal directly with suppliers or clients. But the situation seems easier for those who work in "Christian' companies"[2] or established companies with a good corporate culture. As these companies are more concerned about displaying a good image to the public, they are more willing to go through proper and often expensive ways to avoid the risk of penalties or scandals. Also, they want their employees to abide by rules and laws so as to ensure that their values are highly visible to their clients. This is true for those "Christian" companies that are concerned about being "salt and light" among nonbelievers. Consider, as an illustration, a situation that happens in a "Christian" company: a salesperson entering a "Christian" company would quickly spot a cross, a mission statement or a biblical quotation display in the office. He might be invited to participate in the companies' religious activities, such as the Christmas party and so forth. These interactions and the organizational culture would be more likely to stem his intention of conducting improper activities, such as providing kickbacks to the company's procurement manager, even if he would want to do so. This corporate culture would then help the company's employees to behave in an ethical way and keep its reputation, which might in the long run bring a competitive advantage to the company.

Innovativeness

In order to survive, Christian businesspeople need superior creativity to combine their values and business in a way that can help them to excel, and not to impede them, in the market. This can be highly challenging as moral values often imply more self-imposed restrictions and "seriousness about tasks,"

---

2 The idea of a "Christian" company will be explained in the following chapter on corporate culture.

which, tellingly, are in contrast to the current prevailing Chinese custom of earning quick money through shortcuts.

Nevertheless, such difficult environments have compelled some to bring the initiative and transformative spirit inherent in their faith into full play. This is not surprising because entrepreneurship essentially involves innovation and risk-taking behavior. As has been suggested by economic sociologists such as Joseph Schumpeter (1961), entrepreneurship is the creative combination of factors of production in new commodities or markets. Also, there is the concept in Christianity that views creativity as God's very image in a human being; it is a characteristic that sets humans apart from the rest of God's creation. It is thus expected that people who see themselves as "Christian entrepreneurs" would have double incentives to conduct their business with a creative combination of elements, including the invocation of values and religious incentives in their commerce.

Born in Hong Kong and having completed his study in the United States, MP is the Chinese president of one of the biggest cosmetic chains in China. This international company arrived in China in 1995 and has since brought in US$300 million in Chinese sales in 2005. One important factor responsible for his success is the company's distinctive and creative Christian business ethos. In my interview, MP said:

> We often mention about doing good things, doing ethical things, we talk about sacrifice unselfishly; we mention all these in many companies. Here we too talk about "go give," give your help to others, we say the golden rule, do unto others as you would expect they should do unto you, we talk about heart, how we can make others feel important, talk about priority in life. All these principles are from the Bible. But we will not say this is from the gospel of John or what. We set a clear boundary. We see it as problematic to mix religion and business. But the principle is the same, whether you mention the Bible or not. The most important thing is, often time people talk about give, just giving, but here, in our business model, we make it a point that if you do these things, you will be rewarded. Not only spiritual reward or psychological reward, but your giving will be recognized in a monetary form, including the growth of your business. Everything is linked together. In our company, it is only when you do business based on these values you will see the growth in your business result. If you are only concerned about your income, you don't mind stepping on others to move upward, you will not be able to stay long. Because we have designed our business model in ways that reflect our values, and only if you follow the values you will see success in this business.

> If you ask our 400,000 sales why they prefer our company, I trust their first reason is not because they can earn a lot; I think they will say because they like this corporate culture. We are a big family.

During my stay in Shanghai I talked to at least three of his employees on various occasions who mentioned that they were converted to Christianity after joining the company. But note that they were first interested in Christianity not because someone in the company had shared with them but instead because of its unique corporate culture. The following quotation from Melody, a 24-year-old local Chinese from Guangzhou who started to work part time in the company when she was an undergraduate student, serves as an illustration.

> When I first heard about the golden rule and go give and other business values in this company I was very surprised and impressed. I never learned that. Even if I had learnt that I would never know why I should do that. I fell in love with this company when I first attended its meeting. My mother was against it but I was so firm in my heart because it actually gave me meaning in life and work…he [MP] is very humble and I think he is really a servant leader. He is in such a high rank but he will help in small things like carry thing and serve others. How can he do that if it is not because of his faith? I also came across many nice people here who gave me striking examples of how to be successful and yet loving. There are many humane and good policies here; it makes you feel respected as a human being. When I dig further, I am surprised to know that those people that impressed me are actually Christians and the principles are from the Bible. I decide I want to have the same faith as them.

MP's example is outstanding, but he is not the only or unique one among my respondents who expressed a creative combination of faith and business. Several people like him not only exhibited their creativity in developing a whole range of products and services that were suited specifically to the Chinese market, but also had a creativity constructed for their unique corporate culture that was in line with their religious ethos in the China context. Many Christian businesspeople indicated that they had come to attach central importance to the idea of innovation after they came to China. Besides the reason that being innovative is eagerly being sought so as to excel in the tight market competition, the uniqueness of the Chinese situation, including its business and religious environments as mentioned, is clearly an unavoidable factor, as was explained by the Malaysian manager Shawn, "You can never expect things that work elsewhere will work here; this is China and it is always special!"

In sum, while this chapter does not aim specifically to compare the values and practices of Christians to those of others, some of the discussion has already pointed to differences between the two groups, especially in the areas of how they justify success and relate to the issues of corruption and sex if we recall the accounts of the general Overseas Chinese as mentioned in the previous chapter. This chapter has endeavored to show one main reason for their moral values and lifestyles: a religious motive.

Chapter 5

BUSINESS–FAITH INTEGRATION: THREE TYPES OF CHRISTIAN-BASED COMPANIES

For businessman, it is not a choice between mammon and God, but a challenge to make the one serve the Other.
—Thomas C. Campbell, Jr. (1957)

There are a growing number of self-described "Christian" companies in China today which are owned by both overseas and local Chinese Christians. These companies have declared their conviction to operate with an explicitly evangelical Christian corporate ethos, a phenomenon which is surprising given that China is ruled by an atheist government with a long history of hostility toward Christianity. To a certain extent, these Christian bosses' efforts, in particular those of the Overseas Chinese, can be seen as influenced by a new and worldwide mission movement which emphasizes that business in and of itself is a ministry and instrument of God. The core idea is about motivating "the entrepreneurs and business professionals within the church to transform the world through their business activities" ("Business as Mission" 2004).

Intriguingly, if we refer to *The Protestant Ethic*, Weber focuses on individuals and not on business firms. His book has more to do with the spirit or mentality of the atomic economic actors than with the concrete organization of society. Certainly, Weber's methodological individualism, the idea that sociology begins its analysis with the individual along with the meaning that the individual attaches to his or her behavior, has contributed significantly to his approach in *The Protestant Ethic*. But this should not lead us into thinking that Weber ignores the role of social interaction and organization in explaining action. Quite the contrary, Weber has in his economic sociology understood individual behaviors and choices, that is, economic *social* action, as embedded in organizations as well as within a wider social context (Swedberg 1998). This means that, the actor's worldview includes other people in it in the forms of expectations of how other people are going to behave. This worldview is expressed more obviously and overtly in settings where expectations are formulated as rules and regulations such as corporations. In light of this understanding, this chapter attempts to examine the issue of Christian business ethics from the perspective of a type of economic organization, namely a business firm (owned or managed by Christians), by examining its collective values, its culture and its role as a bearer of ethics. The result will be an organizational/corporate expression, or ethos, of the "Protestant ethic."

Research conducted on the organization has suggested that corporate cultures are extensions and reflections of the personalities, as well as the aggregate of the shared beliefs, of their chief executives or "founding fathers." For example, Davis (1986) observes that in many corporations, the management styles and guiding principles are usually set by the chief executive and transmitted down through the organizational ranks. Employees in the corporation tend to follow and internalize the rules through observing management's behavior and reading management's pronouncements. Norms, values and personalities that filter down through the organization are established over time. Yet, in saying that the founding fathers' or chief executives' beliefs are critical in forming institutional behavior(s), the importance of the institution per se is not to be neglected. Recent research on organizational values has suggested approaching the issue from a broader perspective of organizational policy and strategy. Organizational values are defined in the same way as individual values "except that the end states are those that are preferred by the organization and shared by organizational members…cultures of successful organizations see a good match between individual and organizational values" (Umstott 1988). As the connections between the values and beliefs of individuals, and the kinds of organization they construct, can best be demonstrated in the consistent patterns of those organizations, I shall in the following sections establish several patterns of organizational values and practices in examining this issue.

Three Types of Business–Faith Integration

Christian-owned or -run corporations are important to this study as they provide an institutional base for an understanding of the interaction between faith and business behaviors. Also, they might be a demonstration of the result of the "Protestant ethic." This means that the virtues of industriousness and frugality and self-discipline might have helped the companies to survive and make money in a bottom-line place such as China.

Exactly how faith and business should be put together, if it is ever possible, is always a delicate and controversial issue. Like the long debated issue of "faith vs. culture" among more liberal and conventional Christians, some would argue that faith and commerce are complementary or inseparable, while others would see these two concepts as totally contradictory. Most people would nevertheless walk a fine line between the two extremes. Yet we should not assume that all

Christians are interested in linking their faith to business. Obviously to many this idea seems inconceivable, unrealistic or at best irrelevant. But as this study is about faith/business interaction, I focus mainly on those who are concerned about this issue. For this group of people, there are certainly various ways and levels of examining this issue. I shall now trace the intriguing dynamics, patterns and implications of their views and practices. This chapter will proceed by considering three types of business–faith integration: (a) *business as mission* – one that intends to integrate totally the religious and business functions of a business entity, namely, running a company like a church; (b) *business or mission* – the contrary position that intends to separate business and religion; (c) *mission in business* – one that intends to incorporate certain Christian values into corporate culture, a creative integration of Christian elements into a business entity.

I discuss these three types through examining the following aspects: (1) their views on calling, (2) the interactions between faith and business, (3) work ethic, (4) profit ethic, (5) management style (including recruiting, promoting and firing) and (6) corporate culture. Yet in categorizing Christian companies into these three types, it would be an error to mistake this picture for a complete and definite picture of all the cases I have come across in the field. It also should be clarified here that these types are not mutually exclusive, as their stories will tell.

Business as Mission (A "Christian" Company)

Among the 60 cases that I interviewed, about fifteen of them could be placed under this category. Most of them were self-employed Taiwanese. Their businesses were relatively small-scale and unstructured, which means there was more centralization of decisions and their personal values and decisions were the coordinating principle of their companies. This also means that there was a remarkable degree of flexibility in their companies since they had central power in recruiting, discipline and dismissal procedures. Such characteristics principally explain how they managed to turn their businesses into a church and run them as ministries. The following paragraphs focus on the role of faith and values and how this moves these organizations rather than about their detailed mechanisms. Entrepreneurs that belong to this category are typically people who see doing business in China as fulfilling a spiritual calling and who see their business as a ministry, or to be precise, a church.[1] As mentioned by AT, a Malaysian in his fifties, who earned his engineering degree in

---

1 The church is at once a very familiar and a very confusing concept. Here it means, from what I gathered from my respondents, a local house of worship, where believers get together to study the Bible, pray, share fellowship and conduct sacraments such as baptism and Holy Communion. Its mission is basically to evangelize and to have an influence on society through its existence.

New Zealand and worked as a manager in Malaysia before he became convinced that he should go to China when the doors reopened in 1978:

> If I want to earn money I can be anywhere. I came to China with a conviction. It is not that I think I am better than them. I know I am here so that I can influence people with what I think is the right thing to do… it is easier to go to church than to be a church yourself. What do you go to church for? You want to see God, you want to meet God and you want to see a value system. Now you have to live up to that, in a model rather than to teach. You know here it is not so convenient to find a church, or to attend a church, so we need to be a church so that the local Chinese can see God and a value in us.

For people like AT, their calling is inseparable from "China"; it is to be an effective Christian and an entrepreneur in "atheist China," where the gospel is hardly heard and evangelism is restricted. As significant as the calling is, it frequently comes with a supernatural or special experience. The story of WD, the middle-aged Taiwanese CEO of a mobile phone corporation, illustrates this:

> I didn't want to leave Taiwan but I knew God wanted me to come to China. Yes, China. Like Jonah I escaped many times. But an opportunity appeared in May 2006, followed by many dramatic events, such as I was forced to leave my company within that month. The most important one occurred one day at 6:40 a.m. As I was reading my Bible, I was suddenly filled by the Holy Spirit and began to speak in a new tongue. I never knew how to speak in tongues before. I saw a vision of a paddy field that looked exactly like a China map. And I heard a voice saying to me, "You are not alone." Actually before that I argued with God that I didn't want to come to China because it's lonely and tough. I saw my wife and I were working joyfully in that field. I was awake and it wasn't a dream. I can't escape as God had come to me personally.

Such a direct and personal experience does not always happen. What is more common among Christian bosses under this category is instead a "second level" experience, such as a prophecy or a prayer by someone, which is a demonstration of God speaking to them indirectly through a spiritual authority or a pastor. As mentioned by AX, a 45-year-old Taiwanese woman who owned a trade company:

> I sensed that God wanted me to launch my business in China, in Shanghai. I had good reasons for that but I wasn't very sure. Then I took

a leave from my work and flew to the US for a Christian businesspeople's conference. During one of the sessions, while I was praying and asking God, the speaker came to me and started prophesying, she said, "You are here to ask for a confirmation. God wants to tell you that the answer is already in your heart. Your heart's eager desire is his desire for you." I know it is about coming to China.

Once people are committed to running a church-like business, the tendency is for their behavior to be dedicated, bold and consistent. Their strong sense of calling and seriousness about it creates a whole arena where they can display their faith openly in the business. Faith is expressed through office activities, mission statements, corporate culture and sometimes, a unique name (e.g., God's Love, Revival, Agape, Glory) and logo (typically a cross) for the business. In AT's case, a mission statement is posted on the main entrance of his office stating, "This is a company functioning on Biblical principles." In another case, Christian values are printed in the employee booklet which is distributed to each employee on his or her first day of work. Most importantly, faith is instilled through religious activities that are structurally integrated into the business. AX, the Taiwanese female boss, moved her office from Taiwan to Shanghai after her divorce. She now has four employees, all local Chinese in their twenties. They came to the office at 9 a.m., gathered in front of a computer at 9:30 a.m. and initiated a synchronized prayer through Skype with other staff members at the branch in Taipei. Soft Christian music was played in the office throughout the day. They clocked out at 5:30 p.m., but they could choose to remain for more activities. The options provided included prayer meetings on Tuesday, Bible classes on Wednesday, a fellowship group for nonbelievers on Thursday as well as Sunday services. AX even conducted baptisms and Holy Communion regularly. Each of these meetings, which were organized at the office site, attracted more than thirty young people, including her employees, their friends and other non-Christian contacts. As the group grew in size, AX hired a full time pastor from Taiwan to take care of religious activities so that she could concentrate on her business. Most of AX's employees came as nonbelievers, but they were converted over time. AX's neighbor, DS, the owner of an accounting firm, divided his office into three compartments: a working area with cubicles, a fellowship room and a prayer room. Sitting in the cozy prayer room, DS said, "This office belongs to God. We pray before our work and our board meeting. Also, we give tithes from our profits." The story of DY, a salon owner from Hong Kong, was more startling; he implemented a "24-hour prayer link" among his employees and hired "full time intercessors" to pray in his office. His employees were recruited directly from house churches in villages outside of Shanghai. HI, a girl who had studied in a local seminary, explained why she wanted to work in the salon: "I needed to find a place to serve although I never imagined that place to be a salon. At least I learned a skill [foot massaging] here besides my ministry. When I serve my customers, I have a lot of time to share my faith." These examples illustrate how a "Christian company" is understood by its employers and employees in a literal way and not merely as a metaphor.

Nevertheless, a Christian company is a real business. It exists to generate wealth and thus must be profitable. As mentioned by ZD, who owned a human resource company and led a businesspeople's fellowship group, "Profit is like blood in the body. Every company needs it to survive and function. But no one gets up in the morning and says, 'I live for my blood.' But if our blood goes away we stop living." These Christians do not view profit seeking as inherently bad or unbiblical. Quite the contrary, they see profit as desirable and beneficial as long as it is not derived from dishonest business practices.

Their double mission, namely, to earn money and to minister, probably account for most of their work ethic, which is typically claimed to be based on Biblical principles with a divine ethical authority. As mentioned by AT:

> I said to them these are not "Christian's" values, it is "Biblical" values. We have about 10 values in our vision. Basically there is trust, and we spell it clear that what trust is. Trust is integrity, trust is competency and trust is also care. Without one of them you can't be given trust. We talk about fun, talk about hard work, talk about taking risks.

Integrity is one of the most common traits mentioned by individuals. It is a sense of responsibility which is based on people's commitment to put their faith in God into practice. Yet in a society where everybody is attracted to earning quick money and where unethical practices are common, a company which attempts to maintain a clean record is generally under intense social and economic pressure. But perhaps it is under such tremendous stress that this faith in a transcendental God and reputation as a Christian company can be best expressed. According to AT,

> Nobody [his employees or vendors] can argue that integrity is bad. What they can mostly say is that it is impossible to practice. It is indeed impossible. Yes, you have rules and regulations, but the effect is limited unless you embrace it with your heart, unless you have this dignity. It is like a good artist; you can't simply make a piece of work just because people pay you, because you have the dignity. Similarly, if you embrace

the value of integrity from the bottom of your heart, you don't want to tell a lie because it goes against your dignity. That's why we need God. We can't do it on our own.

Also, the dedication to working hard is inherited in the corporate culture. It is common to hear Christian employers saying something like, "We have a higher expectation of Christians. Don't think because we are brothers and sisters in Christ we can be slack. On the contrary, it is precisely because we are Christian; we have to set examples to the rest. We have to work harder." As to what CC, a Singaporean manager, said it seems that more is expected from Christians than non-Christians. Christian employers under this category, who often play the role of pastors to the employees, are quick to emphasize the practice of high standards of moral behavior as an essential part of Christian as well as business life. Besides diligence and integrity, they frequently emphasize morality – honesty, obedience, humility and restraint – in their inspirational exhortations and official pronouncements. At Hong Konger DY's salon, for example, employees were required to attend a study group which focused on building Christian character. During my visitation, they were reading a book on humility, written by a Chinese pastor called Jiang Xiuqin, under the guidance of DY's wife.

Also, as mentioned in the previous chapter, some of these entrepreneurs (seven of them) sought to institutionalize these values within their corporate policies to various degrees. For instance, to emphasize self-discipline, one company has made it a policy that an employee will be fired or demoted if he is caught in an extramarital relationship. Others make sure that corporate managers will not have to travel on a business trip for more than a week each month. Also, as a restraint against corruption, one company stipulates in its policy that employees are not allowed to give kickbacks to clients. To observe the Lord's Day (Sunday), they close their factories, even if the majority of their workers are not Christians. This is not the custom for most factories in China, which are open seven days a week. It was often said by my respondents that strict moral guidelines, which derive literally from the Bible, regardless of their practicality and results, are what distinguishes this type of Christian company from other companies in the nation.

Entrepreneurs of this type often argue that a useful means to enhance the ideal of "business as mission" is the recruiting of the right people. Most of them prefer to recruit Christians, as it is easier to manage them if they have the same values. But since it is not as easy as in, say, Singapore or Hong Kong to find Christians in the job market, most can only operate on the basis that certain positions, which relate to more critical aspects of a company's management system such as finance or human resources should be filled by Christians. Yet it is common also to hear some people say they would purposely recruit non-Christians as they see this as an opportunity to evangelize. As mentioned by AX:

> I sought help from a human resource company owned by a Christian brother to look for suitable people. When I had a list of them I actually prayed to God that only those that were prepared by God would agree to come for an interview. I didn't want to waste my time. I also searched for suitable people through some websites and through the recommendations of a local pastor. But as I wanted to get into contact with non-Christians, I put church as my last choice…for those who came for an interview; I first looked at their ability through tests. Then I focused on their character, especially loyalty, their values and hobbies.

WD, the previously mentioned CEO of a phone company, had a slightly different focus in his recruitment strategy. He aimed to have 1,000 branches in China. In expanding his business, he always participated in interviewing new managers despite his tight schedule: "I look first in a résumé how frequently he changes his jobs. I told them, 'You're looking for a higher pay, and I expect you'll leave my company within one or two years too. Why should I invest in you? I might just squeeze you before you leave. But this'll be a transaction.' I try to share honestly during the interviews. Some of them cried when I said, 'I can't hire you because I don't want to use you. I'm looking for people who want to achieve something greater and longer. When you are ready, you may come again.'"

Interestingly, a few months after I met WD, I came across a Christian who had been through WD's job interview. I asked him about the interview and he said, "WD was sincere and he made me think. I didn't see that in other employers. I wish to get into his company but the competition is tight." His friend echoed, "He really wants that job. He has been looking for a fatherly figure, now he found one!" This was said half-jokingly, but there was no denying the truth behind it; many Chinese Christians prefer to work in a Christian company as they, like those Christian entrepreneurs, see it as a platform from which to serve God. They expect a Christian company to grant them the privilege to practice their values and to provide a shelter that can protect them from the prominent "wolf culture" of China's business world. This is important given that in some places in China, conversion to Christianity might bring social ostracism and occasionally persecution. My interviews with people working for Christian entrepreneurs have demonstrated that they generally became Christian or more pious believers after joining these companies.

In understanding this type of entrepreneur, it is necessary to point out that some of them did not set out to do everything they are doing today when they first launched their business. This was the case of Linda, who moved her design business from Singapore to China in 2000. Linda said she came to China as a "100 percent businesswoman" and ran her business in a "normal" way. But when she was converted four years later, she wanted to transform certain structures of her company, including setting new rules and replacing old managers who were scornful about her changes with new ones to practice her new values. Like Linda, some of these entrepreneurs realized, or perceived, their business as God's calling only in retrospect; that is, over time they noted that they had been affirmed, or challenged, to look anew at their business as an instrument for extending God's kingdom and they thus made some adjustments accordingly to meet the calling.

Also, intriguingly, the majority of these individuals had a certain charismatic influence. This is perhaps unsurprising given that there has long been a movement within charismatic circles that endorses and promotes entrepreneurship and business activities. A few well-known leaders in charismatic circles have initiated international networks and trained businesspeople, the so-called "marketplace pastors," to have a positive impact on society through their businesses. Networks such as the Full Gospel Businessmen's Fellowship International as well as books such as the Chinese versions of Ed Silvoso's *Anointed for Business* and Rich Marshall's *God @ Work* are among the popular resources preferred by these charismatic businesspeople. A key message that is continually emphasized through these networks is that Christian entrepreneurs should envision themselves as influential, successful and "anointed" business leader for God and their business as "God's powerful vehicle to bring his kingdom to the marketplace and eventually the city" and their business authority as "entrusted by God to struggle effectively against the evil empire" (Silvoso 2002). While such a vision is not to be understood literally or as having any political connotations, its spiritual significance and real life implications are nevertheless clear to those who believe in them.

Nevertheless, the tensions inherent in integrating business and religious goals can be obvious and have been noticed by some of my respondents. There are examples where business has been closely associated with the advancement of the gospel, or vice versa, which have resulted in confusion and exploitation. These are reasons why some Christian entrepreneurs prefer a different type of business–faith combination, as we shall shortly discuss.

Business or Mission

About twenty-six of my respondents could be categorized under this type. We might assume that in a country such as Communist China, where religion is still legally controlled, most companies would prefer a business or mission type of structure. Indeed, China's religious laws have prevented Christians, especially foreigners, from preaching the gospel outside of the officially sanctioned church buildings, so these laws have made conducting religious activities in the office or factory illegal. Also, the business environments where corruption is rampant have created added practical difficulties for most businesspeople who want to envision or describe their business as "Christian" and one which is expected to adhere to a higher moral standard. It is therefore understandable that some Christians would see religion as a hindrance and thus would want to keep it within the church so that they can play by the same business rules as do others in Communist China. Nevertheless, some of these individuals purposely keep their faith and business in separate compartments, not so much because they want to ignore religious requirements, but rather because of religious principles. As suggested by MN, an Asian American bookstore owner, "I'm frustrated at Christian employees who don't understand that working is working, faith is faith. Many good Christians are bad workers; they should know that the best way to be a good Christian is to be a good worker."

For Christians like MN, "religion and business do not mix." This is especially evident where they view business as merely a vocation or a way of making money and do not consider it as something to be "overspiritualized." They see their companies as earthly institutions, which definitely imposes certain strictures or limitations in terms of some unavoidable sinful or unethical practice, in a broken and fallen world and thus should not be equated with a church. This perhaps symbolizes their desire to be as far away as possible from the first type of Christians. As MN expressed, "Operating a company is totally different from operating a church. Who should be accountable if the business fails? Since God is the 'board director,' shall we blame God?"

Others have shifted to this type after they experienced frustration in a previous experience. BL, owner of a headhunting company, once employed a Christian whose real interest was evangelism and church activities as opposed to truly working at his company. He found her reading the Bible and performing church activities during office hours. After asking her to leave, BL purposely avoided emphasizing religion at work. Generally, people under this category tend to be skeptical about the supernatural dimension or, more accurately, the charismatic discourse of religion. Most of them come from conservative churches that prioritize Biblical teachings and downplay experiences. This is clearly seen in the viewpoint of LG, a business consultant from Malaysia, who comments on the concept of a calling: "You don't need something mystical to be a businessman. As long as you have the ability, experience and resources, you can be one. If you want to do business in China, then as the Bible says, sit down and calculate if you have the good resources and abilities." The experience of Elsa, a human resource director, illustrates LG's idea of a calling: "My boss asked if I'd consider transferring to Shanghai. My husband said, 'It is a good adventure, why not?' If he agreed, I agreed. My pastor asked me, 'Did you seek God's affirmation?' No, I just feel peace in my heart."

Nevertheless, a reference to the separation of business and faith does not necessarily accord with a low standard of morality or with aloofness in religion. Rather, this should be seen as the business owner's deliberate and rational decision. As some would argue, the Bible requires Christians to submit to the authorities and laws of their governing nation, so they would prefer that businesspeople abide by China's religious regulations, which prevent them from either evangelizing the local Chinese or from operating religious activities at the office. They would argue that businesspeople should step lightly in the corporation in terms of their religious identity. For them, it is therefore more important to "walk like a Christian than talk like one." As explained by Elsa, "I don't say I'm a Christian, but still people know. If I do anything good, like I value my family time, or I don't believe in *feng shui* but trust in hard work, they'd say, sometimes in front of me, 'You Christians are different.'"

In essence, these people are fully aware of their Christian identity and how that should affect their business practices, but they understand it more as a personal obligation and challenge for their faith, and not for corporate conduct. For example, unlike some of the first type of businesspeople who enact a policy against entertaining clients in bars, these people regard activities that go against their faith as an individual responsibility. As stated by ZM, a middle-aged manager in a Taiwanese company, "I don't like to entertain clients but I don't make it a rule. Others might enjoy it. I do join them occasionally. I think it is OK to drink as long as you don't get drunk or do things that you know are clearly wrong. I don't mind saying I'm a Christian if they ask. So it depends on how firm your faith is."

As the example shows, entrepreneurs of this type also intend to follow Biblical principles in their work, but sometimes they can be more pragmatic and relativistic in selecting what they can do based on the particular environment. Another example of this is that, unlike some people in the first type, they do not see giving money to the church out of the company's profits as their obligation. But they can be generous in giving money as a personal contribution to support church work. I discovered from their narratives that their generosity in giving money was more substantial than Christians of other types because they often see this as the only way for their business to contribute to God's kingdom directly, as they do not couple their faith with their business. Also, even though they do not close their factories on Sunday, they themselves would avoid working so that they can attend church. Also, they might encourage their Christian workers to make arrangements such as changing shift schedules so that they too can attend church. But they do not make this a policy as they think doing so will translate into lost revenue.

For most entrepreneurs of this type, religion and business are activities mainly to be conducted in separate realms, but their identity as a "Christian businesspeople" cannot be divided. For them, there are certain personal religious duties to be fulfilled in the workplace.

Mission in Business

The third type of faith–business integration stands in between the total integration of sacred and mundane business and the total separation of the two; it is a negotiation of the two types of business structures. Among my respondents, 19 espoused this business–faith approach.

Christians who hold this view are mainly CEOs of global corporations that work under non-Christian employers. Most of them are male, in their late forties or fifties, with a tertiary educational background. Most have been Christians for a long time. As they are not owners of the business, they are certainly not able to turn the company into a church. And since they see themselves as representing their bosses, they tend not to display their personal religious identity or to institutionalize religion in their companies. Nonetheless, they have the authority to decide upon a course of action and policies that reflect their moral convictions; they are in many situations accountable for forming the corporate culture. Therefore, they can systematically incorporate Christian values into the corporate culture without engineering a "Christian company." In this regard, the seeming limitation of not being the owner of their business could actually result in an advantage if they are capable of manifesting their beliefs in the office in innovative ways. Some of these individuals use Christian materials as resources for management and employee training, as they see religion as a useful moral source for tackling the many ethical problems occurring in the marketplace. Others encourage their managers to attend business workshops organized by churches and Christian businesspeople's fellowships or occasionally to invite Christian management leaders to their companies to do in-house training. They see conducting "Christian" management training as a useful means for instilling good values in the company and for making management decisions more easily. Most people see this as a feasible and safe way to live out their Christian faith in China as entrepreneurs – this does not violate China's religious regulations and yet does result in introducing some people to Biblical values.

JL's example illustrates this type of corporation. The 48-year-old CEO of a multinational corporation, JL went to China in the early 1990s with his wife and three children by way of a calling from God "to make a difference." When asked about his calling, JL provided an answer that integrates intuitive feeling and rational decision making, which is a combination of the previous two types: "How do you know it's the direction that God wants you to take? You just sense, you just know, this is where the Lord is speaking to you, you should be in China. I discussed it with my wife as we always made decisions together. She agreed and it is confirmed. If God gives you a calling, he will call your family too."

JL said he has endeavored to make his company a "Biblical," rather than a "Christian" one, in contrast to the first type. For JL, spiritual and material aspects of business are not paradoxical and thus, not to be dichotomized. He sees them as complementary, serving different functions, yet different from blending them into one structure. For example, JL does not conduct any religious activities in his office, as he said, "Because not everybody is Christian here. Once you start a Bible study here, people will feel that they are obligated to attend. I don't want that. But I always talk to people about faith." Nevertheless, he sees high morality, which derives heavily from Biblical principles, as the core of the company's ethos. As he said, "I ran everything by Biblical principles and nothing else. But I don't tell them this is from the Bible. I try in as much as I can to do everything according to what Jesus would do if he was here." It is of course a very difficult job for anyone to run a business as Jesus would; many of JL's salespeople left after learning more about his corporate culture. Yet he persisted in constructing a corporate culture that is uncommon to the Chinese business culture. For example, he implemented a Christian program called *Character First*, which has been teaching 48 character qualities such as humility, responsibility, sacrifice and benevolence, since 2000. Everybody, including himself as the CEO, attends the course. He also requires his managers to make decisions based on "what is right and not what is expedient or popular." His financial manager shared a recent example that illustrated this: After the May 2008 earthquake in China, the company intended to donate a significant amount of money to the victims. Like many Chinese businesses, his managers wanted to publicize the news in the media to attract public attention. Yet he insisted that the donation be made anonymously, as the Bible (in Matthew 6:3) says, "When you give to the needy, do not let your left hand know what your right hand is doing." His manager concluded, "Like it or not, this is his style." JL prefers to hire people who believe in these values, and after 8 years of implementation, this set of beliefs is evident in the people in most of the high-ranking positions in the company. He said, "From hiring to firing, we base it on character. Let's say someone has better character, with fewer skills; whereas this person has bad character but good skills, we'll promote the former. He'll make a better leader. But this doesn't mean that we promote a bunch of incompetent people in the company. We demand that they improve the skill set all the time. We're character first, but it doesn't mean character only." Over time, those that remain begin to appreciate the uniqueness of their corporate culture, one that prohibits: giving under the table, treating vendors unfairly, delaying in paying suppliers, working on Sunday and using pirated software. All these values seem to be at odds with the prevalent ways of conducting business in China, yet they seem to lead to a better business performance. JL mentioned that his company has been successful in keeping a group of loyal clients as "they know we don't sell things that they don't need to them. They know whatever questions they have, we resolve."

JL demonstrates how faith is transmitted via diverse processes, such as recruiting, managing and customer service, to help maintain a company's ethos. But these values are often not conveyed in Christian rhetoric; the Christian flavor has been intentionally downplayed. What is emphasized and internalized in the company's structure are the moral codes and virtues that govern daily decisions and interactions. It is significant to note that the economic benefits of such practices are telling. JL's company is one of the top in the industry, with a 30 percent net profit after tax over the past few years so that even his non-Christian boss in the United States has adopted the *Character First* program for his many offices worldwide. JL attributes his success to the structured ethical guidelines and congruent enforcement that have helped maintain the predictability and stability of the company. Individuals know the company's expectations and can predict each other's future behavior. This corporate structure also helps to build trust and loyalty as the individuals within the company feel that they share a principle of solidarity. JL's company had a 14 percent turnover rate in 2007, which is considerably lower than the 25 to 30 percent turnover rate experienced by most companies in Shanghai. Additionally, his company has been able to maintain a group of senior managers who have been working in the company for more than 10 years. This again is an uncommon situation for multinational corporations in Shanghai.

Through three types of business–faith combinations, this chapter has highlighted how faith works through the formation of certain attitudes of the working individuals toward corporate goals, means and culture. It has also discussed how faith helps provide some Christians with management skills and moral resources to establish a corporate culture that promotes behaviors compatible with religious values. To conclude, the three types may be summarized as follows:

Table 5.1. Three types of business–faith integration in Christian-based corporations

Type	Main characteristics	Role of Christian values in corporations	Number of cases among 60 respondents
Business as mission	A corporation is run like a church, with religious activities and purposes, on the one hand, and business goals and means, on the other.	Values are emphasized as Biblical, and they are enforced or institutionalized as norms or policies.	15 (25%)
Business or mission	Business and faith are separate to protect the unique function of each.	Values are practiced as an individual expression of piety and duty.	26 (43%)
Mission in business	There is a selective and creative implementation of Christian values within the business, especially in the areas of character building and work ethic, but without emphasizing their religious source.	Values are diffused in the corporate culture. They are used as moral resources in supporting business goals.	19 (32%)

These types of business–faith integration outline the ways religious values are integrated and implemented into corporate settings. Each way is unique in its application and manifestation of Christian faith and values. While some choose to institutionalize these values within corporate policies, others prefer to keep them as a personal expression of piety. Yet each type does, in one way or another, exhibit the influence of religious beliefs on corporate life.

Chapter 6

COMMUNITIES OF FAITH: FELLOWSHIPS FOR OVERSEAS CHINESE CHRISTIAN BUSINESSPEOPLE IN SHANGHAI

According to Weber, the early Protestantism in America increased economic productivity in two ways. One direct way was through inculcating in its believers a more rational lifestyle, a more ethical working discipline and a stronger motivation to accumulate economic capital, an issue that we discussed in the previous chapters. The other way, which is more indirect, was through the formation of universal trust, norms and regulations which were built on what Weber called a "superior community of faith" such as the Puritan sects in the West. Weber's essay on "The Protestant Sects and the Spirit of Capitalism" ([1906] 1946b), the companion piece to *The Protestant Ethic*, is useful for an understanding of this. Weber highlights the way in which membership in a voluntary organization provides a guarantee of moral qualification and therefore, of credit. Moreover, networks as such provide "a means of contact, a source of mutual assistance and information" (Martin 1995, 341). This chapter will deal with the formation and outcome of these communities of faith. It will highlight how religious faith helps generate networks for its believers and will also outline the effects of religious communities in shaping values and inducing moral obligations for the believers.

How Religious Community Affects Economic Behaviors: Networking and Mutual Accountability

In recent decades, social scientists have become interested in the important role of personal networks in the economic arena. Stimulated by Mark Granovetter's (1985) critique of a pure "market" approach to economic action, the sociological perspective has been reinforced by the introduction and subsequent use of the concepts of "social capital"[1] (Bourdieu, Newman and Wocquant 1991; Coleman 1988; Putnam 1993, 2000) and the structure and dynamics of social networks (Marsden 1990; Laumann and Knoke 1986; Mintz and Schwartz 1985; White 1970). According to Granovetter (1985), all economic transactions are *embedded* in individuals' social relations; such bonds then shape the choices of people's economic actions and affect the outcomes of their economic activities. The construction sector has been cited as an example of this socioeconomic structuring. It is noted that there are long-term relations between contractors and subcontractors, who are embedded "in a community of construction personnel, generate standards of expected behavior that not only obviate the need for but are superior to pure authority relations in discouraging malfeasance" (Granovetter 1992, 68). Although there are various alternative subcontractors available in the market, most general contractors only rely on a few subcontractors in any trade. Granovetter argues that this stability may be explained by the desire of individuals to derive pleasure from interacting with old and familiar work partners in their daily lives. In effect, economic transactions depend on and form various degrees of mutual association and obligation.

While the emphasis on the economic outcomes of social networks became more popular in the 1990s, the origin of the concept is to be found even further back in time (Cornwell 2007). In "The Protestant Sects and the Spirit of Capitalism," Weber already argued that social networks were important in facilitating entrepreneurial activities. He mentioned that during his trip to the United States in 1904, he took part in a baptism ceremony among Baptists. The people waiting to be baptized had to enter the icy water of a mountain stream in their clothes. One of Weber's relatives who had been living in the United States for some time pointed out a young man who was taking part in the ceremony and explained that this young man was eager to be baptized as he wanted to open a bank account and needed significant credit. Membership in a Baptist sect was crucial for proving his moral qualifications, not only to the sect but also to outsiders, which was necessary for him to earn credit or a reputation to attract clients. Weber suggested that voluntary associations as such, which were based on achieved and not prescribed brotherliness, exercised a strong peer control over their members as they had to adhere to the standards imposed for admission into the said group. This example demonstrates that a network of personal relations of a noneconomic and nonfamilial nature, in this case religious membership, can facilitate the formation of trust, a quality

---

1 The most widely used definition of social capital is Coleman's (1988), which speaks of social capital as the set of resources that "inheres in the structure of relations between actors and among actors," and "is productive, making possible the achievement of certain ends that in its absence would not be possible" (S98).

that is necessary in reducing opportunism and malfeasance, and can therefore lead to significant economic consequences (Trigilia 2001).

This chapter is inspired by Weber's argument on the relationship between voluntary (religious) membership and economic development. Recent studies have focused more on the role of social networks and economic behavior. Besides Granovetter's renowned research as indicated, much research has further demonstrated how social networks can contribute directly to economic advantages: These networks provide important and up-to-date information that permits one to spot business opportunities (Hendry et al. 1991, 16; Mulholland 1997, 703–6); they offer opportunities and access to resources (Burt 1992); they help provide access to financing (Bates 1994, 674) and they help secure loyalty and commitment from customers and workers (Bates 1994, 674–7).

Nevertheless, there are negative effects of social networks on economic activities, which include abuse and unequal access to the advantages of social networks (Granovetter 1985; Portes 1998). Again, we might find Weber's essay (1946) helpful in shedding light on this issue. In the case of Protestant sects, Weber argued that the strong bonds of solidarity based on common religious beliefs, and the conviction that the members were chosen by God, had helped to create certain standards of economic ethics such as integrity in business, which had therefore limited the abuse of the network (Bendix 1998). This type of network can therefore be a vehicle of social control; it works through in-group punishment and the moral obligations felt by its members to lead them to behave in a certain way.

While Weber's concern was about voluntary associations and modern capitalist development, his argument nevertheless provides an important implication for this research; it suggests that we might take a close look at the various ways in which religious communities *might* have contributed to fostering economic ethics. While ethical responsibility is and remains with the individual, the individual in today's business world does not operate within a social vacuum. A person's economic ethics are firmly embedded in her personal connections and the communities to which she belongs. This chapter is thus an attempt to explore the relationship between religious groups and their influence on entrepreneurial ethics and performance. I will set out a detailed analysis of the religious communities that exist among the Overseas Chinese Christians in Shanghai to help explain the issue.

Communities of Overseas Chinese Christian Entrepreneurs in Shanghai

In Shanghai, there are currently about four official Christian churches for foreigners: The oldest are the 700-attendee Shanghai Community Fellowship, the Abundant Grace International Fellowship, the 800-attendee Thanksgiving

Church and a new church in the Hongqiao area. The Shanghai Community Fellowship, which is commonly called the International Church, was established in 1925 to cater primarily to the needs of the American community. It was shut down during the Cultural Revolution and was reestablished in 1981 after 15 years of being closed down. It is a multidenominational community that holds services for foreign passport holders and is now the best known of Shanghai's churches among foreign residents and visitors, and is also the largest in attendance.[2] The Abundant Grace Church was started in 2005 using the Chinese Hong-en Church for its worship site. It has an identity of a "Pentecostal, Trinitarian congregation" in that it acknowledges "the importance of the working and ministry of the Holy Spirit and His gifts in our lives today including the need to receive the fullness of the Holy Spirit with the evidence of speaking in an unknown tongue in accordance with the book of Acts".[3] The Thanksgiving Church was originally established and funded by Richard Chang, the Taiwanese American chief executive of China's largest chipmaker, Semiconductor Manufacturing International (SMIC). This church claims to be independent of governmental control, but it remains heavily supported by the Shanghai government (it has a government-approved pastor in charge of its administrative and preaching duties) and is thus regulated by the government to a great extent.

Obviously, these official churches do not have enough room to house, not to mention to minister to, the large group of foreign people in Shanghai. Moreover, as these churches are under governmental control, a great number of foreigners are skeptical toward them, seeing them as "impure." Consequently, there are numerous unofficial, and thus illegal, nondenominational Overseas Chinese fellowships which have been established by lay leaders with or without the support of foreign organizations (e.g. Gideons International) and churches (e.g. the Taiwanese Lingliang church) that have emerged in Shanghai. These groups were formed randomly based on their members' nationality, denominational background, and residential area in Shanghai and the like. Religious communities as such are growing fast to accommodate the needs of Overseas Chinese in Shanghai. Many Overseas Chinese businesspeople, who were not Christians in their home countries, have started joining religious communities and become more religious after moving to China. This is especially obvious among people who are under great stress in their business or in their adjustment to a new life. Christian business groups have served as a source for resource mobilization by enabling businesspeople to get to know like-minded people and to be involved in certain networking. Such a

---

2 See http://www.scfenglish.com (accessed 22 August 2008).
3 See http://agfwheatridgeco.com/default.aspx (accessed 22 August 2008).

phenomenon is neither new nor unique – studies of diasporic communities have showed that religious organizations are important to migrants' adaptation to a new environment (Hume 2003; Hagan and Ebaugh 2003; Cottrell 1999). In the United States for example, new migrants typically participate in religious activities to a greater extent than in their home countries because religious affiliation provides meaning and a supportive environment to help sustain their new lives (Yoo 1998).

I observed at least nine Overseas Chinese Christian fellowships during my fieldwork in Shanghai. They vary greatly in their membership; one with international support claims to have a million affiliate members nationwide, while another that consists of Mandarin and Cantonese sections has a total membership of around one thousand. Others have a membership of a handful or a few hundred. This chapter will focus on two of the more popular Christian communities for Overseas Chinese in Shanghai, namely, the Chinese Businesspeople Fellowship and the Full Gospel Businessmen's Fellowship International. But before moving to a case study of these two groups, I will mention briefly other forms of social networks, namely, *guanxi* and family networks, which have been commonly associated with Overseas Chinese businesspeople in previous research (see for example, Liu 1998; Ong 1999; Ong and Nonini 1997; Redding 1990; Leo Douw 1999).

Previous studies (see for example Hamilton 1991, 1996; Redding 1990; S. Wong 1988) have argued for the critical importance of social networks, namely *guanxi*, in forming and operating Overseas Chinese businesses. These networks are mainly based on family and all kinds of *tong* ("same") ties – *tong xiang* (same native place), *tong xue* (same school), *tong xing* (same family name) and so on (Weller 1999). These studies describe *guanxi* as a unique type of networking practice that is crucial to Chinese business circles, especially to Overseas Chinese, although they agree that the Chinese are hardly the only people whose social networks play a significant role in their economic life. Since the definition of *guanxi* is generally ambiguous, here I adopt the concept that it refers to personal connections that are deliberately developed and nourished through mutual obligation and exchange and are often used to achieve instrumental goals such as job hunting (Gold, Guthrie and Wank 2002; Lin 2001). For the most part, the effectiveness of one's business in China depends largely on the strength of one's *guanxi* network, which in turn depends on one's ability to organize family members and friends to form useful ties with potential business partners and local bureaucrats.

Judging from this definition, it would be unreasonable to deny the crucial importance of *guanxi* to any Christian investors working in China. In fact, most of my respondents commented that they went to China after they had attempted to mobilize possible resources for business opportunities; personal ties, business contacts and religious networks are all important resources to use in receiving advantageous resources such as market information. Networks of various types have helped my respondents to be in a preferable position for more business opportunities. However, in contrast to most research which emphasizes dialect and family links as the most important form of *guanxi* among Overseas Chinese businesspeople in Asia, my fieldwork finds that the advantages of such *guanxi* in providing business benefits, when compared to friendships made at church, are at least equally important among the Christians in Shanghai. For example, among the 60 business owners, CEOs and managers whom I interviewed, only one had extended family links in Shanghai, and none of them hired family members to work in their companies. Yet, on the other hand, about seven of them had recruited Christian friends from the same religious group to be the primary stockholders of their companies. Some of them had kinship ties in other parts of China, especially in the place of their parents' origins, but that distant network did not have a direct effect on the resource generation for business establishment in a global city such as Shanghai. Perhaps this result affirms Weller's (1999) suggestion that Chinese people are now relying less than ever on traditional interpersonal connections.

I shall now turn to another aspect of the *guanxi* network; there is a popular understanding about, or rather a possible application of, *guanxi* which sees it as a type of "deviant" or "irregular" social network practice resulting from a certain institutional environment. Researchers have argued that the particular historical and institutional conditions in China, such as its transitional economy with scarce resources and weak legal regulations, have encouraged the practice of *guanxi* by which people utilize social networks to bypass legal channels and gain access to resources (Walder 1986). Activities such as social eating, gift giving and money giving, which are linked to bribery, are therefore widespread in China and are seen by many unique in the Chinese type of networking. This is where business ethics, the focus of this chapter, comes into play. If *guanxi* building has to involve unethical behaviors, how would Christians respond to it? Would religious networks, presumably a more ethical and healthy type of networking, help Christians to respond in a better manner? Is the community of faith capable of guaranteeing ethical standards and limiting the practice of bribery in business transactions?

Two Case Studies: Chinese Businesspeople Fellowship and Full Gospel Businessmen's Fellowship

I will now provide two case studies of the unofficial fellowships of Overseas Chinese Christian entrepreneurs in Shanghai. The first group is called the Chinese Businesspeople Fellowship and is one of the oldest and most popular

Overseas Chinese Christian communities in Shanghai. It is interdenominational and noncharismatic in nature. Self-initiated by two businessmen, it is now functioning as a church, that is, an institution that ministers and dispenses sacraments to its members. The second group is the Businessmen's Fellowship, which is one of the many chapters of the Full Gospel Businessmen's Fellowship International in China. It is known for its charismatic teachings and its "businessmen" only ministry. Both groups have attracted a sizable number of Overseas Chinese businesspeople of various backgrounds and are relatively well known among Overseas Chinese Christians in Shanghai.

Chinese Businesspeople Fellowship

This group has two sections, Mandarin (Taiwanese) and Cantonese (Hong Kongers), each having numerous cell groups with a total population of roughly one thousand members. Each cell group, which contains from twenty to thirty people, is in fact, a small church in the sense that it organizes weekly Sunday services for adults and children, several ministries during week days (a group in the Songjiang area that I observed, for example, organizes monthly meetings for core members on Monday, prayer meetings on Wednesday, women's meetings on Thursday, family meetings on Friday or Saturday and youth meetings on Saturday) as well as evangelistic meetings. It also practices the rites of baptism and Holy Communion, respectively. Moreover, each cell group provides programs catering to the needs or interests of its members, which include: social activities for singles, golf programs for enthusiasts, summer camps for youths and marriage conferences for couples. Some of the groups also collaborate with seminaries outside of China in organizing courses and flying in lecturers to provide systematic training for their members.

The Chinese Businesspeople Fellowship was initially set up in Shanghai in 1990 by two men, a Hong Konger and a Singaporean. Before going to China they both studied and later worked in the United States. Also, they served together as leaders of a Bible study group in a local church in the US. As both of them shifted their businesses to Shanghai in the early 1990s, they decided to start a weekly Bible study group, with a mix of Chinese and English languages spoken, in their neighborhood. As the founding leader from Hong Kong mentioned:

> We didn't intend to make it big or formal; it was initially designed to serve the needs of the expatriates like us. Bible study is an essential part of our Christian life. Also we need to have fellowship with other Christians. But when we first came to Shanghai in the early 1990s we couldn't find any suitable church or fellowship groups. And so we have to start it by ourselves.

It was mainly about our two families. This was how we started the group. More and more people joined us later, it grew, and this is the process.

Later as more Taiwanese businesspeople joined the group, the leaders began to conduct the Bible study solely in Mandarin. Over time, they started a women's ministry, youth ministry and children's ministry. In a few years, the membership grew dramatically to about three hundred people, forcing them to shift their meeting place from individual homes to factories owned by members of the group. Beginning in the mid-1990s, this group began to focus in particular on two constituencies, Taiwanese and Hong Kongers. The latter became a stronger constituency toward the end of the 1990s. This meant both a linguistic change compared to the earlier Mandarin ministry and a structural one: The group was split into two partly because some Taiwanese wanted to incorporate charismatic elements into their worship but this idea was resisted by some of the Cantonese-speaking people from Hong Kong.

Considering the fact that many of the members would attend weekly small group meetings and Sunday services regularly, this religious community has been one of the most frequent places for Overseas Chinese Christians to meet and network. For example, among my 60 interviewees, one found his business partners through the recommendation of his fellow group members and yet another found a manager for her factory from this group. This finding echoes what Backman (2001) found in his study on Overseas Chinese in Indonesia. In his study, Backman suggested that church membership is now a new mode of networking among the younger generation of Overseas Chinese in Asia. Many Chinese families with business backgrounds send their children to Western universities to enable them to build connections with the sons and daughters of other Asian business families as well as with Western elites. According to Backman (2001, 217), "Classmate connections are important, but one of the most important venues for fervent networking among Overseas Chinese in Asia has become the church." In the case of Overseas Chinese in China, church membership has also become one of the helpful modes of networking. As compared to local Chinese, there are fewer opportunities available for them to build enduring and trustworthy friendships in a foreign land. Many of the Christians among them were already aware of the existence of these religious communities from their contacts even before they went to China. One informant explained that his choice of investing in Shanghai was due partly to knowledge of the existence in that city of active Christian groups, besides Shanghai's relatively clear guidelines and expectations regarding foreign business activities.

Another example of religious networking and business profits is shown through ZD, a key leader of the Chinese Businesspeople Fellowship and an owner of a human resource company. His well-established company, which is shared with two other Christians, acquires a great deal of business from the businesspeople in the group. Yet the benefits are mutual. The following comment that was made by ZM, a Taiwanese manager who was baptized by ZD and has stayed in ZD's group for a long period of time, illustrates what other group members think of ZD's business:

> It saves us a lot of energy and money to find a suitable candidate to fill the post in our companies. It is easier to trust him because we know him personally. You inform him what you want, and he can find a suitable person for you. I think he is not only helping us to find employees, but he is also matching Christian employees with Christian bosses; it is like sending and putting people into the right places. So I see it as a ministry, not only a business.

This comment illustrates how a religious group can also help reduce the transaction costs. In essence, because of the trust established among them, the Christian businesspeople need only go through a minimal number of steps, which makes their job of advertising less expensive. This is also shown through the case of DS, who was a church deacon in the Lingliang church in Taipei but has now moved his accounting office to Shanghai. He decided to launch his accounting business in Shanghai in 2005 following Taiwanese businesspeople's outflow to China:

> I came here mainly because of the business opportunities. Many of my church members and clients have shifted their businesses from Taipei to China and they challenged me to come over. They said if you come to Shanghai, we will continue to be your clients, and we will introduce more Taiwanese clients to you since we already know you can provide trustworthy and more economic accounting services for us. Also, they frequently told me, you should come and start a fellowship here. We need a pastor that can lead us and you can be the man.

As has been suggested by Bates (1994), securing loyal customers and finding new ones is a regular benefit among the members of a network. This is especially true for people with businesses in the service sector (such as restaurants, real estate, travel agencies and the like). Some of my interviews were conducted at a so-called "Christian café" owned by a female member of the fellowship. I frequently bumped into my other interviewees in that cafe; they were there meeting clients, planning for religious activities or simply gathering with friends. One of my respondents provided the reasons why he preferred to have his meetings, including my interview, at this café. Because of this preference, we were then forced to change our meeting time to accommodate the business hours of the café.

> You see all the familiar faces. I come here almost every week. I don't even need to place my order; the waiter knows what I want. I like this kind of feelings–Christian songs, the Taiwanese foods, no alcohol, oh, no smoking; I can't stand people smoking in the restaurant, and the foods are not too expensive.

Interestingly, just opposite the cafe, there is a travel agent company owned by the same female boss, who specializes in settling visa and flight issues for Taiwanese. Such a convenient arrangement obviously provides both businesses with a competitive advantage in attracting and keeping customers, mainly Christian Taiwanese businesspeople who are in need of both services.

Equally important, a religious community can be an effective and open place for people to have access to information of all kinds including business tips. At one of the marriage conferences organized by the fellowship in a hotel function room in Shanghai in April 2008, I overheard a conversation between two men sitting next to me. A man in his fifties asked another man, who seemed to be new to the group, about the trend and growth rate of the stock market. Then the pastor announced a break before the next teaching session started. Hesitantly the newcomer responded, "Is it good to discuss this kind of issue here?" After a short silence, I heard as this newcomer continued apologetically, "We can talk about it later." As I walked to the back of the room to get a cup of coffee, I again overheard another conversation which sounded interesting to me. This time it was between an American Chinese man and a Chinese woman who had just moved back to Shanghai from France. As she inquired about the job market, the man replied to the woman, "My son just got a job in the Citibank in Shanghai. He is very happy. Has your daughter also planned to come to Shanghai?" The woman replied, "She is trying to find a job in Shanghai. Maybe I should bring her here so that she can talk to your son?" The man immediately agreed. I highlight these two stories which occurred randomly in the Fellowship as they provide a concrete picture of how information is conveniently shared and networks are formed and utilized in a religious community.

Also, because of the common faith and the close relationship among the members, religious communities have the ability to develop and disseminate a system of shared norms and values and to build stronger trust. AD, a Taiwanese man in his early forties and a very active leader of the Fellowship, has recently formed a small company with the help of two Christian friends, also from the group, who generously provided him with financial support. AD graduated from a seminary in Taizhong, Taiwan and went to Shanghai decades ago as a businessman and missionary. He started as a part-time pastor and an acoustic engineer in a small company. Over time, he picked up from his friends and his surrounding environment an interest in establishing his own business. Knowing his intentions as well as trusting his character, two men from the fellowship took the initiative to invest in his business without any legal contracts. As XG, one of the two shareholders and a retired entrepreneur, mentioned, "He [AD] brought me to Christ and I've known him for many years. Although he didn't have any experience in doing business, I have it and I can help him. This is not only about investing in a business but more about investing in him and in our friendship. Of course I want this business to be profitable, but that is not the only thing that I care about." XG's response not only shows the trust and shared values that exist among members of the group but is also an interesting example of how one's motivation is moved from the narrow pursuit of immediate economic gains towards the enrichment of relationships through trust and reciprocity (Powell 1990). Clearly, the process of establishing emotional trust, as well as that of the common norms and understandings, is time consuming and requires great effort, but when this trust is established, it can be successfully sustained over a long period of time and bring about significant effects.

My examples so far have shown some direct economic benefits from participating in religious groups, but this is not the overall picture. As the interviews reveal, for most people, participating in a religious group does not provide immediate business opportunities but is mainly intended for participants to "keep in touch," which might or might not turn into a resource for their businesses in the future. Further, there is another function of the religious network that is associated with most people, that is, dealing with corrupting *guanxi*. Most respondents in my study emphasized that they now value integrity and Christian ethics more seriously than before they joined the group. One reason is, of course, the consistent teachings on Biblical ethics in the group. Another reason is the mutual support mechanism that exists in the group. For example, the Fellowship has since 2008 had a monthly "men's discussion group," led by two businessmen, mainly to deal with issues related to bribery and other forms of corrupt practices in China. There are about twenty to thirty participants at each meeting. People who are more senior in their businesses or have been in China longer are assigned to be in charge of the discussion sessions; know-how techniques, principles and consequences are shared and discussed. Two of my respondents who attended the meeting mentioned that they benefited from the open transfer of information and the joint problem-solving arrangements, which were helpful in providing them with moral support and techniques to deal with problems faced in business. When asked why they were interested in joining the group since they were both already regarded as successful and experienced entrepreneurs, they both explained that they perceived helping those younger in their faith or business as a moral and religious obligation. We can then expect that, because of this sense of solidarity and duty that derives from a common faith, information and resources that are exchanged among members of religious networks can be seen as more credible, imbued both with qualities and values that the group emphasizes.

Businessmen's Fellowship

Businessmen's Fellowship is a subgroup of the Full Gospel Businessmen's Fellowship International (FGBMFI), an international religious association which focuses on doing evangelism and discipleship among businessmen. FGBMFI claims to have 182 international directors and 698 field representatives worldwide as well as over three thousand local chapters in 160 countries and about a million affiliate members in its China branch alone.[4]

FGBMFI was started in the United States in 1952 by a dairy businessman of Armenian origin named Demos Shakarian, who began the businessmen's fellowship in a cafeteria in Los Angeles. He received a vision from God in which he saw countless people around the globe raising their hands praising God together through his ministry. This vision was confirmed when Mordecai Ham, the man who led Billy Graham (a well-known contemporary American evangelist) to Christ, told him, "The Full Gospel Businessmen's Fellowship International is God's instrument to awaken the laymen – the sleeping giant of evangelism."[5] With this vision to motivate lay businessmen to be involved in world evangelism, FGBMFI has encouraged hundreds and thousands of businessmen to fly to different parts of the world to give their testimonies and organize evangelistic meetings. And through this way, many businessmen have been brought to Christ and motivated to start new branches in various cities around the world. In the case of China, it has been mainly through the initiative and support of the Hong Kong and Taiwan branches that many new chapters have come into existence in recent years. In China, groups of Chinese Christian CEOs, both local and overseas, now meet regularly under the ministry of FGBMFI in various cities such as Shanghai, Wenzhou, Guangzhou and Shenzhen. Similar to FGBMFI worldwide, they frequently organize evangelistic meetings through dinner parties held at hotels, attracting hundreds of businessmen and their families each time.

---

4 See http://fgbmfi.net/4 (accessed 22 August 2008).
5 See http://fgbmfi.net/4 (accessed 22 August 2008).

As indicated, most of its ministries and activities are confined to men only, with the exception of a few meetings where wives can participate. According to XK, director of a construction firm and the founding leader of the Shanghai branch, "Men and female have different struggles. For men, the greatest struggles are always about money and sex. But sex is always the first and foremost struggle. We want men to be able to focus on spiritual things when they are joining our meetings and don't want to complicate the issue by allowing women participants."

Unlike the previously mentioned fellowship that welcomes Overseas Chinese of all walks of life, the Businessmen's Fellowship is more focused on its target and is thus more restrictive in its membership. Its members consist mainly of churchgoing charismatic Christian businessmen who are eager to link up with other Christian businesspeople around the city.

Having said this, besides being exclusive on gender and occupation, Businessmen's Fellowship does not normally reject people from its circles. It is in fact inclusive in the sense that any man can join, although it prefers businessmen with good moral and business standing. In this regard, although it aims to build up godly and influential businessmen with strong morals and a good reputation, its membership should not be seen as a "social guarantee" to others as in the Protestant sects in early America. In Weber's writing, the Protestant sects were highly selective in recruiting members as they saw themselves as among the "saved." To protect their good name, the sects gave intense scrutiny to each member's conduct and character. For those members who did not meet their requirements, they would be sanctioned both socially and financially. But it is quite different in the case of FGBMFI: Although it emphasizes Christian ethics and moral requirements, it is not in the group's best interests to be too exclusive or punitive, for otherwise it would not have the opportunity to reach out (that is, to do evangelism and discipleship) to as many businessmen as it could. It has norms of behavior, but they are more a means of protecting the members from exploitation although such could also serve to protect the name of the group. As mentioned by WC, a Taiwanese businessman who is an active and senior participant in the group:

> According to our international policies, we can't do advertisement or sell our goods to others in our meetings. We can't turn our group gathering into a promotion party or board meeting. If we find out somebody intends to do so, he will be disqualified to join us next year. Our membership is renewable annually.

It is obvious that, given the different nature, the group could not maintain the ethical standards of its members at a similar level to that of the Protestant sects in Weber's writing. But it does strive to provide a certain close monitoring of the business and ethical behaviors of its regular attendees and committed members. For example, the Shanghai branch used to practice a system of accountability to prevent its members from sexual temptation during their business trips. It had a peer system that assigned each member who indicated willingness to participate with a peer to call his partner to ascertain that person's whereabouts. If the partner was on a business trip, the peer would make a daily call to his hotel room so that they could share their needs and pray together over the phone. A few people who participated in this system mentioned that such a close network had indeed helped them greatly in avoiding sexual temptations as well as in preventing poor business decisions when they were away from home and church. It thus appears that one of the possible outcomes of this group membership is about *building* its members into good Christians, and eventually good Christian businessmen, according to Biblical principles and the examples of others rather than *proving* their competence in moral and business conduct.

In line with this, the group might be able, to a certain extent, to show a member's credibility to his fellow group members although it might not be able to do so to outsiders. As religious networks are tied through faith – a faith in God and in fellow believers – the reliability of a member as a person and as a potential business partner is inseparable from his seriousness in his faith and his level of commitment to the group. Often the tangible evidence of a person's religiosity lies in his attendance at the meetings and his willingness to participate in the ministry, which is shown in the following remark by a Taiwanese American boss:

> Of course I hope I can have a Christian partner; it makes things easier and simpler if we've the same values. But still you've got to be careful to find out if he is a real Christian! What he says does not count; you have to observe how he prays, his participation in the group, and through his sharing of thoughts. If he says he is a Christian but he is always absent from the group meeting and never wants to serve in the ministry, I don't trust his words.

The reason offered during my conversation with this respondent for such a thought seems to be straightforward: Only a "real" Christian will want to be accountable to God and to his fellow believers, which thus makes him a potentially trustworthy partner. The heart of the matter is trust and dependability. This is especially important in a situation such as in China today where the laws are conspicuously lacking in protecting foreign businesspeople's rights and where officialdom's behavior is changeable and not always benign. This situation tends to heighten the importance of knowing people that can be trusted, and of course strengthens the centripetal pull of a religious community.

It is significant to note that the sense of mutual reliance among fellow believers is displayed not only locally, but also globally. Within both networks mentioned above, especially the Businessmen's Fellowship, members often travel from one country to another to help establish new groups, to network and to attend training. A few of both groups' leaders have traveled locally and internationally to share about the potential role of Christian businesspeople in modeling high business ethics in China. Regular contact is maintained with fellow believers from other parts of the world. Also, overseas members often visit Shanghai on vacations or mission trips to help in the ministry, giving the congregation a feeling of global brotherhood. In view of the global links that exist closely among members of the group, it can be expected that a certain trust, as well as market-generating social capital, might be generated globally.

In short, this chapter has attempted to explore how religious groups provide a platform for networking and a means by which the ethical teachings of Christianity can be promoted and disseminated to their members. It intends to contribute to the sociological understanding of networking by using two empirical examples from my fieldwork in Shanghai to examine the ways in which Christian communities, those which are based on trust in a transcendental God and are not economic in nature, can affect economic actions. However, the effects of Christian networks are still weak in China. A more effective working of the network requires the unfavorable religious conditions in China to change. Having said this, it is expected that as Christianity grows, the networks will expand and carry increasing significance in business activities.

Chapter 7

FEMALE ENTREPRENEURS: FOUR STORIES

Research has shown that more Chinese women are becoming entrepreneurs. A recent report by the Xinhua News Agency on 4 July 2002 claims that women entrepreneurs make up about 20 percent of all the entrepreneurs in China. It has also been estimated that in China, among the micro-entrepreneurs, fully half are women (McEwen 1994, 340). This is a phenomenon that is happening in many developing countries. Legal changes in marriage rights and a higher level of literacy have granted women access to markets and networks traditionally closed to them. Lower birth rates and changes in gender role expectations have also impacted women's long-term career development. More recently, the restructuring of industry, urbanization and the emergence of new service industries, such as tourism, health care and insurance, have also given women more opportunities to become entrepreneurs (Cooke Fang 2004).

While such numerical significance of women in the business field is a new phenomenon, this has long been the case in the religious field. Gender imbalance in religious participation is often the case in many societies. In China, for example, it is estimated that 80 percent of Christians are women; this ratio is approximately the same in the house church networks and state-sanctioned churches or networks of urban fellowship groups (Aikman 2003). The consequence of this fact, that is, the growing importance of women in both business and religious fields, is the great importance of women in our discussion on Christian businesspeople in China.

However, perhaps unsurprisingly, knowledge about Chinese businesswomen in general and Chinese Christian businesswomen in particular remains very limited. One main reason is that the number of female entrepreneurs was initially small. Equally important, the deep-rooted legacy of male supremacy in Chinese societies has often drawn scholars to focus their attention on male actors. To fill the gap in our knowledge, I will in this chapter provide a detailed account of the lives and personalities of four female Overseas Chinese Christian entrepreneurs in China. It is hoped that such an account will shed light on the following questions: How are "ascetic practices of the self" expressed through these businesswomen? What are the unique challenges that they face being female Christian entrepreneurs in China? Are there any distinctive expressions and features of a "female Protestant ethic"? Weber did not have gender in his mind when he wrote about the Protestant ethic. This discussion, therefore, should shed light on a neglected aspect of an old topic.

During my fieldwork in Shanghai I interviewed 20 female entrepreneurs through snowball sampling. Among them, 17 were below 50 years of age. Most of them were well educated (16 of them had tertiary degrees and at least 3 had MBA degrees). All except one established their businesses in China after 1998 and all were in privately owned enterprises or were self-employed. If we follow Ng and Ng's (2003) definition of micro-entrepreneurs, that is, business owners who are self-employed or who employ fewer than 10 employees, then about ten of them were in such "petty" businesses, while the rest were in middle or large businesses employing 30 to 300 workers. To capture the fabric of the business and faith lives of these female entrepreneurs, I will focus on four stories in this chapter. These four cases were selected because of their different nationality, type of business, work experience, position in the business and working environments and thus, ethical challenges, so as to provide a more comprehensive understanding of Christian female entrepreneurs in China. As the interviewees were not randomly chosen, they are not meant to be representative of the population of female Christian businesspeople in China. But this is not to say that their stories are unique; in fact, theirs were typical among the 20 interviewees I met.

Gender Differences in Ethical Performances

There are a growing number of studies dealing with gender differences in corporate and ethical behavior (see for example Borkowski and Ugras 1998; Whitley et al. 1999). The gender socialization approach has argued that gender creates different moral orientations, resulting in different decisions and practices (Gilligan 1982; Kohlberg 1984; Luthar and Karri 2005). For instance, men are trained to seek success and are more likely to break rules, while women are more concerned about having harmonious relationships and are thus more willing to abide by sociocultural rules. Some studies seem to affirm this idea. They show that women are more concerned about ethical issues (Collins 2000) and possess significantly different and less tolerant ethical values than men (Hoffman 1998). They also show that women are more likely to view certain questionable acts as unethical, unlike men, who have more instrumental traits such as strong independence and competitiveness, making them less ethical. Women are then perceived as more sensitive, emotional, not very competitive and not particularly goal oriented (Beu et al. 2003; Dawson 1997; Mason and Mudrack 1996; Ritter 2006). For the purpose of this research, we might go on to ask, if women are more likely than men to evaluate questionable acts as unethical and to take action to reduce their personal guilt, would they also be more likely to display a moral reasoning corresponding to Weber's "Protestant ethic," a work ethic that values both integrity and an accountability toward God?

Weber, of course, did not give us an answer to this question. In fact, *The Protestant Ethic* only touches once on women when Weber used unmarried women workers as an example to explain a type of backward traditional form of labor (1992, 62). Nevertheless, we can identify a subtle yet crucial influence of women on the formation of the thesis of the Protestant ethic through a study of Weber's life. Weber's academic and emotional life was strongly influenced by a few women, in particular his mother, his aunt and his wife, Marianne. Marianne, subsequently an author of a feminist history of marriage, had a very intimate intellectual relationship with Weber. In fact she had, according to Peter Thomas (2006), "in a very real sense 'authored' the Weber we know today" as she assembled Weber's studies, *Economy and Society* and *The Protestant Ethic and the Spirit of Capitalism*, into posthumous collections and edited the unpublished texts. Also, Weber's mother, Helene Fallenstein, was an example of a Calvinist believer with a sense of religious commitment and obligation, showing "an iron will, activity, a heroic moral stance, excitability and fiery dynamism" (Weber 1975, 17). Weber's aunt, Helene's sister Ida, had an equally strong influence on Weber through leading him to enjoy religious reading, especially her favorite moral theologian, William Ellery Channing, who emphasized rational control over the instincts rather than emotional experiences of divinity (Mitzman 1971, 29). It can be argued that Ida's forceful personality and her strong commitment to social responsibility, as well as Helene's uncompromising religious standards instilled in Weber's heart and works a strong sense of interest in the Protestant virtues (Thomas 2006).

It does seem reasonable to suggest that women's influence underlined the creation of the Protestant ethic thesis although Weber largely ignored this in his writings. But as Weber observed, "Women had everywhere shown a particular susceptibility to religious stimuli," (quoted in Lichtblau 1995, 189), which might provide us with a ground for exploring if women would also show a higher sensitivity to religious obligations and moral duty.

Women, Rational Business Behavior and Social Networking

Much research on women in management has focused on women accommodating work with family responsibilities (Won 2005). A preliminary study on women in Chinese societies has shown that younger women in particular may have to choose between family and career and has suggested that a higher divorce rate exists for young married women (McEwen 1994, 162, 254). Indeed, my empirical work shows that only 25 percent of my female respondents were still in their first marriages, while 94 percent of the male respondents were (see Table 1.2). Social expectations regarding women's role and family responsibilities usually require that women assume a greater responsibility for their household, childcare and dependent care, all of which can be a burden for women trying to manage and balance these responsibilities while trying to develop their businesses. This happens to be the case for divorced businesspeople in my study; among the six divorced businesswomen, five were single mothers, whereas none of the male divorcees had assumed the custodial parental role.

Besides having familial duties, research has also found that female entrepreneurs typically encounter a primary barrier of acquiring financial and social capital in starting a business (Verheul and Thurik 2001). The glass ceiling phenomenon could be more entrenched in a Chinese society in which women normally have less social support for career development and less access to business opportunities (Weller 1998). Traditional patriarchies still persist to some extent in stereotyping the roles of men and women and in delimiting their social spaces in Chinese society. Men have the natural duty to be breadwinners and they are expected to participate in social life and networking. But this is not true for women; the image of women joining the male-dominated networking environment does not fit neatly into social expectations. In my interviews, for instance, women often commented that they tried to avoid as much as they could the opportunity to build rapport with male clients through taking them out. Most of these entertaining activities take place after working hours in karaoke clubs, bars or massage parlors, where the women felt it either inconvenient or uncomfortable to join because of family commitments or because of personal values. They were aware that taking part in such events, which often involve competitive social drinking or even sexual activities, would not only call their character into question, as any Chinese women would encounter, but also contradict their faith in the case of Christian women. Yet they were also aware that being left out of some of those loops, they would not have access to as many business resources, which might influence the human and social capital endowments which were necessary for their business growth. Furthermore, some might have to avoid business travel, too, if they could, not only because frequent travel would reduce their family time, but also because this travel would invite rumors and family problems. Ida, the designer and manager of an international hotel company, told me that her fiancé, also a professional, had always complained about her traveling too frequently. At one point, he even suspected that she was having an affair with a client because of her overnight weekend trips. Although she promised to cut down her trips and even brought him along occasionally, his suspicions grew stronger. He finally forced her to change her position to one which was less challenging and at a lower level and therefore required no travel. Interestingly, it was after she became more serious about her Christian faith, because of this relationship crisis, that her fiancé changed his view toward her business travels and began to trust her more.

In general, in order to compensate for the multiple restrictions in acquiring business connections, these women tended to be extra diligent, professional and creative in their business to accomplish their tasks. For example, in Ida's case, she has to work extra hard in her office as well as during her business trips, or to use internet conferences or Skype to contact her overseas clients so as to minimize the time spent traveling. Moreover, to allow for the lack of social functions in which to participate, these women were eager to demonstrate their competency or friendliness in order to cement long-term ties with clients through professional and satisfactory business performance that may lead to verbal recommendations from clients. Women in such situations are more likely to have a rational and disciplined business style; they need to exercise rigorous self-control and management if they want to survive in the male-dominated business world. Of course, if they still intend to keep their families intact while excelling in business, a rational lifestyle is then a necessary skill instead of a choice. In this case, these women's relative disadvantages in entering the business world have led them to promote a Weberian version of rational market behavior (Weller 1998).

We have, in previous chapters, indicated various contexts in which social networks and communities help to bring about business development. Yet we need to be aware of the internal inequalities of gender within the communities (Field 2008). Obviously, gender has led to differences in building networks and relationships. One example from my fieldwork to illustrate this issue is that among Christian communities in Shanghai, there are a few businesspeople's communities, such as the Businessmen's Fellowship that was mentioned in a previous chapter, with membership limited to men. This international business group is capable of providing wider networks of friendship, support and resources for Christian businesspeople. Yet it excludes Christian businesswomen mainly because it wants to "reduce the risk of sexual temptation," as one of the leaders explained. Such practices have contributed to network poverty for women, who are already at a disadvantage.

Having said that, it is notable that women have their own advantages too in networking, particularly where networks are characterized by affective ties and emotionally valued skills (Field 2008). While women's spheres of connections are generally much more limited than men's, they can also be more reliable and close. Religious communities, as long as they are open to women, might be among the few that can provide them with strong solidarity. For instance, in most religious groups that I observed in Shanghai, women generally have had more active engagements and stronger connections with others although men always held the leadership positions. It seems that women have more eagerly made use of such networks and emotional resources, perhaps because they help to extend existing networks. Also, because of women's openness in personal sharing and their strong social skills, they tend to create more intense bonds and feelings of trust among their peers. For example, a businessman told me that he might sometimes question a woman's ability to accomplish certain jobs, but that he generally trusted women's credibility: "You just trust that they will not cheat on you; maybe it is the chemistry between different sexes." Thus, in cases where fair opportunities are given, women can have their own advantage too in the business networking race.

Therefore, based on previous studies on women's ethical behavior, it is interesting to examine how Christian businesswomen would subscribe to Christian ethics, including actual practices and the cultivation of such ethics. Equally important, because of women's relative lack of access to networking opportunities, as well as their heavier family responsibilities, it is important to see if they will develop a rational market behavior similar to or stronger than that of the men, an argument which is quite counterintuitive. But this suggestion probably should not have been too surprising. Scholars such as Roslyn Bologh (1990) have argued that Weber's conception of rationality is patriarchal in the sense that it is freed from the constraints of emotion as well as tradition and community.[1] But to the extent that women live their lives within the family, neighborhood and community, their lives are subject to the constraints and empowerment of community and tradition. Bologh instead suggests a female rationality, one which characterizes the domestic sphere of the home, family and personal relationships and which assumes an embeddedness in communal life and a concern for the effects on community (see Bologh 1990, particularly chapter 15). While it is important to suggest female actions are rational, the

---

[1] Weber has also been criticized by Bologh for adopting a "masculinist" orientation to sexuality in which "brother love" provides the model for interpersonal relationships. But according to Turner (1998), such a criticism is probably inappropriate as Weber's emphasis was on power and violence, which was clearly not related to women, and it also underestimates Weber's involvement, with his wife, in the women's movement.

businesswomen in my study nevertheless did not simply exhibit a "female rationality," according to Bologh's definition. Of course, they are deeply involved in their communities and families and are concerned about other's emotions and the consequences of their actions; these businesswomen have undoubtedly strived to realize certain values related to "female rationality." But unlike traditional women in Bologh's study, their place was not merely confined to the home. They played a crucial role in the public sphere, that is the business world, and were thus familiar with calculating and technical rationality. Their roles situated them in two worlds, a modern business world dominated by men and a family world reserved for traditional women. If both worlds need different rationalities in which to survive, successful businesswomen might need a good combination of both to excel in their dual roles. The following section will examine these ideas by analyzing four case studies.

Formations and Expressions of "Female Protestant Ethics"

Linda

Linda moved her interior design company from Singapore to Shanghai in 2000. She has now opened two branches in Beijing and Chengdu and has over thirty employees in Shanghai alone. In our interview, Linda, a single woman in her early fifties, frequently referred to the year 2004 as the turning point in her business life. On a trip back to Singapore in January 2004, she accompanied a friend to church on Sunday, an incident that changed her life. After the service, she decided to begin reading the Bible, and within a month, she found herself in a baptism class and was soon baptized. When she went back to Shanghai a few months later, she realized her religious conversion had changed her into a different person; as she put it, "When I came into China in 2000 I was not a Christian; I was then a 100 percent businesswoman." It is common for people, religious or not, to think that ignoring ethical principles is vital to earning money in China, as corruption at all levels in the public sector is almost unavoidable. The conflict between ethical or religious principles with the business culture is overwhelming. As one of my respondents commented on a friend from Hong Kong who recently started a joint-venture consultant firm with some bureaucrats from a state sector enterprise, "He came in as Mr Christian, but now ends up as Mr Chinese!" It seems therefore quite common for people to think that these two terms, Christian and Chinese, are contradictory and cannot coexist in the business world.

But Linda was hardly an unethical businesswoman even before she was converted. She said, "Being raised in Singapore, though I didn't have any specific belief, I possessed a strong sense of norms and morality; it was always quite clear in business, what to do and what not to do. Before I came here I could hardly imagine I would have to go to the extreme of buying my business." Yet in a new business environment where competition was fiercer, and rivals were paying bribes to get their business, Linda had adopted a new attitude, "I will not say no if people ask for under-table money. I was told this is how things are done here. It is a normal custom or Chinese culture or whatever. So if people approach me, do you want this project? But there is a condition. Well, I won't say no."

Nevertheless, she determined to conduct business in a different way after her conversion. First, she was convinced that she should no longer give bribes as this was an unbiblical principle. Also, she decided to ask for an organizational transformation, pushing for more transparency and predictability in the operation. She also attempted to make job distributions and managements more systematic and controllable. But her new decisions were not well accepted; her capable GM resigned as he could not accept these new changes, and to replace him, she had to recruit four new managers. She remembered her first meeting with the managers, "I told them straight, first, I don't do this; second, I don't do that. I won't bribe in order to get a project; I don't take bribes from my supplier either and so forth. The immediate response of the four new men was, 'Madam, you will ruin the company with your personal beliefs! If we do business as you said, we can't survive in the market!'" True enough, before long, her beliefs encountered one serious battle after another. One of the toughest decisions came a few months later. Her company has had an endemic problem in striving to have the clients clear their bad debts. But the situation was particularly serious that year. As her manager persuaded her, "If you don't pay speed money (unofficial payments for getting things done) to those officials, they will not help you to settle the bill. They don't have the incentive to clear this debt." Others even suggested that she resort to force in solving the problem. It was not easy for Linda to see her company running into financial crisis or to merely ignore the suggestions of her staff, but she felt the urge to try working within her faith. In justifying her decision, she persuaded them: "I gave them an illustration. Remember the many big cases of high-level wrongdoings coming to light recently; the mass-contaminated milk powders scandal, fake foods, and so forth. This was nothing new. I said, do you know why those people do such evil things? You think they are sick and selfish. But here we have exactly the same mentality. Why do we want to use force or give bribes? Because everybody is doing the same, we have no choice; people assume you do bad things even if you don't. So why be good? Why don't we do the same to survive? But sorry, no, my final answer was no."

She knew people were uncomfortable with her rationale and would be more reluctant to follow her instructions if the same were not derived from her management prerogatives. But fortunately, to the surprise of many, the incident ended on a happy note. A few major clients took the initiative to pay off their balance before the end of the year, with the exception of some minor cases related to privately owned enterprises. Everybody was happy with that miraculous result, albeit with different interpretations; her staff took it as a "lucky thing [that] happened in a lucky year," but she obviously had a different understanding, stating: "I used legal ways to settle the case. Also, I shared my problem with my church group and asked for intercession. It is a miracle, but not totally unexpected." For Linda, it was "a work of God," in essence, both a prayer answered and a faith honored, which strengthened her faith in God, and equally importantly, in the Christian community. She commented that her long cultivated business habits or instinct might have helped her to avoid bribery in situations where she could, but it was her Christian belief in a transcendent and omnipresent God that empowered her with a stronger motivation to face the consequences of not complying with corrupt practices.

However, when we touched on matters related to tax payments, Linda showed less confidence. She readily admitted that this was an uncertain and confusing zone that "gives her headaches." Regional differences in law enforcement due to variations in local leadership made it difficult for her to decide what to do. She complained that the policy was unreasonable, if not transparent, and imposed unbearable burdens on a small law-abiding company like hers. She was extremely upset at the fact that the law inevitably put her at a competitive disadvantage to more ruthless operators. Thus, when someone informed her that the tax was actually negotiable and she could ask for a reduction, although it sounded unrealistic to her initially, she decided to give it a try. So she managed to get the company tax cut from 18 percent to 15 percent. The financial result was good but it caused new headaches; how should that 3 percent, returned to her later, be used? She was presented with disturbing choices: she could either spend the money on buying gifts for related officials or share the money in a direct way, or she could do nothing but prepare for a higher tax rate the next year or something worse. She felt increasingly uncomfortable with the tax reduction option and the choices that followed, feeling as if she "has cheated the country." Linda said she was fearful of being caught by local officials for mistakes made by herself or her subordinates, but she was even more frightened that because of her nonbribery actions, she would receive more inspections from supervising institutions, which could cause more trouble for the company. Therefore, to protect herself from any possible problems, Linda imposed a regular check on her accountant, asking questions such as: "Did you put in that unlawful, cheating stuff into our account? Can you explain the items if we are under scrutiny?" The accountant long complained that she was overcautious, but she insisted on making every detail transparent and clean.

Linda commented that it was these day-to-day practices that constituted the biggest challenges to her values. She said, "I have learned to pay no heed to what others think of me. Most importantly, I have learned to take money more easily. Of course earning money is my first job here, but not through stepping on my faith. I will try my best to make as much money as I can, but life is not just about that. If I keep on calculating how much I can earn or I must earn this year or this month, then it will be very tempting for me to give in. If you have a bad precedent, it is easier for you to have a second one. It is a trap. Honestly speaking, I must confess that until today, I still have a few clients who constantly ask for under-table money. We have paid them since I first came to China and that was before my conversion. I can't get rid of that! If you ask me about my struggle, I tell you, it happens every day! It is like teetering on a fine line every day."

When asked why she persisted in her principles despite all of the risks involved, she mentioned that the only reason was her faith, although I could see that legal considerations were obviously on her mind. "I think it is just normal for a Christian to want to follow your beliefs especially when you understand God's principles more. In some cases the instructions are clear and straightforward. You know the consequences; if you don't follow it, you will reap the fruits when you see God one day. I don't think it is worth risking my eternal salvation for short-term profits. The risk is just not worth taking. But of course, as I said, the pressure of conformity is difficult to resist. Like any businessperson, I used to do many wrong things, but now at least I try not to repeat it. When I first became a Christian I had this wrong thought; I wanted to test God. I didn't bribe when everybody bribed. I wanted to see how God can help me in such situations…and for the whole last year I have seen him helping me in many unexpected ways. This gives me the courage to stand my ground. The point is, if he can bless you with great profits without you trying to be clever, then why do you want to use human ways to do your business?"

This nonnegotiable attitude toward business practices characterizes her management and it is a signal to her staff and clients that making money is what she wants and that principles must be upheld. Linda's calculation and her rationale are obviously different from those of other nonbelieving businesspeople. She works as hard as anybody, but the company's profits are not her only concern; rather, the moral sanction of salvation and damnation seems to be higher on her priority scale too.

Elsa

For many businesspeople, managing people continues to be one of the most challenging tasks in business. This is especially true in the case of China.

As China reforms and modernizes its economy, human resource issues have become one of the biggest problems that keep it from moving as fast is it can. Some of the ongoing issues faced by employers include attracting and retaining staff, working with the changing labor laws, deterring and detecting fraud in the company and motivating people with "modern attitudes" such as personal efficacy. Managing people thus plays a central role in determining a company's competitiveness as well as a Christian manager's ethical performance.

With this challenge in mind, Elsa, a Taiwanese woman in her fifties, accepted her company's invitation to take over the role of human resources director for greater China in 2002. This is a family-owned company, based in the US, with approximately six hundred employees in its Shanghai headquarters. She brought with her 20 years of experience in the areas of human resources, training and policymaking. The company had been embroiled in a period of bitter emotion as it had just gone through an internal restructuring that left many employees both frustrated and mistrusting. Her first experience happened a few days after she took on her new position. She received a call from the company's factory workers asking her for an informal meeting. So she went alone without a second thought. But she was surprised to see angry workers surrounding her immediately and bombarding her with inflammatory complaints. It was only with the help of a few others that she managed to appease their anger and have a talk with them. The workers told her that she was the first high-ranking manager, in fact, she was the first HR director who could even speak Chinese, who went to the factory alone and who had shown an interest in their problems. But her boss was shocked to learn of her seemingly "careless" actions; he thought any meetings with the workers would definitely end up in disaster. Elsa's reply was surprising to her boss; she said instead of feeling upset by such a confrontation, which she interpreted as a reflection of worker's insecurity in the face of a changing environment, she felt sympathetic towards the workers.

Although Elsa had earned the trust of the workers, the situation did not improve overnight. For the next few months, still there were workers who, on various occasions and for various reasons, surrounded her office, slammed her office door, lashed out at her or even went on strike and camped in front of her office for days. She tried to explain to them on more than one occasion, "I told them you have shouted at me for an hour and I am sitting here to listen. If I can solve the problem by giving you an extra 100 yuan for your salary, or by keeping this person or that person, why should I say no? The problem is not as simple as you put it. I have my own difficulties; that's why I am here to listen to you, to find a solution." The headquarters in the United States complained about her attempts to demonstrate too much compassion when solving issues. But she thought that as a director with responsibilities for all workers, her duty was not just to please the headquarters but also to build genuine, honest and candid relationships with her workers. She sighed, "I am sure I lost credibility with my boss, but it is hard to always make everybody happy with what you do."

Elsa carefully avoided sharing her faith at work, as she thought that this could invite stereotyping and defensiveness. But she was eager to live out her faith. One way to do that was through cultivating a self-questioning habit in her daily decision making, "What would Jesus do in this situation? What would he do in my position?" By checking on her own behavior and motivations, she hoped her life could meet the demands of being a good Christian. Indeed, she saw her job as a most suitable platform for her to practice life as a good Christian. As a policymaker, Elsa was basically dealing with the delicate balance between accountability and compassion, which according to her was the core of Christianity. She faced constant questions such as "Should the company be compassionate towards a low-performing employee, or should the company fire her so as to hold other employees to account?" The decisions were always difficult but in each case she hoped to deal squarely with reality and then carry out these with compassion. The company's love fund, for example, was one of her efforts to provide support and subsidies to laid-off workers before they could find a new job.

Elsa found her job satisfactory as she had ample opportunities to integrate her values and her work. One illustration was her attempt to promote a culture of integrity within the company, which, tellingly, is not a common Chinese way of doing business. She not only required employees at all levels to attend training, but also standardized rules and employees' practices, including gift giving to clients, across dispersed units. New rules inevitably stirred negative responses from the staff: "They said there must be something wrong with me for trying to promote integrity in China." But this was not an ad hoc decision on her part; in fact, Elsa carefully weighed the policies against the pros and cons with her boss and came to the conclusion: "It is a gain to sacrifice short-term profits for long-term reputation." But she admitted it was painful when she first grappled with the effects of such change. She said, "It seems a culture of integrity just does not fit neatly into the bigger environment. But we can't ignore the fact that this is the right thing to do. The outcry of the staff was swift. The salespeople, in particular, see me as an alien. But over time, I can now see a ray of hope in the snail's pace progress."

Another illustration of integrating faith and work might be her family-friendly policies. In order to create a culture of caring, Elsa started an internship program which catered mainly to the employees' children. She made it clear that as long as they were the "company's children," regardless of their parents' positions in the company, they would be eligible for the program.

She hoped to benefit the staff through providing internship opportunities with some monetary benefits for their children and by adding future value to their children's résumés. She also expected such policy to benefit the company as it would attract young talent at a lower cost and help to build the company's reputation as trustworthy and charitable. Such a win-win result is really what Elsa hoped to achieve in her career.

Furthermore, Elsa's feminine acumen, assisted by her profound experience in management, helped her to initiate a flextime system in the company so as to make life easier for working mothers because, as she said, "being a working mother myself I know their struggles." She explained this system of honesty, one which would allow people come to the office and leave at their own convenient time without having to report to any system so long as they met the 8-hour requirement, as a method to inculcate a habit of self-discipline. This attitude was to her one of the most important qualities that needed to be developed in her staff. Elsa has since gone even further by proposing a work-at-home system. Her survey found that general traveling hours for each employee amounted to 2–4 hours per day, which she saw as a waste of time and a counterefficient activity. She said she does not believe that long hours mean better productivity but instead thought that a "work–life balance" would be a better way to maintain the company's productivity in the long run.

When I asked her about her motivations for working, Elsa said half-jokingly that, first, she needed a monetary reward, a job, to maintain a comfortable life for her family. This was her natural duty as a wife and a mother. But second, as more of a religious duty, she wanted to have an impact on the quality of people's lives through her job. She defined success as having "no regret" in what she did. And what she wanted in life was a balance among her family, job and faith: "I might not be the most successful person in this company, but I can say I am one of the people who have a balanced life, and I have no regrets. I am happy with my present life and I think I am successful in this regard." Indeed, it was intriguing to see how women such as Elsa have developed a particular set of skills over time; they are good at juggling and completing many tasks simultaneously because that is the story of their daily existence. She was a rare case among my female interviewees. She had not only remained in her first marriage but also had a healthy family life. But her success had not come so easily; in the midst of the rush and tumble of business life, she had designed a rigorous schedule which is effortlessly predictable. She recalled immediately the fixed schedule of her daily activities when her children were still young – it was 25 years ago – when the many activities such as taking her son to sports, running errands and helping with homework were all planned. She also came out with a fixed menu for her children's daily meals, rationally calculating the nutrition in each. Everything seemed to be perfectly calculated in theory and extraordinarily rational and systematic in practice. She said proudly that her son, a lawyer, and her daughter, a bank manager, both reside in the United States and have adopted her effective methods in raising their own children.

Sun

Sun was born in 1966 in a small city in Malaysia. After growing up there, she later moved to Singapore, then the United Kingdom, where she earned a bachelor's degree in architecture and later an MBA. She is now a director of an international construction company based in Shanghai.

When she first went to Shanghai four years ago to join the company where she now works, she took it for granted that fraudulent activities "should not bother me because we are a multinational company!" She tried hard to prove others wrong when people told her that corruption was a normal practice, even in her company. Despite her strong confidence in her corporation, it did not take too long for Sun to discover how her colleagues accepted bribes shamelessly. She was stunned and found it hard to face, and she was forced to answer a difficult question, "Why shouldn't I take the money too?" She eventually made up her mind to reject the temptation as it not only concerned her reputation and character "as a professional and a Christian," but inevitably affected her standard for high quality work: "If people know you can be bought by money, they will think they can buy you over in the rest of the things too. Then I have to compromise my standards. How can I insist on the quality of work if their money is in my handbag?" Sun says her identities of being a professional, a Christian and also, interestingly, a woman, have empowered her to be firm with her morality: "I learned to say no when I need to; when I say it, I mean it."

It seems to be not unusual for people to expect that most female entrepreneurs or managers, in attempting to perform their tasks well, have adapted themselves to male characteristics such as competitiveness and aggression in a male dominated work setting. Such a view suggests that there is no significant difference between male and female businesspeople. A typical example can be found in one report by Xinhua News Agency on 4 July 2002. In the report on women entrepreneurs in China, a female general manager of a technology development company commented, "There is not much difference between female and male entrepreneurs compared to ten years ago. Those who make the most of an opportunity, whether male or female, will be successful." Such remarks can be right as there are obviously some common attributes that are required in the business field; those who have them, men or women, will tend to be more successful in their career paths.

Yet closer scrutiny reveals a subtle distinction created by gender differences. Women managers such as Sun, who have a strong gender consciousness, are capable of turning their characteristics such as sensitivity and expressiveness into particular advantages by being caring and communicative, which can be very useful in doing their tasks. Perhaps also because of their sensitivity toward their gender constructions, they are more likely to avoid the alleged weaknesses of a woman boss, who might be viewed as overly emotional or having a "small heart," in a sense being seen as narrow-minded. For instance, in the case of Sun, in doing justice to her feminine people-oriented and caring personality, she purposely took the initiative to "disciple," to use her word, new managers in her company, making it her priority to help them not only in their career development but also in the area of personal growth. This role has been time-consuming, admittedly, but in doing so she has been efficient in building profound relationships as well as retaining her employees. She perceived such an approach as her superiority in leadership style because most of her male counterparts lacked the patience to build long-term relationships or play a pastoral role in the job.

Likewise, Sun was aware that women's involvement in management can bring a more empathetic and nurturing perspective to problems: "As a woman myself and a person working with employees of both sexes, I can see how women add value in a way that is distinctively combined with a woman's way of thinking about problems and solving the problems." She recalled in many incidents her spontaneous jokes, a casual and understanding tone or remark or an eagerness to create dialogue had broken the ice between two rival parties in a meeting and prevented infighting. Sun explained, "If you are pushy and demanding, the first thing a man will think is 'what a bitch,' but if you 'flirt' with them – I mean being pushy in a soft and sweet way – it is hard for a man to say no." She knew well that her feminine touch was an advantage in her leadership capacities. Yet she was aware that not everybody agrees. She said that to counter the bias against women, she works exceptionally hard: "Precisely because you are a woman and a Christian, you don't want to let people look down on you." But yet, despite her professionalism, she constantly encountered skepticism of all kinds – from the collaborators who practiced bribery and thus saw her nonbribery commitment as strange or from men who did not take her decisions seriously and comfortably. Such a bias burdened her with an obligation to achieve greater heights in order to prove herself. In fact, Sun is not alone in her struggle; research has shown that women often face barriers in rising to higher executive level management positions. My fieldwork shows that most women executives remained managers and did not reach the level of CEO or general manager. A significant number of them decided not to work for someone else and started their own businesses (see Table 1.2).

Sun's position as a director in a male-dominated construction company was thus an outstanding one; perhaps her tremendous drive to succeed has helped her in this regard. Nevertheless, she explained that working hard is not only, nor mainly, to prove herself, although that was her ultimate motive before her conversion to Christianity. But after becoming a Christian, new elements were added to her motivations; she wanted to achieve her best because the ability and opportunities for making money are given by God. She reflected, "Do you think you could sit in this position if God didn't allow it? The Bible says for those to whom much is given, from them much will be expected."

Sun seemed confident and charming with her stylish dress, beautiful earrings, remarkable sense of humor and cheerful expression. She was very attractive. When I complimented her on her beauty, she laughed and said she was upset at the fact that not many men dare to ask her out, probably because of her high position and her assumed high tastes. It might also have been because she was neither young nor free for a relaxing date. It was hardly surprising that her faith had also caused her to be more selective in pursuing a marriage partner. Putting the Bible as her supreme moral authority she was eager to have a same-faith partner, which obviously further reduced her already limited pool of choices. However, Sun was open-minded enough to admit readily her struggle to maintain an ascetic, inevitably lonely, life in a city such as Shanghai, where the nightlife can be very active, especially among expatriates. Thanks to the strength of her religion and the concerted support of the religious community, she had, as she said, gradually developed a stronger incentive to maintain a self-controlled life although it did not come as naturally or easily as she might have desired. To help herself to stay "on the right track," she persisted in having a Bible reading and prayer time every morning as well as in attending Sunday services every week. She said she made a hard decision at the beginning of the year 2008 that she would not entertain any work-related call or business trip or meeting on Sunday: "At first people didn't take me seriously; they kept on calling on Sunday. I ignored their calls and finally they gave up. Now they believe me… I want at least to be able to concentrate on my worship. This is the bottom line that I need to keep."

Jenny

Jenny moved from Taiwan to Shanghai in 1999 with her husband to start a tent business. But the business collapsed terribly after a few years and her husband ran away with his secretary. Out of the ruins of despair, she went to Hong Kong to seek help from one of their big clients. She told him that although she had no knowledge of the business, she was prepared to hit the ground running if he would give her the first contract.

She spent three days persuading the client, waiting hopelessly and impatiently at the harbor for an answer, entertaining final thoughts of giving up. Yet to her surprise, the client eventually decided to transfer an assignment of 300 million yuan to her for a try. This great mercy on the part of the client was a turning point in Jenny's life. With this ray of hope, she decided to stay in Shanghai with her five daughters to restart the business. With 200 more newly recruited temporary workers working day and night, she managed to meet the deadlines and earn the trust of her client. What was equally important is that during that period of time, she converted to Christianity, together with her five children, through the Hong Kong client. She said she could not think of a second reason why the client gave a contract to a person like her, who obviously knew nothing about the products and business, if not out of the mercy and love of God. For her, the contract was thus both a spiritual and material blessing from God, and her decision to stay in Shanghai was undoubtedly a calling from God.

Yet it has been a demanding and tiring effort for Jenny to reconstruct the business virtually from the ground up. She took steps to recruit people, to systematize the system, to set objectives and to distribute roles. Also, she conducted leadership programs for her managers, and equipped the lower ranking workers with technical skills and character courses. On top of that she hired professionals to design more models for her production. When asked how she built the networks without giving bribes or attending banqueting as most businesspeople do, she smilingly replies, "I get many business contacts through my church network. I do business with Christians or non-Christians, but of course if they are church friends I feel more secure. Also I spend a lot of time in praying; I really think God can bring suitable clients to me. In fact I have always had some clients who find my company in the directory and they walk in. Of course I have to give a very reasonable price and professional service to keep them."

However, given the uncertainty and high-risks in the business environment, Jenny has struggled to make the company profitable. I met her on three occasions during my fieldwork in Shanghai and each time I saw her wrestling with different, but equally challenging, problems. The first meeting was in February 2008, a week after the Chinese New Year. Shortly after we started our interview at 8 a.m., she suddenly stood up and explained to me that she needed to go to the factory, located at the back of the office where we were "to check how many workers are still here after the New Year's break." Twenty minutes later, she returned to the office joyfully, exclaiming to me, "One third of them came back! Not bad!" The extremely high turnover rates of workers and middle-ranking managers, the rising wages, and the serious and constant rifts in the factory among people from different provinces, among other problems, have led a lot of foreign factories to shift away from China in favor of other Asian countries such as Vietnam. Jenny too was considering if she should shift away from China. But she was hesitating, afraid that hundreds of skilled employees would be laid off and management terminated. Two months later, we met at a spiritual revival conference organized by and for Christian businesspeople in a hotel in Shanghai. She told me that it had become increasingly tricky to maintain the flow of workers. The factory was haunted by the possibility of bankruptcy. But she remained optimistic, and sometimes even joyful, during our three days spent together at the hotel. "Since God is the one who brings me here, he is responsible for my company," she said. I asked her, "But what if the business fails again?" "That will be his decision and responsibility too!" she replied immediately, pointing up and smiling. The last time I saw Jenny was in July 2008, a few weeks after the earthquake occurred in Sichuan. The situation in the office was totally different this time; it was busy and she was occupied with visitors and calls. Her tent production business was soaring and it was a stunning turnaround for the company. She had managed to transform the leisure tent into a special kind of tent designed specifically for earthquake refugees within a short period of time; her creativity and efficiency had made her one of the main suppliers of refugees' tents to Sichuan. Even the Shanghai Civil Affairs Bureau and the Shanghai Bureau of Quality and Technique Supervision had credited her for her highly useful tents. People floated into her office offering to help in various aspects – even to provide loans with very low interest rates. She said, "I'm very glad that I've been faithful to my calling, I've kept my factory, and it is now helpful to the country." Seeing her business as a manifestation and fulfillment of her calling, Jenny was therefore very concerned about the quality of her products; all her company's tents were under quality control. Yet the pressure to produce quick results was unceasing and she constantly ran the risk of either compromising the quality or losing the business. "I told them [the customers] I won't let the tents go out of my factory if they are not good. So don't push me; if not, I will cancel the business. Some people are only concerned about saving face. They want their tents to be done as soon as possible so that they can report to the company and public that they have met their targets, how many tents they have contributed to the refugees and so forth. Who cares what dangers the refugees will face staying in this kind of tent?" True enough, a few weeks later the newspaper reported that hundreds of tents which were used to set up a temporary exam site in Sichuan collapsed under the strong winds, while hers were among the few that stood firm.

Conclusion

This chapter attempts, through the case studies of four women entrepreneurs and managers' lives which are based on a sample of 20 women, to portray how religious values are justified by these businesswomen and translated into ethical conduct in their business life. Their examples show how religious faith, when combined with female acumen, characteristics and the experience of working in a male-dominated field, has inculcated a set of virtues that shape these women's personality and behavior. Their stories display their high, or sometimes higher, sensitivity toward problematic conduct compared to their male counterparts. I have frequently faced these questions (only from women!) when interviewing entrepreneurs in my fieldwork: "Am I right in doing this or that? What have other respondents said about it? Will it be considered as a sin?" The questionable issues that worried them ranged from paying a bribe in a difficult situation, not paying full taxes, going to karaoke, or even, absence from church because of business activities. Their anxiety about questionable practices, their willingness to diminish guilt, as well as their more people-oriented attributes, have perhaps resulted in their exhibiting a more noticeable (although not necessarily stronger in essence) business ethic than men. Furthermore, insofar as women are more open and willing to share with each other their life stories and experiences, their personal memories of conversion, of being called into China, of "help from above" in a business crisis have all combined to reinforce the inner conviction within them.

As an ethnographic study, this chapter does not aim to prove gender differences in relation to business ethics. It is mainly concerned with depicting how businesswomen display a moral reasoning which essentially corresponds to Weber's Protestant ethic. However, it is clear that none of the personality elements these women have demonstrated are limited specifically to women; the previous chapters in this book have shown how men may also have similar ideas. One possible reason might be since there are characteristics essential for entrepreneurial success, successful businesswomen, like men, are typically those who have acquired certain traits in order to do well within the business field. The nuance of differences between the sexes is thus more in degree than in kind. This chapter is an attempt to shed light on one neglected aspect, namely, the female and business ethic, aiming to increase our understanding about the issues and challenges facing Christian women entrepreneurs and to identify their responses in the Chinese business field.

Chapter 8
CONCLUSION AND RESEARCH IMPLICATIONS

This research has attempted, through a qualitative study of 60 Overseas Chinese Christian entrepreneurs in China, to shed light on three salient issues regarding Christianity and business life in China. First, it shows how Christian faith is taken seriously by those entrepreneurs and also shows the ways in which this faith influences their daily business practices in a very secular society such as China in an ethical and rational direction. The study implies that Christianity has been and can be one possible source and actor of a new business morality in China. Second, unlike the typical assumption that links Overseas Chinese businesspeople with Neo-Confucian entrepreneurs, this research joins other studies in demonstrating the heterogeneity of the Overseas Chinese community. It shows that there is a significant and growing number of Christians among Overseas Chinese who are actively involved in Christian networking and pursuing management strategies based on Christian principles. Instead of shying away from revealing their faith, they are keen to integrate their faith into their business practices. Although it is difficult to disentangle totally Confucian values from Christian values with these businesspeople, the conduct and rationales behind their choices seem to have become more an implementation of certain interpretations of Christian values than a straightforward result of Confucian values. Third, the case studies on Overseas Chinese businesswomen imply that women are not only active in the church, as many have noticed, but are also steadily involved in entrepreneurship. Their stories show how they have developed, perhaps counterintuitively, a rational market behavior corresponding to Weber's Protestant ethic that is similar to or sometimes stronger than that of the men, due mainly to the gender restrictions that have been imposed on them. The voluminous studies on the Protestant ethic have generally ignored the gender issue; the tentative findings of this study suggest that our understanding of Weber's thesis might be enhanced by taking into account gender differences.

In short, to answer the question about belief and action, this research has attempted to show that Christian beliefs have affected businesspeople's day-to-day work manners in the following ways: Christianity works through inculcating a rational personality and certain attitudes toward business, ethics and profit. It also works more overtly through providing a community and network that regulates as well as supports Christians' business activities. It helps to provide some Christian employers with the moral resources to establish a corporate culture which promotes behavior that is compatible with religious values. Yet, as religious influences are woven into the fabric of daily life, it is difficult to measure exactly the degree of depth to which religious values penetrate people's behaviors. Of course, the impact of religion varies according to the circumstances. In certain situations, such as when a shelter is offered to distressed businesspeople from the rigors of very rapid social change, the impact of religion is immediate and tangible. But at another time when it helps adherents to form a certain attitude or a new worldview, its impact may be subtle and slow but also more substantial. Although the roles of religion are often mosaic and indirect, they can nonetheless be important in our understanding of business behavior.

Implications of the Research

It is not surprising if some scholars, inside and outside of China, think a study that introduces religious questions into Chinese business can be regarded as intrusive and irrelevant. It is also not surprising if some scholars assume that what is happening in China now is a form of materialistic dog-eat-dog capitalism, which leaves no room for religion or ethics whatsoever. The response of an economics professor in Shanghai toward my questions regarding his comments on Overseas Chinese business ethics might illustrate this sentiment: "Christian business ethics? I don't think you can find any good examples from local as well as established multinational companies here. Some MNC might have Christian backgrounds or clear ethical policies but they intentionally lower their standards when they come into China. They do the same things as local people do. All crows are equally black."

These comments and common assumptions are part of the reality, for in general, it is true that the overall situation in China has been unusually hostile toward Christianity. Past experience, fierce suppression and atheistic education have all combined to make Christianity a dangerous, or at best irrelevant, foreign ideology. It is also true that the economic changes in China have been mainly caused by institutional conditions such as private-sector dynamism, a relatively supportive financial environment and increasing property rights security, which have nothing to do with religion.

To be sure, Christianity is neither a causative force in the formation of China's market economy nor the ethic to guide that formation. It is also certain that Christianity will remain a minority religion in China, although it is emerging rapidly and some might even argue that "China may be on its way to becoming a Christian nation" (Eastland 2002). Recognizing these factual constraints, this research nevertheless suggests that useful connections might be made between religion and economic life in China. There are many implications from this research.

First, generally, the explanation of economic action requires an expansion beyond the common approaches that focus on the role of interests or social interaction and social structure to include meaning and values. During the twentieth century, mainstream economists have focused primarily on interest-driven behavior, while sociologists have tended to emphasize social behavior. Inspired by Weber's work, this research and its findings instead suggest that one fruitful approach to the study of economic actions is through an examination of the meaning and reasons actors invest in such actions. It is true that economic actions are typically prompted by interests, as suggested by economists. Yet, for an interest to become one, as argued by Weber, it has to be justified with a distinct meaning by the actor. That is, interests are directed by worldviews and values, which in turn are products of certain beliefs. In other words, most people behave according to what they think is both reasonable and meaningful. The sources of this sense of meaning are largely religious. Weber argues that religion is important as it affects people's thoughts and emotions and defines both what is right and wrong and what is worth living one's life for. Even if some people might not be aware of it, their sense of meaning may be traceable to religious influences that were long ago woven into the fabric of daily life. Further, as discussed above, interests propel people to act. Weber divides interests into material and ideal interests. Many studies on economic actions have either been an economic analysis emphasizing the role of material factors and utility or a sociological approach giving prominence to social structures. Both generally downplay ideal interests, which include nationalism, ethnic honor and, particularly, religious benefits – that is, an assurance of salvation or rewards in the afterlife. It is thus crucial to examine, as we have seen in the case of *The Protestant Ethic* and this study, what happens when individuals' economic actions are driven mainly by religious benefits, when material and ideal interests are combined or conflict, and the like.

Despite the many criticisms against Weber, this research argues that his approaches are applicable to our understanding of religion and modern economic activities in China. In particular, what he has to say regarding the relevance of values in understanding economic social actions, which is the "meaning" and purpose of actions, deserves more attention. In essence, his thesis concerning Protestantism and Confucianism might be controversial and inaccurate, especially in the latter case, but he is right to see values as crucial to modern capitalism. The current study shows empirically that in order to understand fully the economic actions of individuals, we need to take into consideration their understanding of meaning and values. Furthermore, if Weber is correct that religiously shaped moral and cultural patterns were keys to economic development in the West, then it might be the case that similar beliefs or values can have some stimulating effects on development elsewhere. By the same token, if we want to understand modern capitalism or to reform a market economy morally, we may have to search more directly into the religious meaning or spiritual foundation on which it rests.

As discussed, China's unprecedented economic boom has given rise to a critical debate about the market and morality. The preponderance of different forms of corruption and value crises have forced many, intellectuals and government officials alike, to realize that the establishment of a market economy and an improvement of business ethics will strongly depend on each other. The debate has attracted a surging research interest but a consensus has yet to develop. John Hanafin (2002) summarizes the debate as below: Some, especially Marxists, believe that the introduction of a market economy has had a negative effect on public morality. Others argue that it has had only a positive effect. Besides this particular debate there are two others. It is argued on the one side that market behavior is amoral and transactional in nature, while on the other side that general ethical norms apply equally to the economy. For those who hold the latter view, some believe the market creates its own norms, while others argue that the moral categories articulated in a moral philosophy are applicable to economic behavior. It is perhaps not surprising that in this debate, religion in general and Christianity in particular have no significant role to play. Most previous researchers have not considered Christianity as a particularly relevant factor. However, this research shows the many ways that Christian values can be applicable and are able to contribute to market behaviors from this analysis of Christian entrepreneurs who are attempting to integrate two life orders or value spheres, that is, religion and economics, through assimilations and accommodations of the latter with the former.

This research has taken place as the global economic crisis has been unfolding, the consequences of which continue to grip the world. The crisis emerged in September 2008 with the failure of a few big United States–based financial firms, and it spread with the insolvency of additional companies, governments in Europe and declining stock market prices around the globe. The impact has been global and immeasurable as banks and companies around the world have collapsed and tens of thousands of people have lost their jobs and homes. China has not been exempt from this global crisis. People worldwide are asking, who or what should we blame for this credit crunch? What is wrong with capitalism? What can we do with this pathological market? Some are going further to search for its root causes and ask, "Is there a moral or spiritual lesson to be learnt?" (Melik 2009). Perhaps one of the main underlying problems, as mentioned by the US president Barack Obama at his historic inaugural in Washington, is that we are now living in an era "of greed and irresponsibility." According to Obama, although the market's power "to generate wealth and expand freedom is unmatched… without a watchful eye, the market can spin out of control" (Obama 2009). Indeed, few would disagree that "the culture of greed has created an individualism, selfishness – a society looking for compensation – a society we don't want to live in," as suggested by Shaunaka Rishi Das of the Oxford Centre for Hindu Studies (Melik 2009).

What is more significant from the point of view of this analysis is, in response to our main question, the role of beliefs and morals in this credit crisis. As argued by Dr Richard Chartres, the Bishop of London, "A financial crisis is not something which can be fixed in a technical way because there is the spiritual dimension of trust and confidence. All financial markets are based on confidence – the root of that word is to have faith together" (Melik 2009). This comment implies that the current economic crisis is in fact a moral or a faith problem; its solutions will therefore involve more than technical methods. This reminds us again of Weber's arguments concerning the significant connections between religious ethics and modern economic life. *The Protestant Ethic*, for example, is perhaps relevant in our attempts to make sense of the current crisis: For Weber, what is "modern" in modern capitalism is an ethic that says that people find meaning in their work in a disciplined and dedicated economic activity. It is precisely the ethical component of the spirit of modern capitalism that distinguishes it from "the instinct of acquisition," which is characterized by ruthless acquisition and bound by no ethical rules whatsoever. Therefore, without the ethical component, modern capitalism is reduced to an adventurer's capitalism. What this research suggests is that, in short, further investigations along these lines may prove more illuminating if religious issues are taken into account.

Second, a more comprehensive understanding of religious developments in modern China requires taking into account its relations with economics. By the late 1990s, religious research in China had grown significantly and become a solidly established discipline (Yang 2005). Many researchers have made the effort to reveal and reflect upon the desecularized reality of China, a phenomenon which goes against the Western experience that suggests religion has declined at the macro-, meso- or micro-levels. They have brought attention to the growing prominence of religion, including Christianity, in Chinese society. Yet, very few studies have focused their attention on the influence of Christianity and the seriousness that its adherents, especially entrepreneurs, attach to it in modern China. To be sure, there have been a growing number of studies on religion and its related aspects of culture and society, such as the arts, philosophy, literature, education, politics, archeology and science, but few studies have emphasized the relationships between Christianity and economics. One prominent reason, as mentioned by Fenggang Yang in his work on religious research in China (2005), is the uneven development of historical studies versus contemporary studies concerning religious issues in general and Christianity in particular. As mentioned in Chapter 1, Christianity has been treated differently in China's religious policies and research because the study of Christianity might cause greater political risks. But despite the reality of this practical difficulty, this study nevertheless suggests that it is crucial to approach Christianity from the angle of its relationship to the economy as the links between the two are becoming ever more established and obvious.

Third, we might have to come to terms with the possible influences Christianity has had on the Overseas Chinese community and its economic achievements. It has been observed that the Overseas Chinese are composed of a group that "have far too long been acknowledged as intriguing, seen as possibly powerful, but never really been understood outside their own sphere" (Redding 1990, 227). But there have been signs of change. We have seen impressive growth in the study of the Overseas Chinese economies since the economic growth in Hong Kong, Taiwan and Singapore has become prominent. More recently, the significance of both the Overseas Chinese and their capitalism has taken on a new aspect because China has become increasingly aware of their economic dynamism; they are now new examples for China's economic development as it moves away from the Stalinist model.

Yet, again, despite the voluminous literature on Overseas Chinese which has been published, almost no attention has been given to Christianity. Most research has linked the ethnic Chinese businesspeople to Neo-Confucian entrepreneurs (Hicks and Redding 1983; Berger 1988; Hicks 1989; Redding 1988, 1990). One typical example was put forward by Ambler and Witzel (2003, 190), "Overseas Chinese are far more concerned with Confucian values, especially respect for tradition. As noted above, the Overseas Chinese are far more concerned with traditions and respecting the past than are their mainland counterparts – 'more Chinese than the Chinese.'" Scholars dealing with the Overseas Chinese have assumed that their culture stems only from Confucian tradition, Chinese legacies and old values, but by assuming this, these scholars have virtually ignored the existence of the Christian community and the influence of Christian values.

Similarly, scholars on Chinese society who have been studying the impact of open-door policies, especially foreign investment, on its socialist economy have equally neglected the possible impact of foreign Christian investors in China. While most of this research focuses on economic aspects, there are some scholars that have pointed to the impact of globalization and the internet on Chinese society, especially in the areas of values, beliefs and behaviors (Naylor 1996). They argue that China's participation in the international community has been inevitably accompanied by the penetration of foreign cultures. They see that the influx of Western economic practices, technology and trade into China has also brought Western political ideas and values into China. But, despite the emphasis on the unprecedented knowledge transfer and cultural learning, this research does not consider the possible influence of Christian values and moral principles, which serve as the bedrock of Western values, on Chinese culture and business behavior. We might expect that as China embraces modernity and foreign cultures and is integrated effectively into the world economy, Christianity might be playing a more obvious role in its economic sphere, and thus deserves our attention.

Finally, this research also found that women are playing an increasing role in business. Women's desire to be economically independent has led them to participate heavily in entrepreneurship (Koper 1993). Also, societal factors, such as growth in education levels and changes in gender role expectations, have increased the access women have had to entrepreneurial opportunities (Brush and Hisrich 1999). This suggests that the ethics of the business community might be affected because of increasing female involvement. Much research has predicted this based on the belief and some empirical results that females are more ethical than males (for examples, Dawson 1995; Farrell and Skinner 1988; Jones and Gautschi 1988; Lane 1995; Whipple and Swords 1992). Others suggest that empirical results cannot prove women's ethical superiority, but only show their difference in ethical attitudes (Borkowski and Ugras 1998).

Research on Weber's thesis on the Protestant ethic has generally neglected the gender dimension. Weber himself did not mention the female in his work on economics in general or in *The Protestant Ethic* in particular. Not surprisingly, then, Weber has been criticized as being "masculine, masculinist and patriarchal" by scholars such as Bologh. According to Bologh (1990, 1), Weber's work is "masculine, because it unself-consciously expresses ideas and values that are associated with masculinity; masculinist, because it self-consciously champions these values and denigrates or ignores others considered feminine; patriarchal, because many of its ideas and values assume and require a social order in which women and women's ways continue to be dominated, repressed and defined by subordination to men and men's ways." While some scholars have seen this charge against Weber as historically inappropriate (Turner 1998a), it is nevertheless certain that Weber's thesis can be supplemented if the gender dimension is considered; this is especially so as the advancement of women in management and entrepreneurial ventures has been progressing recently, albeit at a slow pace.

As argued by Linda Woodhead (2008), "The sociology of religion is not blind to gender, yet its central paradigms remain relatively untouched by an awareness of its significance." This is most obviously true of studies on religion and economics, on the one hand, and religion in China, on the other. In this research, women are either ignored, or they are presupposed to behave like men. This is partly because of the fact that the numbers of female entrepreneurs in general and in Asian societies in particular were initially small and insignificant. Most female-owned businesses have come into existence only in recent decades. However, whether or not women will behave similarly in their attitude and behavior is a matter that needs to be verified empirically and not just assumed.

In conclusion, there is plenty of scope for more research along the topic of religion and economics. This research has laid the foundation for more inquiry into corruption and ethics, religious freedom and foreign investment, civil instability and the Christian presence as well as for the possibility of greater interaction between Confucianism and Christianity. It is, therefore, my desire that these research efforts will introduce new insights and should help in supplementing the interest-driven and structural approaches to understanding the economic actions in China.

BIBLIOGRAPHY

Aikman, David. 2003. *Jesus in Beijing*. Washington DC: Regnery Publishing.
All-China Women's Federation. 2000. "The Situation of Women Entrepreneurs in Non-public Sectors." *Research in Women* 2: 34–9.
Ambler, Tim, Morgen Witzel and Chao Xi. 2003. *Doing Business in China*. London and New York: Routledge.
Antonio, Robert J. and Ronald M. Glassman. 1985. *A Weber-Marx Dialogue*. Lawrence, KS: University Press of Kansas.
Aron, Raymond. 1970. *Main Currents in Sociological Thought*, vol. 2. Harmondsworth: Penguin.
Backman, Michael. 2001. *Asian Eclipse: Exposing the Dark Side of Business in Asia*. Singapore: John Wiley and Sons.
Baehr, Peter R. and Gordon C. Wells. 2002. *The Protestant Ethic and the 'Spirit' of Capitalism and Other Writings*. New York: Penguin.
Barbalet, Jack. 2008. *Weber, Passion and Profits: 'The Protestant Ethic and the Spirit of Capitalism' in Context*. Cambridge: Cambridge University Press.
Barro, Robert J. and Rachel M. McCleary. 2003. "Religion and Economic Growth." National Bureau of Economic Research (NBER), Working Paper No. 9682. http://www.nber.org/~rosenbla/econ302/lecture/barroreligion.pdf (accessed 1 November 2011).
Barton, Cliff A. 1983. "Trust and Credit: Some Observations Regarding Business Strategies of Overseas Chinese Traders in South Vietnam." In Linda Y. C. Lim and L. A. Peter Gosling (eds), *The Chinese in Southeast Asia*. Singapore/Ann Arbor: Maruzen/University of Michigan, Center for South and Southeast Asia Studies.
Bates, Timothy. 1994. "Social Resources Generated by Group Support Networks May Not Be Beneficial to Asian Immigrant-owned Small Businesses." *Social Forces* 72.3: 671–89.
Bays, H. Daniel. 2003. "Chinese Protestant Christianity Today." *China Quarterly* 174: 488–504.
———. 2008. *Protestantism in Modern China as 'Foreign Religion' and 'Chinese Religion': Autonomy, Independence, and the Constraints of Foreign Hegemony*. Conference paper for the Beijing Summit on Chinese Spirituality and Society, Peking University, 8–10 October.
Bell, Daniel. 1996. "Afterword: 1996." In *The Cultural Contradictions of Capitalism: Twentieth Anniversary Edition*. New York: Basic Books.
Bell, S. Linda. 1994. "For Better, for Worse: Women and the World Market in Rural China." *Modern China* 20.2: 180–210.
Bellah, N. Robert. 1957. *Tokugawa Religion: The Values of Pre-Industrial Japan*. Glencoe, IL: The Free Press.
———. 1963. "Reflections on the Protestant Ethic Analogy in Asia." *Journal of Social Issues* 19.1: 52–61.
Bendix, Reinhard, 1998. *Max Weber: An Intellectual Portrait*. London and New York: Routledge.

Berger, L. Peter. 1963. "Charisma and Religious Innovation: The Social Location of Israelite Prophecy." *American Sociological Review* 28: 940–51.

———. 1988. "An East Asian Development Model." In Peter L. Berger and Hsin-Huang M. Hsiao (eds), *In Search of an East Asian Development Model*. New Brunswick, NJ: Transaction Books.

Beu, Danielle S., Ronald M. Buckley and Michale G. Harvey. 2003. "Ethical Decision-making: A Multidimensional Construct." *Business Ethics: A European Review* 12: 88–106.

Bjorkman, Ingmar, Adam Smale, Jennie Sumelius, Vesa Suutari and Yuan Lu. 2008. "Changes in Institutional Context and MNC Operations in China: Subsidiary HRM Practices in 1996 Versus 2006." *International Business Review* 17: 146–58.

Bologh, W. Roslyn. 1990. *Love or Greatness: Max Weber and Masculine Thinking – A Feminist Inquiry*. London: Unwin Hyman.

Bolt, J. Paul. 1996. "Looking to the Diaspora: The Overseas Chinese and China's Economic Development, 1978–1994." *Diaspora: A Journal of Transnational Studies* 5.3: 467–96.

Borkowski, Susan C. and Yusuf J. Ugras. 1998. "Business Students and Ethics: A Meta-Analysis." *Journal of Business Ethics* 17.11: 1117–27.

Bourdieu, Pierre, Channa Newman and Loïc J. D. Wacquant. 1991. "The Peculiar History of Scientific Reason." *Sociological Forum* 6: 3–26.

Bramall, Chris. 2008. *Chinese Economic Development*. New York: Routledge.

Brouwer, Steve, Paul Gifford and Susan D. Rose. 1996. *Exporting the American Gospel: Global Christian Fundamentalism*. New York and London: Routledge.

Brush, Candida G. and Robert D. Hisrich. 1999. "Women-owned Businesses: Why Do They Matter?" In Zoltán J. Ács (ed.), *Are Small Firms Important? Their Role and Impact*. Boston, MA: Kluwer Academic Publishers.

Burt, Ronald. 1992. *Structural Holes: The Social Structure of Competition*. Cambridge, MA: Harvard University Press.

"Business as Mission." 2004. Lausanne Occasional Paper No. 59. www.lausanne.org/documents/2004forum/LOP59_IG30.pdf (accessed 10 October 2008).

Campbell, Thomas C. Jr. 1957. "Capitalism and Christianity." *Harvard Business Review*, July–August: 37–44.

Cao, Nanlai. 2007. "Christian Entrepreneurs and the Post-Mao State: An Ethnographic Account of Church-State Relations in China's Economic Transition." *Sociology of Religion* 68.1: 45–66.

Chan, Kim-Kwong. 1992. "A Chinese Perspective on the Interpretation of the Chinese Government's Religious Policy." In Alan Hunter and Don Rimmington (eds), *All Under Heaven: Chinese Tradition and Christian Life in the People's Republic of China*. Kampen: J. H. Kok.

Chen, Cunfu and Tianhai Huang. 2004. "The Emergence of a New Type of Christians in China Today." *Review of Religious Research* 46: 183–200.

Chen, Q. and S. Hu. 1997. "An Analysis on China's Utilization of Foreign Investment." *The Study of Overseas Chinese Affairs* 72.2.

Cheung, Tak Sing and Ambrose Y. C. King. 2001. "A Study of Confucian Entrepreneurs in Mainland China, Taiwan and Hong Kong." In Alvin Y. So, Nan Lin and Dudley L. Poston (eds), *The Chinese Triangle of Mainland China, Taiwan, and Hong Kong: Comparative Institutional Analyses*. Westport, CT: Greenwood.

Chu, Yin-wah (ed.) 2010. *Chinese Capitalisms: Historical Emergence and Political Implications*. New York: Palgrave Macmillan.

Churchman, W. Charles. 1971. *The Design of Inquiring Systems*. New York: Basic Books.

Clifford, R. Nicholas. 1991. *Spoilt Children of Empire: Westerners in Shanghai and the Chinese Revolution of the 1920s*. Hanover, NH/London: University Press of New England/Middlebury College Press.
Coleman, S. James. 1988. "Social Capital in the Creation of Human Capital." *American Journal of Sociology* 94: 95–121.
Collins, Randall. 1985. *Max Weber: A Skeleton Key*. Beverly Hills: Sage.
———. 1997. "An Asian Route to Capitalism: Religious Economy and the Origins of Self-Transforming Growth in Japan." *American Sociological Review* 62 (December): 843–65.
Collins, Denis. 2000. "The Quest to Improve the Human Condition: The First 1500 Articles Published in Journal of Business Ethics." *Journal of Business Ethics* 26: 1–73.
Cooke, Fang Lee. 2004. "Women in Management in China." In Marilyn L. Davidson and Ronald J. Burke (eds), *Women in Management Worldwide: Progress and Prospects*. Aldershot: Ashgate Publishing Company.
Cornwell, Benjamin. 2007. "The Protestant Sect Credit Machine: Social Capital and the Rise of Capitalism." *Journal of Classical Sociology* 7.3: 267–291.
Cottrell, Michael. 1999. "The Irish in Saskatchewan, 1850–1930: A Study of Intergenerational Ethnicity." *Prairie Forum* 24: 185–209.
Davis, Stanley M. 1986. *Managing Corporate Culture*. Cambridge, MA: Ballinger.
Dawson, Leslie M. 1997. "Ethical Differences between Men and Women in the Sales Profession." *Journal of Business Ethics* 16: 1143–52.
Deal, Terry and Allan Kennedy. 1982. *Corporate Cultures*. New York: Addison-Wesley.
Dean, James M. and Anthony M. C. Waterman (eds). 1999. *Religion and Economics: Normative Social Theory*. Dordrecht: Kluwer Academic Publishers.
Dimaggio, Paul J. and Walter Powell. 1991. "The Iron Cage Revisited: Institutional Isomorphism and Collective Rationality in Organization Fields." In Walter Powell and Paul J. DiMaggio (eds), *New Institutionalism in Organizational Analysis*. Chicago: University of Chicago Press.
Dirlik, Arif. 1997. "Critical Reflections on 'Chinese Capitalism' as a Paradigm." *Identities* 3.3: 303–30.
Dore, Ronald P. 1996. "Confucianism, Economic Growth and Social Development." In Josef Kreiner (ed.), *The Impact of Traditional Thought on Present-Day Japan*. Munich: Iudicium.
Eastland, Terry. 2002. "China's Next Great Leap." *Weekly Standard*, 1 October. http://www.weeklystandard.com/Content/Public/Articles/000/000/001/719fczfj.asp (accessed 1 November 2011).
Esquire. 2006. "Shangdi shi Wo de Dongshizhang" [God is the Chairman of My Board of Directors], January.
Evans, P. B. 1979. *Dependent Development: The Alliance of Multinational, State and Local Capital in Brazil*. Princeton, NJ: Princeton University Press.
Eisenstadt, Schmuel N. 1968. "The Protestant Ethic Thesis in an Analytical and Comparative Framework." In Schmuel N. Eisenstadt (ed.), *The Protestant Ethic and Modernization: A Comparative View*. New York: Basic Books.
———. 1985. "This-Worldly Transcendentalism and the Structuring of the World: Weber's *Religion of China* and the Format of Chinese History and Civilization." *Journal of Developing Societies* 1–2: 168–186.
Elzinga, Kenneth G. 1999. "Economics and Religion: Comment." In James M. Dean and Anthony M. C. Waterman (eds), *Religion and Economics: Normative Social Theory*. Dordrecht: Kluwer Academic Publishers.
Fairbank, John K. 1979. *The United States and China*. Cambridge, MA: Harvard University Press.

Fanfani, Amintore. 1935. *Catholicism, Protestantism and Capitalism*. London: Sheed & Ward.
Fang, Tony, Shuming Zhao and Verner Worm. 2008. "Editorial: The Changing Chinese Culture and Business Behavior." *International Business Review* 17: 141–145.
Faure, Olivier G. and Tony Fang. 2008. "Changing Chinese Values: Keeping up with Paradoxes." *International Business Review* 17: 194–207.
Ferrell, O. C. and Steven J. Skinner. 1988. "Ethical Behavior and Bureaucratic Structure in Marketing Research Organizations." *Journal of Marketing Research* 25: 103–109.
Field, John. 2008. *Social Capital*. London: Routledge.
Finnemore, Martha. 1996. *National Interests in International Society*. Ithaca, NY: Cornell University Press.
Fukuyama, Francis. 2005. "The Calvinist Manifesto." http://www.nytimes.com/2005/03/13/books/review/013FUKUYA.html (accessed 23 July 2008).
Fullerton, Kemper. 1928. "Calvinism and Capitalism." *Harvard Theological Review* 21: 163–95.
Geertz, Clifford. 1960. "Religious Belief and Economic Behavior in a Central Javanese Town: Some Preliminary Considerations." *Economic Development and Cultural Change* 4: 134–58.
Gilligan, Carol. 1982. *In a Different Voice*. Cambridge, MA: Harvard University Press.
Godley, Michael R. 1981. *The Mandarin-Capitalists from Nanyang: Overseas Chinese Enterprise in the Modernization of China 1893–1911*. Cambridge: Cambridge University Press.
Gold, Thomas, Doug Guthrie and David L. Wank (eds). 2002. *Social Connections in China: Institutions, Culture, and the Changing Nature of Guanxi*. New York: Cambridge University Press.
Goldman, Merle. 1986. "Religion in Post-Mao China." *Annals of the American Academy of Political and Social Science* 483: 146–156.
Gomez, Edmund Terence and Hsin-Huang M. Hsiao (eds). 2001. *Chinese Business in Southeast Asia*. Richmond: Curzon Press.
Granovetter, Mark. 1985. "Economic Action and Social Structure: The Problem of Embeddedness." *American Journal of Sociology* 91: 481–510.
Granovetter, Mark. 1992. "Problems of Explanation in Economic Sociology." In N. Nohria and R. Eccles (eds), *Networks and Organizations: Structures, Form and Action*. Boston: Harvard Business School Press.
Grimshaw, Jean. 1999. "The Idea of a Female Ethic." In Peter Singer (ed.), *A Companion to Ethics*. Oxford: Blackwell Publishers.
Gu, Zhibin. 1991. *China beyond Deng: Reform in the PRC*. Jefferson, NC: McFarland and Co.
Guthrie, Doug. 1999. *Dragon in a Three-Piece Suit: The Emergence of Capitalism in China*. Princeton, NJ: Princeton University Press.
Hagan, Jacqueline and Helen R. Ebaugh. 2003. "Calling Upon the Sacred: Migrants' Use of Religion in the Migration Process." *International Migration Review* 37: 1145–62.
Hamilton, Gary G. 1984. "Patriarchalism in Imperial China and Western Europe: A Revision of Weber's Sociology of Domination." *Theory and Society* 13: 393–425.
———. (ed.) 1991. *Business Networks and Economic Development in East and Southeast Asia*. Hong Kong: Centre of Asian Studies, University of Hong Kong.
———. 1996. 'Overseas Chinese Capitalism.' In Wei-Ming Tu (ed.), *The Confucian Dimensions of Industrial East Asia*. Cambridge, MA: Harvard University Press.
Hamilton, Gary G. and Cheng-shu Kao. 1990. "The Institutional Foundations of Chinese Business." *Comparative Social Research* 12: 135–151.
Hamrin, Carol L. 2008. *China's Protestants: A Mustard Seed for Moral Renewal?* American Enterprise Institute for Public Policy Research, Papers and Studies, 14 May. http://www.aei.org/publications/filter.social,pubID.27992/pub_detail.asp (accessed 27 Oct 2008).

Hanafin, John J. 2002. "Morality and the Market in China: Some Contemporary Views." *Business Ethics Quarterly* 12.1: 1–18.
Hartwell, Ronald M. 1971. *The Industrial Revolution and Economic Growth*. London: Methuen.
Hawtrey, Kim. 1999. "Economics and Evangelicalism." In James M. Dean and Anthony M. C. Waterman (eds), *Religion and Economics: Normative Social Theory*. Dordrecht: Kluwer Academic Publishers.
Hellman, Joel, Geraint Jones and Daniel Kaufmann. 2002. "Far From Home: Do Foreign Investors Import Higher Standards of Governance in Transition Economies?" Washington DC: The World Bank.
Hendry, C., A. Jones, M. Arthur and A. Pettigrew. 1991. "Human Resource Development in Small to Medium Sized Enterprises." Sheffield: Employment Department Research Paper.
Hennis, Wilhem. 1988. *Max Weber: Essays in Reconstruction*. London: Allen & Unwin.
Hicks, George. 1989. "The Four Little Dragons: An Enthusiast's Reading Guide." *Asian-Pacific Economic Literature* 3.2: 35–49.
Hicks, George and S. G. Redding. 1983. "The Story of the East Asian Economic Miracle." *Euro-Asia Business Review* 2: 3–4.
Hill, M. 1973. *Sociology of Religion*. London: Heinemann Educational.
Hoffman, James. 1998. "Are Women Really More Ethical than Men? Maybe It Depends on the Situation." *Journal of Managerial Issues* 10: 60–73.
Hong Kong Trade Development Council (HKTDC). 2004. "More Hong Kong Residents Work in Shanghai." *Business Alert – China* 12, 1 December. http://www.tdctrade.com/alert/cba-e0412g-3.htm (accessed 12 October 2011).
Hong, M. W. 2008. "Religiousness, Love of Money, and Ethical Attitudes of Malaysian Evangelical Christians in Business." *Journal of Business Ethics* 81: 169–191.
Hsiao, Hsin-Huang M. 1988. "An East Asian Development Model: Empirical Explorations." In Peter Berger and Hsin-Huang M. Hsiao (eds), *In Search of an East Asian Development Model*. New Brunswick, NJ: Transaction Books.
Hsing, You-tien. 1998. *Making Capitalism in China: The Taiwan Connection*. New York: Oxford University Press.
Huang, Cen. 1998. "The Organization and Management of Chinese Transnational Enterprises in South China." *Issues and Studies* 34.3: 51–70.
Huang, Yasheng. 2003. *Selling China: Foreign Direct Investment during the Reform Era*. New York: Cambridge University Press.
———. 2008. *Capitalism with Chinese Characteristics: Entrepreneurship and the State*. Cambridge: Cambridge University Press.
Hume, Susan. 2003. "Belgian Settlement and Society in the Indiana Rust Belt." *Geographical Review* 93: 30–50.
Hunt, A. 1997. "Are Women more Ethical than Men?" *Baylor Business Review* 15: 7.
Hunter, Alan and Don Rimmington. 1992. "Religion and Social Change in Contemporary China." In Alan Hunter and Don Rimmington (eds), *All Under Heaven: Chinese Tradition and Christian Life in the People's Republic of China*. Kampen: J. H. Kok.
Hunter, Alan and Kim-Kwong Chan. 1993. *Protestantism in Contemporary China*. New York: Cambridge University Press.
Huntington, Samuel P. 1996. *The Clash of Civilizations and the Remaking of World Order*. New York: Simon & Schuster.
Ibrahim, Nabil A. and John P. Angelidis. 2005. "The Long-Term Performance of Small Business: Are There Differences between 'Christian-Based' Companies and Their Secular Counterparts?" *Journal of Business Ethics* 58: 187–193.

Ibrahim, Nabil A., Leslie W. Rue, Patricia P. McDougall and Robert G. Greene. 1991. "Characteristics and Practices of 'Christian-Based' Companies." *Journal of Business Ethics* 10.2: 123–32.

Inglehart, Ronald and Wayne E. Baker. 2000. "Modernization, Cultural Change, and the Persistence of Traditional Values." *American Sociological Review* (February): 19–51.

Jackall, Robert. 1988. *Moral Mazes*. New York: Oxford University Press.

Jones, Thomas M. and Frederick H. Gautschi III. 1988. "Will the Ethics of Business Change? A Survey of Future Executives." *Journal of Business Ethics* 7: 231–248.

Kim, Chan W. and Renée Mauborgne. 1999. "Strategy, Value Innovation, and the Knowledge Economy." *Sloan Management Review* 40: 41–53.

King, Y. 1983. "Rujia Lunli yu Jingji Fazhan: Weibo Xueshuo Chongtan" [The Confucian Ethic and Economic Development: Revisiting Weber's Scholarship]. *Linhe Yuekan* [United Monthly] 25: 70–9.

Koh, Byong-ik. 1991. "Confucianism in Contemporary Korea." In Wei-Ming Tu (ed.), *The Triadic Chord: Confucian Ethics, Industrial East Asia and Max Weber*. Singapore: The Institute of East Asian Philosophies.

Kohlberg, Lawrence. 1984. *The Psychology of Moral Development in Essays on Moral Development*, vol. 2. San Francisco: Harper & Rowe.

Koper, Gerda. 1993. "Women Entrepreneurs and the Granting of Business Credit." In Sheila Allen and Carole Truman (eds), *Women in Business: Perspective on Women Entrepreneurs*. London and New York: Routledge.

Ku, Chung-hwa. 2010. "The 'Spirit' of Capitalism in China: Contemporary Meanings of Weber's Thought." In Yin-wah Chu (ed.), *Chinese Capitalisms: Historical Emergence and Political Implications*. New York: Palgrave Macmillan.

Lai, Harry. 2003. "The Religious Revival in China." *Copenhagen Journal of Asian Studies* 18: 40–64.

Landa, Janet. 1983. "The Political Economy of the Ethnically Heterogeneous Chinese Middleman Group in Southeast Asia: Ethnicity and Entrepreneurship in a Plural Society." In Linda Y. C. Lim and Peter Gosling (eds), *The Chinese in Southeast Asia*. Singapore/Ann Arbor: Maruzen/University of Michigan, Center for South and Southeast Asia Studies.

Landes, David S. 1999. *The Wealth and Poverty of Nations: Why Some Are So Rich and Some So Poor*. New York: Norton.

Lane, Jim C. 1995. "Ethics of Business Students: Some Marketing Perspectives." *Journal of Business Ethics* 14: 571–580.

Lardy, N. 1995. "The Role of Foreign Trade and Investment in China's Economic Transformation." *China Quarterly* 144: 1065–82.

Laumann, Edward O. and David Knoke. 1986. "Social Network Theory." In Siegwart Lindenberg, James. S. Coleman and Stefan Nowak (eds), *Approaches to Social Theory*. New York: Russell Sage.

Lee, Ching Kwan. 1998. *Unravelling the South China Miracle: Two Worlds of Factory Women*. Berkeley: University of California Press.

Lehmann, Hartmut and Guenther Roth (eds). 1995. *Weber's Protestant Ethic: Origins, Evidence, Contexts*. Cambridge: Cambridge University Press.

Leo Douw, Cen Huang and Michael R. Godley. 1999. *Qiaoxiang Ties: Interdisciplinary Approaches to "Cultural Capitalism" in South China*. London: Kegan Paul (in association with International Institute for Asian Studies, Leiden).

Leung, Beatrice. 2005. "China's Religious Freedom Policy: The Art of Managing Religious Activity." *China Quarterly* 184: 894–913.

Levi, Michael. 1997. "Stealing from the People." *China Review* 8 (Autumn–Winter): 4–9.
Levenson, Joseph R. 1958. *Confucian China and its Modern Fate: The Problems of Intellectual Continuity*. Berkeley: University of California Press.
Li, Pingye. 1999. "90 Niandai Zhongguo Zongjiao Fazhan Zhuangkuang Baogao" [A Report on the Development of Religion in China in the 1990s]. *Jidujiao Wenhua Xuekan* [Journal of Christian Culture] 1: 201–22.
Li, Xiangping and Fenggang Yang. 2008. *Jidujiao Lunli yu Shehui Xinren de Guanxi Jiangou* [Christian Ethics and the Construction of Social Trust – The Study of Contemporary Chinese Christian Business]. http://www.360doc.com/content/10/1124/17/164198_72080049.shtml (accessed 20 October 2011).
Lichtblau, Klaus. 1995. "The Protestant Ethic versus the 'New Ethic.'" In Hartmut Lehmann and Guenther Roth (eds), *Weber's Protestant Ethic: Origins, Evidence, Contexts*. Cambridge: Cambridge University Press.
Liedtka, Jeanne M. 1992. "Exploring Ethical Issues Using Personal Interviews." *Business Ethics Quarterly* 2.2: 161–181.
Lim, Linda Y. C. 2006. "Overseas Chinese Investments in China." In Lynn Pan (ed.), *The Encyclopedia of the Chinese Overseas*. Singapore: Editions Didier Millet.
Lin, Nan. 2001. "Guanxi: A Conceptual Analysis." In Alvin Y. So, Nan Lin and Dudley Poston (eds), *The Chinese Triangle of Mainland-Taiwan-Hong Kong*. Westport, CT: Greenwood Press.
Ling, Trevor O. 1991. "The Weberian Thesis and Interpretive Positions on Modernization." In Wei-Ming Tu (ed.), *The Triadic Chord: Confucian Ethics, Industrial East Asia and Max Weber*. Singapore: The Institute of East Asian Philosophies.
Liu, Hong. 1998. "Old Linkages, New Networks: The Globalization of Overseas Chinese Voluntary Associations and its Implications." *China Quarterly* 155: 583–609.
Luthar, Harsh K. and Ranjan Karri. 2005. "Exposure to Ethics Education and the Perception of Linkage between Organizational Ethical Behavior and Business Outcomes." *Journal of Business Ethics* 61: 353–368.
MacInnis, Donald. 1994. *Religion in China Today*. Marryknoll, NY: Orbis Books.
Marsden, Peter V. 1990. "Network and Data Measurement." *Annual Review of Sociology* 16: 435–63.
Marshall, Gordon. 1980. *Presbyteries and Profits: Calvinism and the Development of Capitalism in Scotland, 1560–1707*. Oxford: Clarendon Press.
_____. 1982. *In Search of the Spirit of Capitalism: An Essay on Max Weber's Protestant Ethic Thesis*. London: Hutchinson & Co.
Martin, David. 1990. *Tongues of Fire: The Explosion of Protestantism in Latin America*. Oxford: Basil Blackwell.
_____. 1995. "Religion and Economic Culture." In M. L. Stackhouse, D. P. McCann and S. J. Roels (eds), *On Moral Business: Classical and Contemporary Resources for Ethics in Economic Life*. Grand Rapids, MI: Wm. B. Eerdmans Publishing.
Mason, Sharon E. and Peter E. Mudrack. 1996. " Gender and Ethical Orientation: A Test of Gender and Occupational Socialization Theories." *Journal of Business Ethics* 15: 599–604.
McEwen, S. 1994. "Markets, Modernization, and Individualism in Three Chinese Societies." PhD dissertation, Boston University.
Melik, James. 2009. "The moral dilemmas of the financial crisis." BBC News, 25 January. http://news.bbc.co.uk/1/hi/business/7831002.stm (accessed 1 November 2011).

Merton, Robert K. 1970. *Science, Technology and Society in Seventeenth Century England*. New York/Atlantic Highlands, NJ: Fertig/Humanities Press.
Michailova, Snejina and Verner Worm. 2003. "Personal Networking in Russia and China: Blat and Guanxi." *European Management Journal* 21.4: 509–19.
Michalisin, Michael D., Douglas M. Kline and Robert D. Smith. 2000. "Intangible Strategic Assets and Firm Performance: A Multi-industry Study of the Resource-based View." *Journal of Business Strategies* 17: 91–103.
Miller, Donald and Tetsunao Yamamori. 2007. *Global Pentecostalism: The New Face of Christian Social Engagement*. Berkeley and Los Angeles: University of California Press.
Miller, David W. 2007. *God at Work: The History and Promise of the Faith at Work Movement*. New York: Oxford University Press.
Mintz, Beth and Michael Schwartz. 1985. *The Power Structure of American Business*. Chicago: University of Chicago Press.
Mishler, Elliot. 1986. *Research Interviewing: Context and Narrative*. Cambridge, MA: Harvard University Press.
Mitzman, Arthur. 1971. *The Iron Cage: An Historical Interpretation of Max Weber*. New York: Universal Library.
Moore, Robert. 1971. "History, Economics and Religion: A Review of 'The Max Weber Thesis' Thesis." In Arun Sahay (ed.), *Max Weber and Modern Sociology*. London: Routledge & Kegan Paul.
Morawetz, David. 1980. *Why the Emperor's New Clothes Are Not Made in Colombia? A Case Study in Latin America and East Asia Manufactured Exports*. Washington DC: The World Bank.
Morishima, Michio. 1982. *Why Has Japan 'Succeeded'? Western Technology and the Japanese Ethos*. Cambridge: Cambridge University Press.
Mulholland, Kate. 1997. "The Family, Enterprise and Business Strategies." *Work, Employment and Society* 11.4: 685–711.
Nash, Laura L. 1994. *Believers in Business*. Nashville: Thomas Nelson Publishers.
Naylor, Larry L. 1996. *Culture and Change: An Introduction*. Westport, CT: Bergin & Garvey.
Ng, Evelyn G. H. and Catherine W. Ng. 2003. "Women Micro Entrepreneurs in Hong Kong: Balancing the Personal with the Business." In John E. Butler (ed.), *New Perspectives on Women Entrepreneurs*. Greenwich, CT: Information Age Publishing.
Obama, Barack. 2009. "President Barack Obama's Inaugural Address." *The White House Blog*, 21 January. http://www.whitehouse.gov/blog/inaugural-address/ (accessed 1 November 2011).
Ong, Aihwa. 1999. *Flexible Citizenship: The Cultural Logics of Transnationality*. Durham, NC and London: Duke University Press.
Ong, Aihwa and Donald Nonini (eds). 1997. *Ungrounded Empires: The Cultural Politics of Modern Chinese Transnationalism*. New York and London: Routledge.
Overmyer, Daniel L. 2003. "Religion in China Today: Introduction." *China Quarterly* 174: 307–16.
Parkin, Frank. 1982. *Max Weber*. New York: Tavistock Publications.
Peters, Tom and Bob Waterman. 1982. *In Search of Excellence*. New York: Harper & Row.
Portes, Alejandro. 1998. "Social Capital: Its Origins and Applications in Modern Sociology." *Annual Review of Sociology* 24: 1–24.
Powell, Walter W. 1990. "Neither Markets Nor Hierarchy: Network Forms of Organization." *Research in Organizational Behavior* 12: 295–336.

Powell, Walter W. and Laurel Smith-Doerr. 1994. "Networks and Economic Life." In Neil J. Smelser and Richard Swedberg (eds), *The Handbook of Economic Sociology*. Princeton, NJ: Princeton University Press.

Putnam, Robert D. 1993. *Making Democracy Work: Civic Traditions in Modern Italy*. Princeton, NJ: Princeton University Press.

———. 2000. *Bowling Alone: The Collapse and Revival of American Community*. New York: Simon & Schuster.

Pye, Lucian W. 1981. "Foreword." In Christopher Howe (ed.), *Shanghai: Revolution and Development in An Asian Metropolis*. Cambridge: Cambridge University Press.

Redding, Gordon S. 1988. "The Role of the Entrepreneur in the New Asian Capitalism." In Peter L. Berger and Hsin-Huang M. Hsiao (eds), *In Search of an East Asian Development Model*. New Brunswick, NJ: Transaction Books.

———. 1990. *The Spirit of Chinese Capitalism*. Berlin and New York: Walter de Greuter.

Redding, Gordon S. and Michael A. Witt. 2007. *The Future of Chinese Capitalism*. New York: Oxford University Press.

Risse, Thomas, Stephen Ropp and Kathryn Sikkink (eds). 1999. *Power of Human Rights: International Norms and Domestic Change*. New York: Cambridge University Press.

Ritter, Barbara A. 2006. "Can Business Ethics be Trained? A Study of the Ethical Decision-Making Process in Business Students." *Journal of Business Ethics* 68: 153–164.

Robb, Alicia M. 2002. "Entrepreneurial Performance by Women and Minorities: The Case of New Firms." *Journal of Developmental Entrepreneurship* 7.4: 383–397.

Robertson, Menteith H. 1935. *Aspects of the Rise of Economic Individualism: A Criticism of Max Weber and His School*. Cambridge: Cambridge University Press.

Robbins, Stephen P. 1983. *Organizational Theory, Structure, Design, and Applications*. Englewood Cliffs, NJ: Prentice Hall.

Rocca, Jean-Louis. 1992. "Corruption and Its Shadow: An Anthropological View of Corruption in China." *China Quarterly* 130: 402–16.

Roels, Shirley J. 1997. "The Business Ethics of Evangelicals." *Business Ethics Quarterly* 7.2: 109–22.

Ross, R. S. 1988. "China and the Ethnic Chinese: Political Liability/Economic Asset." In J. K. Kallgren, N. Sopiee and S. Djiwandono (eds), *ASEAN and China: An Evolving Relationship*. Berkeley: Institute of East Asian Studies, University of California.

Salomon, Albert. 1945. "German Sociology." In Georges Gurvitch and Wilbert E. Moore (eds), *Twentieth Century Sociology*. New York: Philosophical Library.

Samuelson, Paul. 1979. *Economics*. New York: McGraw-Hill.

Samuelsson, Kurt. 1961. *Religion and Economic Action*. London: Heinemann.

Santoro, Michael A. 2000. *Profits and Principles: Global Capitalism and Human Rights in China*. Ithaca, NY: Cornell University Press.

Schak, David C. 1999. "Culture as a Management Issue: The Case of Taiwanese Entrepreneurs in the Pearl River Delta." In Leo Douw, Cen Huang and Michael R. Godley (eds), *Qiaoxiang Ties: Interdisciplinary Approaches to "Cultural Capitalism" in South China*. London: Kegan Paul (in association with the International Institute for Asian Studies, Leiden).

Schumpeter, Joseph. 1961. *The Theory of Economic Development*. New York: Galaxy Books.

Shanghai Foreign Investment Commission (SFIC). 2001. *A Summary of the Survey on FDI in Shanghai*. Shanghai: Shanghai Foreign Investment Commission.

Shen, Hsiu-hua. 2003. "Making Taiwanese Transnational Business Masculinity: Commodifying Chinese Women." Paper presented at the annual meeting of the American Sociological Association, Atlanta, 16 August.

———. 2004. "The Making of a Transnational Taiwan Capitalist Class in China." Paper presented at the annual meeting of the American Sociological Association, San Francisco, 14 August.
Silin, Robert H. 1976. *Leadership and Values: The Organization of Large-Scale Taiwanese Enterprises.* Cambridge, MA: Harvard University Press.
Silvoso, Ed. 2002. *Anointed for Business.* California: Regal Books.
Stockwell, Foster. 2003. *Westerners in China: A History of Exploration and Trade, Ancient Times through the Present.* Jefferson, NC: McFarland and Co.
Swedberg, Richard. 1998. *Max Weber and the Idea of Economic Sociology.* Princeton, NJ: Princeton University Press.
Swidler, Ann. 1986. "Culture in Action: Symbols and Strategies." *American Sociological Review* 51.2: 273–86.
Tan, Chee-Beng. 1995. "The Study of Chinese Religions in Southeast Asia." In Leo Suryadinata (ed.), *Southeast Asian Chinese: The Socio-Cultural Dimension.* Singapore: Times Academic Press.
Tawney, Richard H. 1926. *Religion and the Rise of Capitalism.* West Drayton: Pelican Books.
———. 1930. "Foreword." In Max Weber, *The Protestant Ethic and the Spirit of Capitalism,* trans. Talcott Parsons. London: Allen & Unwin.
"The Second National Sample Survey of Women's Social Position in China: Project Report." 2001. *Collection of Women's Studies* 42.5: 4–12.
Thomas, Peter. 2006. "Being Max Weber." *New Left Review* 41 (September–October). http://www.newleftreview.org/?getpdf=NLR27509andpdflang=en (accessed 10 Nov 2008).
Tian, G. 1999. "Changing Patterns of FDI in Shanghai." In Yanrui Wu (ed.), *Foreign Direct Investment and Economic Growth in China.* Cheltenham: Edward Elgar.
Tong, Joy Kooi-Chin. 2008. "McDonaldization and the Mega-Church: A Case Study of City Harvest Church in Singapore." In Pattana Kitiarsa (ed.), *Religious Commodications in Asia.* London: Routledge.
Tracy, Noel and Constance Lever-Tracy. 1997. "A New Alliance for Profit: China's Local Industries and the Chinese Diaspora." In Thomas Menkhoff and Solvay Gerke (eds), *Chinese Entrepreneurship and Asian Business Networks.* London: Routledge.
Trevor-Roper, Hugh R. 1963. "Religion, the Reformation, and Social Change." *Historical Studies* 4: 18–44.
Trigilia, Carlo. 2001. "Social Capital and Local Development." *European Journal of Social Theory* 4.4: 427–42.
Troeltsch, Ernst. 1931. *The Social Teaching of the Christian Churches.* New York: Macmillan.
Tu, Wei-Ming. 1984. *Confucian Ethics Today: The Singapore Challenge.* Singapore: Curriculum Development Institute of Singapore.
———. 1985. *Confucian Thought: Selfhood as Creative Transformation.* New York: State University of New York Press.
———. 1990. "Is Confucianism Part of the Capitalist Ethic?" Excerpt from a paper presented at the International Conference on Culture and Development in Asia and the Pacific, held in Fukuoka, Japan, March.
———. (ed.) 1991. *The Triadic Chord: Confucian Ethics, Industrial East Asia and Max Weber.* Singapore: The Institute of East Asian Philosophies.
Turner, Bryan S. 1983. *Religion and Social Theory.* London: Heinemann.
———. 1996. *For Weber: Essays on the Sociology of Fate.* London: Sage.
———. 1998a. "Introduction." In Reinhard Bendix, *Max Weber: An Intellectual Portrait.* London: Routledge and Thoemmes Press.

——· 1998b. *Weber and Islam*. London and New York: Routledge.
——· (ed.) 1999a. *Max Weber: Critical Responses*. New York: Routledge.
——· 1999b. "An Introduction to Max Weber's Sociology." In Bryan S. Turner (ed.), *Max Weber: Critical Responses*. New York: Routledge.
——· 2008. "The Price of Piety." *Contemporary Islam* 2.1: 1–6.
——· 2009. "Max Weber on Islam and Confucianism: The Kantian Theory of Secularisation." In Peter Clarke (ed.), *The Oxford Handbook of the Sociology of Religion*. Oxford: Oxford University Press.
Umstott, Denis D. 1988. *Understanding Organizational Behavior*. St Paul, MN: West Publishing Company.
Van der Sprenkel, Otto B. 1964. "Max Weber on China." *History and Theory* 3.3: 348–70.
Verheul, Ingrid and Roy Thurik. 2001. "Start-Up Capital: 'Does Gender Matter?'" *Small Business Economics* 16: 329–45.
Vermeir, Iris and Patrick V. Kenhove. 2008. "Gender Differences in Double Standards." *Journal of Business Ethics* 81: 281–95.
Walder, Andrew G. 1986. *Chinese Neo-traditionalism: Work and Authority in Chinese Industry*. Berkeley: University of California Press.
Wang, Gungwu. 1988. "Trade and Cultural Values: Australia and the Four Dragons." *Asian Studies Association of Australia Review* 11.3: 1–9.
——· 1993. *Community and Nation: China, Southeast Asia and Australia*. Sydney: Allen and Unwin.
——· 1995. "The Southeast Asian Chinese and the Development of China." In Leo Suryadinata (ed.), *Southeast Asian Chinese and China: The Politico-Economic Dimension*. Singapore: Times Academic Press.
Wang, Hongying. 2000. *Weak State, Strong Networks: The Institutional Dynamics of Foreign Direct Investment in China*. New York: Oxford University Press.
Wang, Hongying and Xueyi Chen. 2005. "Foreign Direct Investment and Host Country Corruption: Preliminary Evidence from China." *Journal of Asian Business* 21.2: 1–28.
Wang, Yeu-Farn. 1994. *Chinese Entrepreneurs in Southeast Asia: Historical Roots and Modern Significance*. Stockholm: Center for Pacific Asia Studies of Stockholm University.
Wang, Zhenghua. 2008. "Overseas Chinese Invest in Shanghai." *China Daily*, 7 October. http://www.chinadaily.com.cn/bizchina/2008-10/07/content_7083466.htm (accessed 12 October 2011).
Wang, Zhile. 2006. *2006 Kuaguo Gongsi Zhongguo Baogao* [2006 Report on Transnational Corporations in China]. Beijing: Zhongguo Jingji Chubanshe.
Weber, Marianne. 1975. *Max Weber: A Biography*. New Brunswick, NJ: Transaction Books.
Weber, Max. 1946a. *From Max Weber. Essays in Sociology*, trans. and ed. with an introduction by H. H. Gerth and C. W. Mills. London: Kegan Paul, Trench, Trübner and Co.
——· 1946b. "The Protestant Sects and the Spirit of Capitalism." In H. H. Gerth and C. W. Mills (trans.) *From Max Weber. Essays in Sociology*. New York: Oxford University Press.
——· 1950. *General Economic History*, trans. F. H. Knight. Glencoe, IL: The Free Press.
——· 1951. *The Religion of China: Confucianism and Taoism*. New York: Macmillan.
——· 1952. *Ancient Judaism*, trans. and ed. by H. H. Gerth and Don Martindale. New York: The Free Press.
——· 1966. *The Sociology of Religion*. London: Methuen.
——· 1978. *Economy and Society: An Outline of Interpretive Sociology*. Berkeley: University of California Press.
——· 1992. *The Protestant Ethic and the Spirit of Capitalism*, trans. T. Parsons with an introduction by A. Giddens. London and New York: Routledge.

Weeks, William A., Carlos W. Moore, Joseph A. McKinney and Justin G. Longenecker. 1999. "The Effect of Gender and Career Stage on Ethical Judgment." *Journal of Business Ethics* 20: 301–13.
Wehrfritz, George and Lynette Clemetson. 1998. "Missionaries Flock to China." *Newsweek*, 29 June. http://www.washingtonpost.com/wp-srv/newsweek/religion.htm (accessed 1 November 2011).
Welch, Patrick J. and J. J. Mueller. 2001. "The Relationships of Religion to Economics." *Review of Social Economy* 59.2 (June).
Weller, Robert. 1998. "Divided Market Cultures in China: Gender, Enterprise, and Religion." In Robert W. Hefner (ed.), *Market Cultures: Society and Morality in the New Asian Capitalisms*. Boulder, CO: Westview Press.
———. 1999. *Alternate Civilities*. Boulder, CO: Westview Press.
Whimster, Sam. 2005. Editorial. *Max Weber Studies* 5.2: 177–83.
Whipple, Thomas W. and Dominic F. Swords. 1992. "Business Ethics Judgments: A Cross-Cultural Comparison." *Journal of Business Ethics* 11.9: 671–78.
White, Harrison. 1970. *Chains of Opportunity: System Models of Mobility in Organizations*. Cambridge, MA: Harvard University Press.
Whitley, Bernard E. Jr., Amanda B. Nelson and Curtis J. Jones. 1999. "Gender Differences in Cheating Attitudes and Classroom Cheating Behavior: A Meta-Analysis." *Sex Roles* 41: 657–80.
Willmott, William E. (ed.) 1972. *Economic Organization in Chinese Society*. Stanford, CA: Stanford University Press.
Wiley, Norbert (ed.) 1987. *The Marx-Weber Debate*. Newbury Park, CA: Sage.
Won, S-Y. 2005. "Play the Men's Game? Accommodating Work and Family in the Workplace." *Asian Journal of Women's Studies* 11.3: 7–35.
Wong, Siu-lun. 1988. *Emigrant Entrepreneurs: Shanghai Industrialists in Hong Kong*. Hong Kong: Oxford University Press.
Woodhead, Linda. 2008. "Gendering Secularization Theory." *Social Compass* 55.2: 187–93.
Wu, Yuan-Li and Wu, Chun-His. 1980. *Economic Development in Southeast Asia: The Chinese Dimension*. Stanford, CA: Hoover Institution Press.
Xiyu, Cheng .1994. "Research Note on the 'Chinese Economic Zone.'" ISSCO Bulletin 2.2.
Yang, Fenggang. 1999. *Chinese Christians in America: Conversion, Assimilation, and Adhesive Identities*. University Park, PA: Pennsylvania State University Press.
———. 2005. "Between Secularist Ideology and Desecularizing Reality: The Birth and Growth of Religious Research in Communist China." In Fenggang Yang and Joseph. B. Tamney (eds), *State, Market, and Religions in Chinese Societies*. Boston: Brill.
———. 2006. "The Red, Black and Gray Markets of Religion in China." *Sociological Quarterly* 47: 93–122.
———. 2007. "Zhongguo de Shichang Jingji Zhuanxingzhong de Jidujiao Lunli" [The Christian Ethic during the Market Transition in China]. In Yao Xiyi (ed.), *Qianlu Qiusuo: Fuyin Xinyang yu Dangdai Zhongguo Shehui Xianshi* [Christianity and Contemporary China Social Reality]. Hong Kong: CGST Press.
Yang, Keming. 2007. *Entrepreneurship in China*. Hampshire: Ashgate Publishing Company.
Yang, Mayfair M. 2004. "Spatial Struggles: Postcolonial Complex, State Disenchantment, and Popular Reappropriation of Space in Rural Southeast China." *Journal of Asian Studies* 63: 719–55.
Yeung, Agnes, Ruby Chau and Sam Yu. 2004. "The Strategies Used by Chinese Managerial Women to Cope with Social Exclusion." *Asian Women* 18: 103–22.
Yoo, Jin-Kyung. 1998. *Korean Immigrant Entrepreneurs: Network and Ethnic Resources*. New York and London: Garland Publishing.

Yu, Ying-shih. 1987. *Zhongguo Jinshi Zongjiao Lunli yu Shangren Jingshen* [Religious Ethics and the Spirit of Merchants in Late Imperial China]. Taipei: Lienjing.

———. 1997. "Business Culture and Chinese Traditions – Toward a Study of the Evolution of Merchant Culture in Chinese History." In Gungwu Wang and Siu-lun Wong (eds), *Dynamic Hong Kong: Business and Culture*. Hong Kong: University of Hong Kong Press.

Zerbe, Wilfred J. and Delroy L. Paulhus. 1987. "Socially Desirable Responding in Organizational Behavior: A Reconception." *Academy of Management Review* 12.2: 250–64.

INDEX

Abundant Grace International Fellowship, Shanghai 66, 109
Aikman, David 3–4, 17, 123
America 28, 39, 56, 59–62, 66, 83–4, 100, 108, 110, 116, 119–20
   American community in Shanghai 110
   American missionaries to China 10
   "Americanized of Sinic world" 47
APEC (Asia-Pacific Economic Cooperation Conference) 58
ascetic ethic 31, 35–8, 40–1, 123

baptism 20, 93n1, 95, 108, 113, 129
Bays, Daniel 4, 11, 14, 16, 68
belief 9–10, 35, 39–40, 42, 45–9, 51–2, 69–70, 76, 129, 131, 144, 149
   and (economic) action 40, 47–52, 144
Berger, Peter 44, 45, 50, 64, 148
Bible study (groups) 20, 72, 103, 113–4
Biblical principles 66, 70, 73, 75–6, 85, 95–6, 101, 103, 120
Bologh, Roslyn 128, 128n1, 149
"boss Christians" 68, 72
bribery 41, 62, 85–6, 112, 117, 130–2, 136–7, 139, 141
Buddhism 10, 11n1, 16, 39, 42, 44, 69
business as mission 93, 97, 105

calling 15, 29–30, 33–6, 39, 41, 51, 74, 76, 78, 80–2, 85, 93–5, 99–101, 103, 138–140
Calvinism (and capitalism) 34–41
capitalism 2, 4–5, 7, 17–8, 30, 33–40, 42–6, 48–51, 63–4, 73, 107–8, 125, 144, 146–8
   with Chinese characteristics 4
   in East Asia 33
   rational 43, 48–9

the spirit of modern capitalism 34, 39, 51, 147
Catholicism 10
   Catholic understanding of calling 36
cell group, small group 80, 113–14
CEO(s) 3, 27–8, 94, 98, 103, 137
   God as 79
Chang, Richard (SMIC) 14, 66–7, 72, 82, 84, 110
character 36–7, 45, 54–5, 72, 98, 103–5, 117, 126, 136, 139
Character First 103–4
charismatics 27–9, 76–8, 99–100, 113–4, 119
China 1, 3–21, 24–31, 33, 40–6, 52–70, 72–5, 79, 81–2, 85, 87–8, 91–104, 110–15, 117–18, 120–1, 123–4, 129, 132–4, 136, 140–1, 143–5, 147–50
   and the adoption of Christianity in its modernization efforts 4, 16
   economic reforms of 1, 5–9, 41, 55
   open-door policy of 9, 28, 53, 81, 149
   religious changes in 1, 9–16
   religious regulations in 12–16
Chinese Businesspeople Fellowship (Huashang Tuanqi) 112–18
Christian churches (in Shanghai) 10, 15, 67, 109–111
Christian ethics, Christian values 1, 17, 30, 33, 46, 52, 64, 70, 72, 93, 95, 102, 105, 117, 119, 128, 143, 146, 148–9
Christianity 1, 3–4, 9–17, 17n4, 19, 25–6, 28–30, 33–4, 52, 65–6, 68–70, 73, 78, 82, 87–8, 91, 98, 121, 134, 138–9, 143–6, 148–50
   in China 1, 3–4, 9–16, 144–5, 148–9

integration with Chinese identity 64, 68–70
"Christianity Fever" 9, 11, 26
Communist Party, Chinese 5, 10, 12, 55
Confucian ethics and values 15, 29, 39, 43–7, 59, 64, 68–9, 143, 148
Confucianism 16, 29, 33, 41–7, 50, 52, 64–5, 68–70, 146, 150
corporate culture 65, 80, 86, 88, 92–3, 95, 97, 102–5, 144
corruption 7–8, 61, 89, 97, 100, 129, 136, 146, 150

Deng, Xiaoping 5–7, 10, 13

"elective affinity" 50
evangelism 82–3, 94, 100, 118–19
and discipleship 118–19

"faith vs. culture" 92
foreign trade and investment (in China) 5, 6, 8, 10, 53, 57–9, 149–50
relationship with religious regulation 10
frugality 30, 39, 44, 64, 74, 83–4, 92
Fukuyama, Francis 1
Full Gospel Businessmen's Fellowship International 99, 111, 118–21

Gideons International 110
gift-giving and money-giving 62, 104, 112, 131, 134, 139
God's kingdom 75, 78, 99, 101
Godley, Michael R. 46, 54–5, 69
"golden rule" 71, 87–8
Guangdong 16, 57–8
guanxi 60, 62, 111–2, 117; see also networking
deviant type of 62

Hamrin, Carol L. 11–12, 14–16
Holy Communion 93n1, 95, 113
Hong Kong 7, 10, 13, 16, 18, 26, 28, 44, 53, 56–9, 62–3, 66, 71, 77, 87, 95, 97, 113–14, 118, 129, 138–9, 148

Indonesia 57, 71, 114
innovativeness 30, 41, 74, 86 –8

institutionalization (of faith in corporations) 8, 80–1, 97, 102, 105
integrity 30, 69–71, 74, 84–5, 96–7, 109, 117, 125, 134
Islam 10, 11n1

Malaysia 26, 28, 56–7, 59, 63, 66, 71, 79, 86, 88, 93, 100, 136
Mammon and God 91
"marketplace pastors" 99
Marshall, Gordon 36, 38, 40–1, 48
ministry 78, 83, 91, 93, 96, 110, 113–15, 118, 120–1
children's 113–14
women's 113–14
youth 113–14
missionaries 10, 13–14, 82
MNCs (multinational companies) 59, 144

Nash, Laura 71
networks, networking; see also guanxi
"deviant" or "irregular" 62, 112, 117
dialect and family 65, 111–12
gender differences in 126–8
negative effects of 109
of Christian businesspeople 15, 65–6, 99, 110, 112, 114–18, 120–1, 139, 143–4

Overseas Chinese 1, 3, 7–8, 10, 13–9, 23, 25–31, 33, 45–7, 53–69, 72–6, 81–5, 89, 91, 109–14, 119, 123, 143–4, 148
business and investment in china 3, 54–8, 61–5
"Chineseness" of 64, 69
Christian community in Shanghai 109–21
definition of 18, 18 n5
economic performance of 53, 55–6
preferential treatment of 54, 56
role in China's economic reform 7–8, 16, 18, 53
in Shanghai 58–60
as "Westernized" Chinese 54–5

prayer meetings 71, 95, 113
24-hour prayer link 95
profit ethic 36, 76, 93, 96

prosperity gospel 76–7
Protestant Ethic thesis 2–3, 18, 33–41, 44, 48–52, 70, 91, 125, 147
"Protestant Sects and the Spirit of Capitalism, The" 30, 37–8, 107–9, 119
Pudong 59, 83
Puritan sects 2, 30, 37–8, 43, 48, 51, 76, 107
and economic life 37–8, 48, 107

rationalization 35, 42, 45
Redding, Gordon 8, 18, 49, 64, 111, 148
religion and economics 1–4, 48–52
religious freedom (in post-1978 China) 10, 12, 14, 150
religious training 4, 72, 113
rongshenyiren 78

salvation 34–8, 43, 50, 76, 132, 145
secularization 2
self-discipline/control 30, 39, 41, 44, 74, 78–80, 92, 97, 127, 135, 138
sexual immorality/temptation 61, 79–80, 120, 126–7
"Shang Tai Ren" 60
Shanghai 7, 10–11, 15, 19–21, 23, 27–30, 53–4, 58–61, 63, 66, 68–9, 73–9, 81–5, 88, 94–5, 101, 104, 109–21, 127–9, 133, 136, 138–40, 144
as China's "global city" 59, 112
foreign investment in 58–9
importance for Christianity in China 19
Shanghai Community Fellowship (International Church) 66, 109–10
Silvoso, Ed 99
Singapore 26, 28, 44, 51, 56 60, 63, 66, 77, 82, 85, 97, 99, 113, 129, 136, 148
social capital 8, 12, 107, 108n1, 121, 126
social eating 62, 112
soft power 4, 8, 16
Southeast Asia 7, 18, 47, 53–7, 59
success, sense and value 34, 36, 74–8, 84, 89, 124, 135
Sunday services 68, 80, 95, 113–14, 138
Swedberg, Richard 37, 91

taibao 60
Taiwan 7, 10, 13, 18, 20, 26, 28, 28n6, 44, 53, 57–9, 63, 67, 75, 77, 94–5, 117–18, 138, 148
Ten Commandments 69, 72, 79
Thailand 56–7
Thanksgiving Church, Shanghai 66–7, 110
Tiananmen crackdown 6, 10, 18, 53
tithing (giving money to church) 72, 76–7, 101–2
trust 8, 30, 44, 70, 96, 104, 107–8, 115–17, 120–1, 128, 133, 139, 147
Tu, Wei-ming 45, 47
Turner, Bryan 2, 37–8, 43, 47–51, 72, 128 n1, 150

Weber, Max 1–4, 18, 33–52, 69–70, 76, 81, 91, 107–9, 119–20, 124–5, 127–8, 141, 143, 145–7, 149–50
study on China and Confucianism 33, 41–7, 50, 146
criticism against 38–41, 44–7
methodological individualism 91
motivational approach 33, 45, 47, 52
"superior community of faith" 30, 107
Weller, Robert 111–12, 126–7
"wolf culture" 98
women
differences in ethical performances 124–5
and Weber's Protestant ethics 125, 127–9
rationality of 127–9
work and family responsibilities of 125–9
work ethic 2, 35, 93, 96, 105, 125
World Expo, Shanghai 58
World Trade Organization 7–8

Yang, Fenggang 9, 12, 46, 66, 69–70, 74, 83, 147–8

Zhao, Xiao 3, 17

www.ingramcontent.com/pod-product-compliance
Lightning Source LLC
Chambersburg PA
CBHW021830300426
44114CB00009BA/396